IMAGES
of America

YORKTOWN AND NORDHEIM

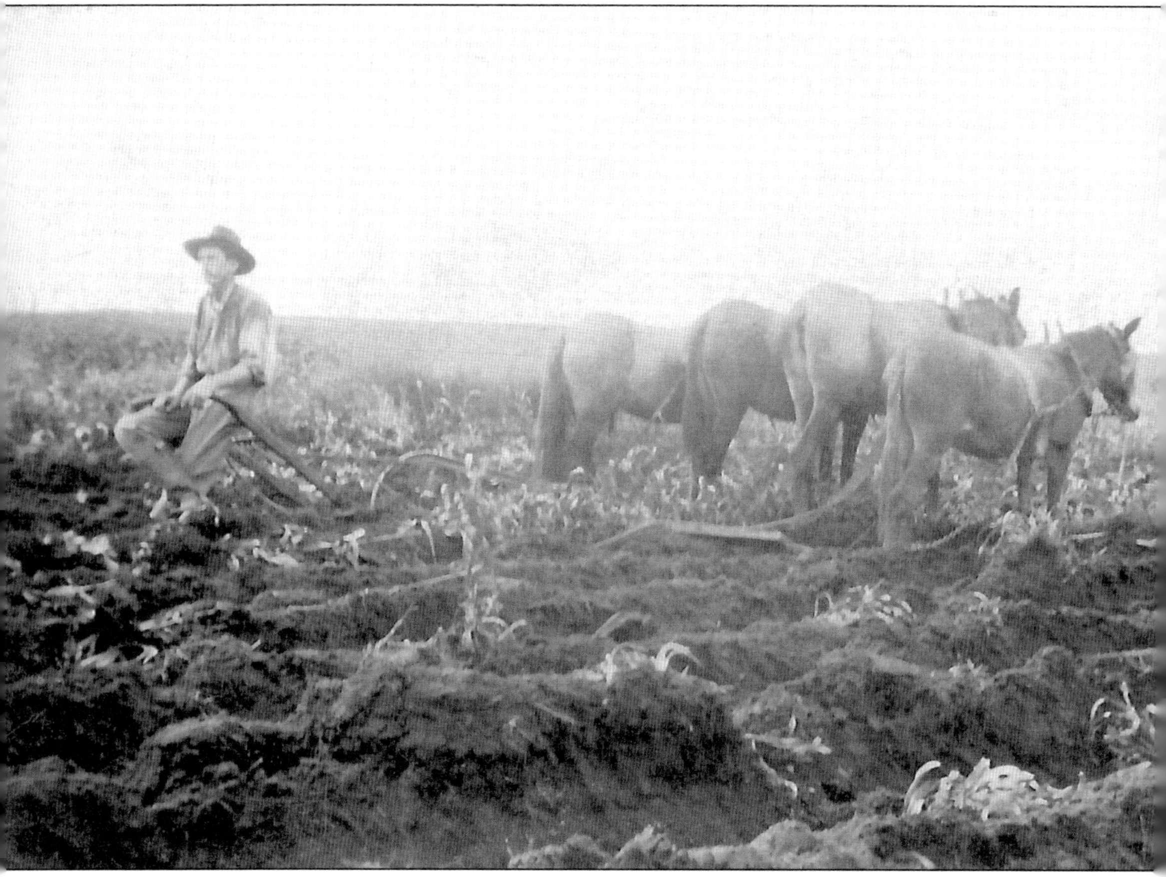

Carl Stirl sits on the back of his middle buster to rest after trudging behind his four horses turning the soil in his field. On this day in 1914 Stirl daydreams of the crops he will plant after the soil has been prepared. He owned a farm between Dahse and Remmers Roads outside of Nordheim. He married Olga Sein, and they produced two boys and two girls. (Courtesy Bernice Geffert.)

On the Cover: Cotton was a staple crop in the Yorktown and Nordheim areas in the late 1800s and early 1900s. Here three wagons loaded with cotton are being driven to one of four gins in Yorktown. Oxen, six-mule teams, or horses were used to pull the wagons because the country roads were often hard to navigate. Depending on the conditions, deep sand or mud hindered the wagons' progress. The building on the left in the background was Noster's Butcher Shop. (Courtesy Yorktown Historical Museum.)

IMAGES
of America

Yorktown and Nordheim

Yorktown Historical Society
and Nordheim Historical Museum Association

ARCADIA
PUBLISHING

ISBN 978-0-7385-7976-4

Published by Arcadia Publishing
Charleston, South Carolina

Printed in the United States of America

Library of Congress Control Number: 2010936918

For all general information, please contact Arcadia Publishing:
Telephone 843-853-2070
Fax 843-853-0044
E-mail sales@arcadiapublishing.com
For customer service and orders:
Toll-Free 1-888-313-2665

Visit us on the Internet at www.arcadiapublishing.com

This book is dedicated to the preservation of the history and heritage of the communities known as Yorktown and Nordheim, Texas.

Contents

ACKNOWLEDGMENTS

Preservation of the past has to come from the diligence of a town's citizenry. The Yorktown Historical Society and the Nordheim Historical Museum Association want to thank those who met the challenge when called upon to contribute photographs for this pictorial history and share memories of Yorktown and Nordheim. Our thanks go to Beverly Bruns, June Buchhorn, Dolores Huck Denman, Della Leister Evans, Bernice Geffert, Jay Heil, Linda Hurta, Iris Mueller Johnson, Kay Klaevemann, Frances Ann Koopmann, Betty Ladner, Bea McKinney, Robert Muschalek, Gilbert and Mary Pargmann, Esther Puente, Jimmy Saldana, Mary Sauermilch, Arlene and Clydelle Schroeder, Karen Swain, Della Ruth Dean Thurman, Lindbergh and Georgie Voelkel, Mark Weischwill, Cathy Wilems, and the Yorktown Chamber of Commerce.

Recognition also goes to Judge Rudolph Kleberg Jr. who wrote *History of Yorktown* for its 50th anniversary and Alfreda Huck for her book *Nordheim's 100th Anniversary 1897 to 1997* and her work to preserve our history.

Unless otherwise noted, all of the images in this book came from the archives of the Yorktown Historical Society and the Nordheim Historical Museum Association.

INTRODUCTION

Yorktown and Nordheim are two small towns located 7 miles apart in south central Texas. The two towns were settled by Germans, Polish, Mexicans, African Americans, and Lithuanians.

Yorktown was built along the Coleto Creek as a rest stop along the Indianola Trail for freight wagon drivers traveling from Indianola on their way to New Braunfels and San Antonio. Charles Eckhardt contracted with John A. King to survey a shorter route that would go through Yorktown. Capt. John York, for whom the town is named, and Charles Eckhardt founded the town in 1848. It was one of the few towns in Texas that was laid out into streets, city blocks, a public square, and cemetery before the first house was built. In May 1848, Peter Metz and John Frank built the first house for Charles Eckhardt. The house was later occupied by Caesar Eckhardt, who took over the C. Eckhardt and Sons Mercantile Company, known for 50 years as a leader of its kind in western DeWitt County. In 1871, Yorktown became the first incorporated town in DeWitt County.

In 1886, the San Antonio and Aransas Pass Railroad was built and passed through Yorktown and Weldon Switch. The name Weldon Switch was changed and officially recognized as Nordheim in 1898. The site of Nordheim's first town block was sold September 18, 1895, to Henry Schlosser, who built the first mercantile business and residence. Nordheim was incorporated in 1918 with L. C. Neutzler as its first mayor.

Religion was an important part of the citizens' lives. Nordheim has two churches: St. Paul Lutheran Church, built in 1908 by donations, and St. Ann's Catholic Church, erected in 1921. Yorktown has 12 churches: St. Paul Lutheran Church, Church of Christ, Holy Cross Catholic Church, First Presbyterian Church, United Methodist Church, Faith Assembly of God Church, Church of Jesus Christ of Latter Day Saints, Open Bible Baptist Church, San Luis Catholic Church, Primera Baptist Church/Primera Iglesia Bautista, New Life Baptist Church, and Rising Star Missionary Baptist Church.

This book will reveal the early beginnings and settlers of each town, and their growth through businesses, schools, homes, churches, cemeteries, music, and celebrations. Incorporated into the book will also be several small rural communities in close proximity of Yorktown and Nordheim. These communities are Gruenau, Garfield, Cabeza, and Cotton Patch. Several of the communities boast shooting clubs/dance halls and were the sites of country schools. Gruenau, Garfield, the Nordheim Shooting Club, and the Yorktown Community Hall host sausage or barbecue feasts twice a year. They make their own sausage, boil it, and serve it along with stuffed cabbage, potato salad, coleslaw, sweet rice, and desserts.

Several historic sites will be highlighted including the C. Eckhardt and Sons building, which is now the Yorktown Historical Museum. This building is on the National Register of Historic Buildings and displays a Texas Historic Medallion. The Upper Town Cemetery has graves dating back to the Civil War and before. It received a Texas historical marker in 2001. The burial site of Capt. John York is located between Yorktown and Meyersville and has a Texas historical marker. Nordheim lays claim to a high hill called Pilot Knob with an elevation of 447 feet, the highest point between Houston and San Antonio. Knob Hill, the Nordheim Shooting Club and Dance Hall, and the Jubilee Park Pavilion have all been honored with Texas historical markers. St. Ann's Cemetery in Nordheim, which is over 100 years old, has also received state historic recognition. These have all been recognized as a part of the communities' continued effort to honor those who came before us and help preserve their history.

Education was a priority among early settlers. This is evident in the country schools built in the rural communities and the schools built within the towns. The citizens have pride in their towns and their history.

One

Yorktown Beginnings

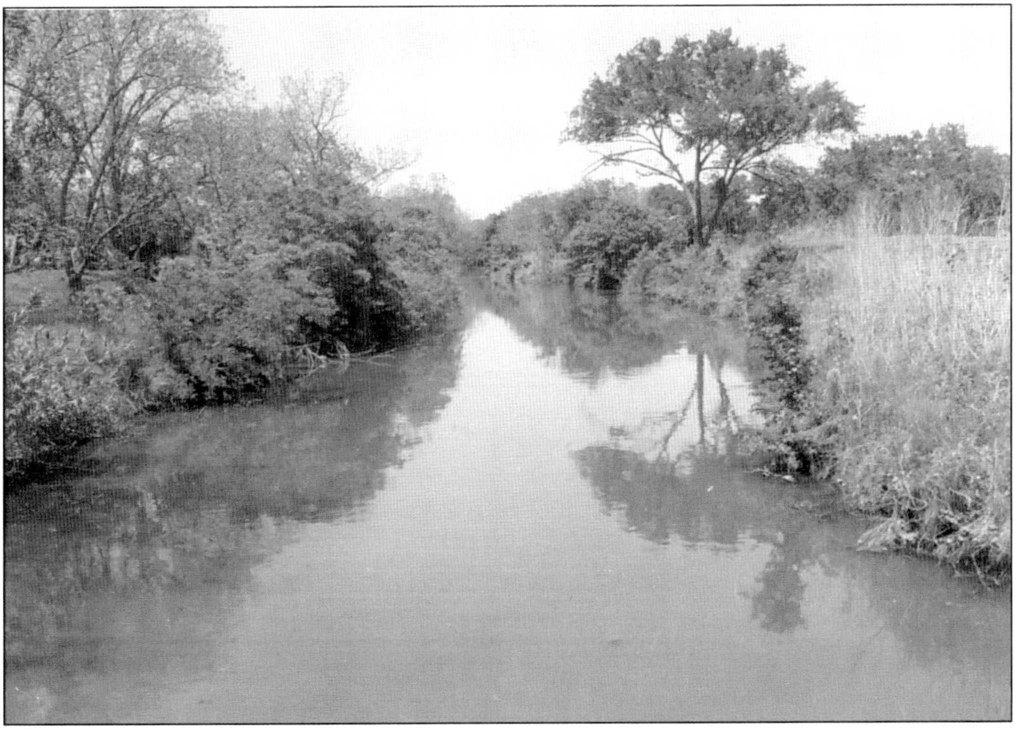

Coleto Creek (originally named Yorktown Creek) was important in the establishment of Yorktown as a way station for freighters to rest and water their horses as they headed toward New Braunfels and San Antonio. This creek originates a mile northeast of Yorktown, runs southeast through the town, and then on for 40 more miles before it empties into the Guadalupe River below Victoria. In 2010, the creek was returned to its original name, Yorktown Creek.

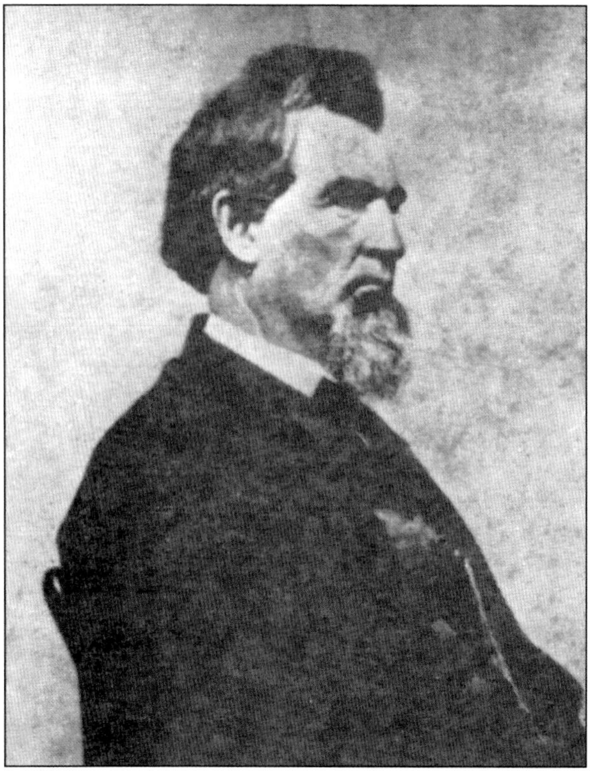

Yorktown was named for Capt. John York who gave the land on which the town was situated. He and Charles Eckhardt, a mercantile owner, founded the town along the Coleto Creek in 1848 as a shorter route and a way station for freight drivers along the Indianola Trail. Yorktown was one of the few towns in Texas that was planned with streets, city blocks, a park, and cemetery before the first house was built. In 1871, Yorktown was the first town in DeWitt County to be incorporated. Robert C. Eckhardt was appointed mayor.

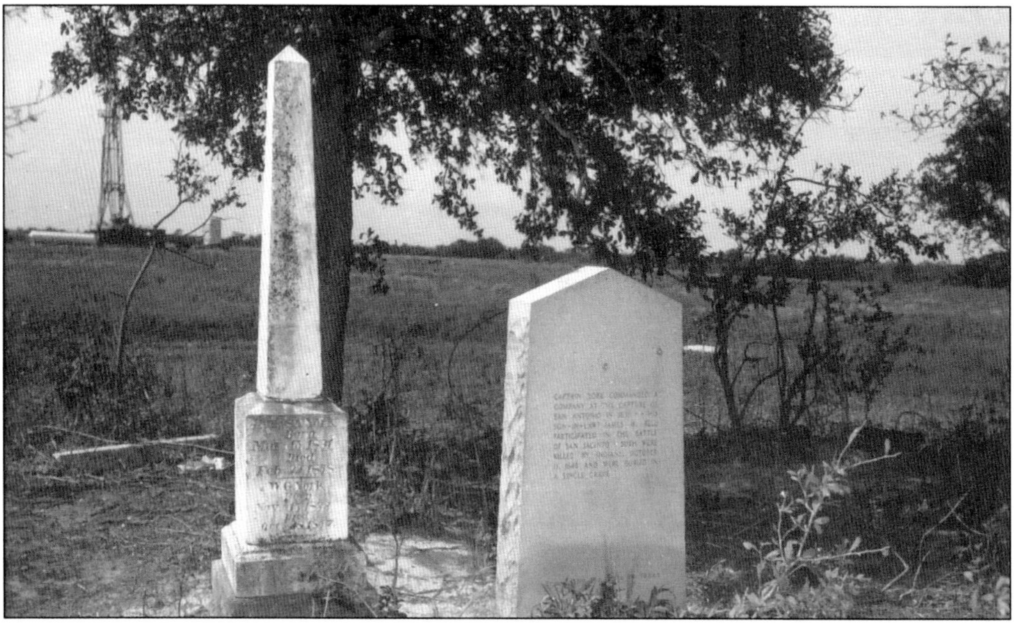

A few months after Yorktown was settled, Capt. John York and his son-in-law James Madison Bell were killed in a Native American fight along the Escondido Creek on October 11, 1848. The Lipan Apache Indians had been attacking area settlers. Bell was married to York's oldest daughter Miriam. York and Bell were buried together in a single handmade coffin approximately 10 miles east of Yorktown on Highway 237.

Upper Yorktown Cemetery was established in 1872 from land donated by Ann Friar. Then in 1949 Barbara Respondek donated 1 additional acre of land to the cemetery. The cemetery has plot areas for people of Anglo, Hispanic, and African American origins. In 2001, the cemetery was recognized with a marker as a Historic Texas Cemetery through the efforts of John Janacek and Darwin Sparck. The cemetery is located north of town off Highway 240.

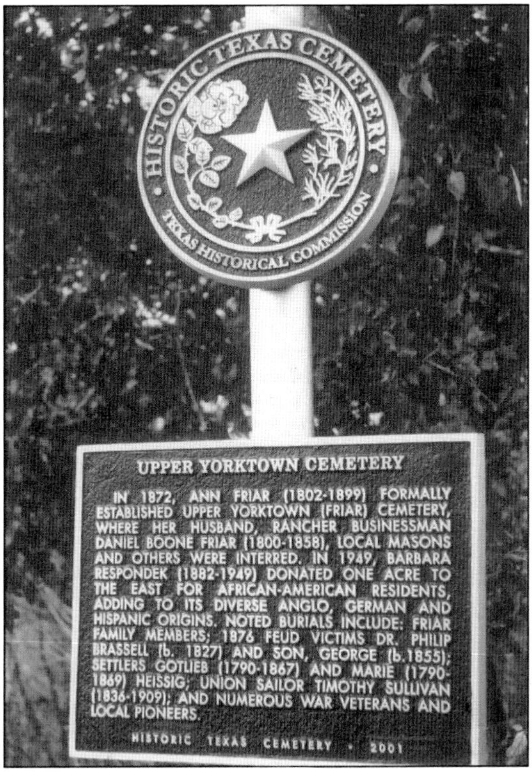

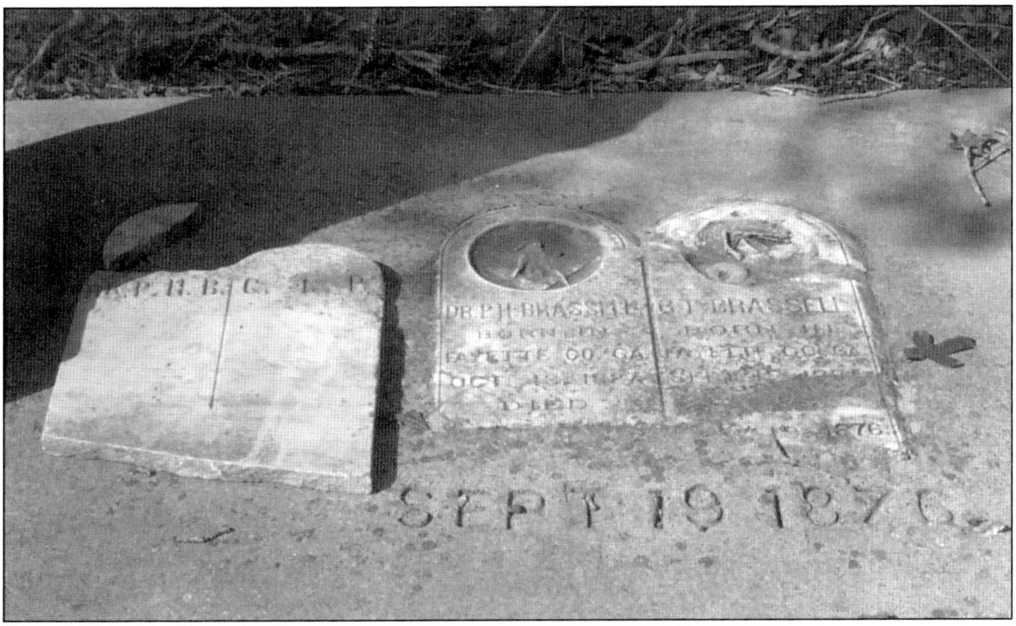

Pictured are the tombstones of Dr. Phillip Brassel and his son George, who were murdered in connection with the Taylor-Sutton feud on September 19, 1876. A posse of Sutton family sympathizers took Dr. Brassel and his three sons out of their home and after a short distance shot Dr. Brassel and George, but the other two sons, Theodore and Sheshane, escaped. Dr. Brassel and George were buried in the Upper Yorktown Cemetery.

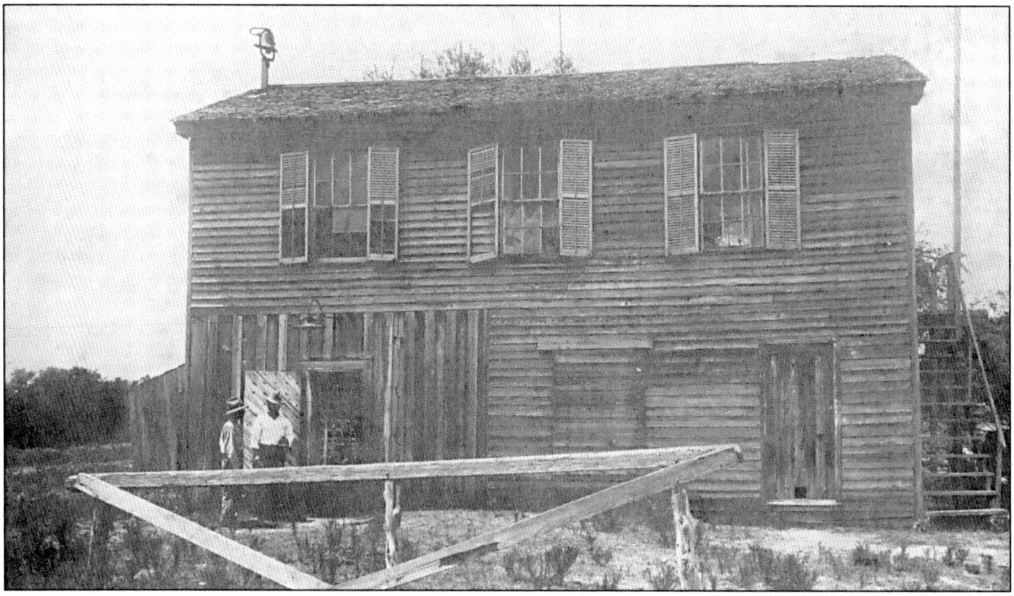

This dilapidated building was at one time Yorktown's city hall. It served until 1914 when a new two-story brick city hall was built across from the park on Eckhardt Street. This old building was also DeWitt County's courthouse when the county seat was located in Clinton. (Courtesy Robert Muschalek.)

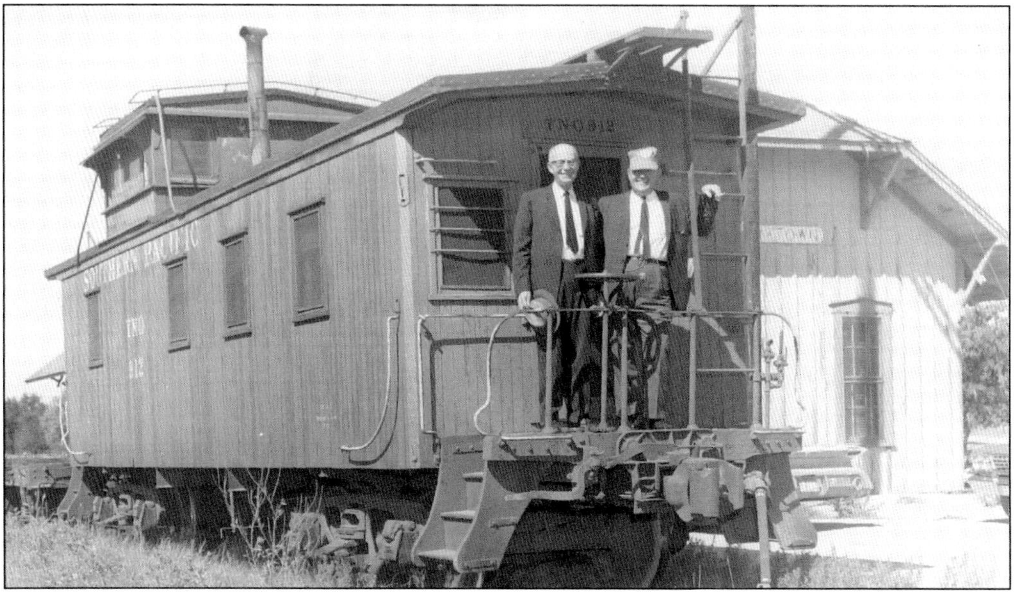

The San Antonio and Aransas Pass Railroad was persuaded to route its tracks through Yorktown in 1886 after William Eckhardt paid them $3,346 to keep the town from being doomed. He only received $588 in repayment from the town's citizens. The train transported products such as cotton, cattle, oil, and passengers for nearly a century. Passengers used the train to ride from one town to another to shop. They called this train "The Dinky." In the 1920s and 1930s, as many as six trains a day came through Yorktown. However, with the rise in automobile travel and the use of trucks for freight, the last train blew its whistle on February 10, 1972, as it came through town. (Courtesy Robert Muschalek.)

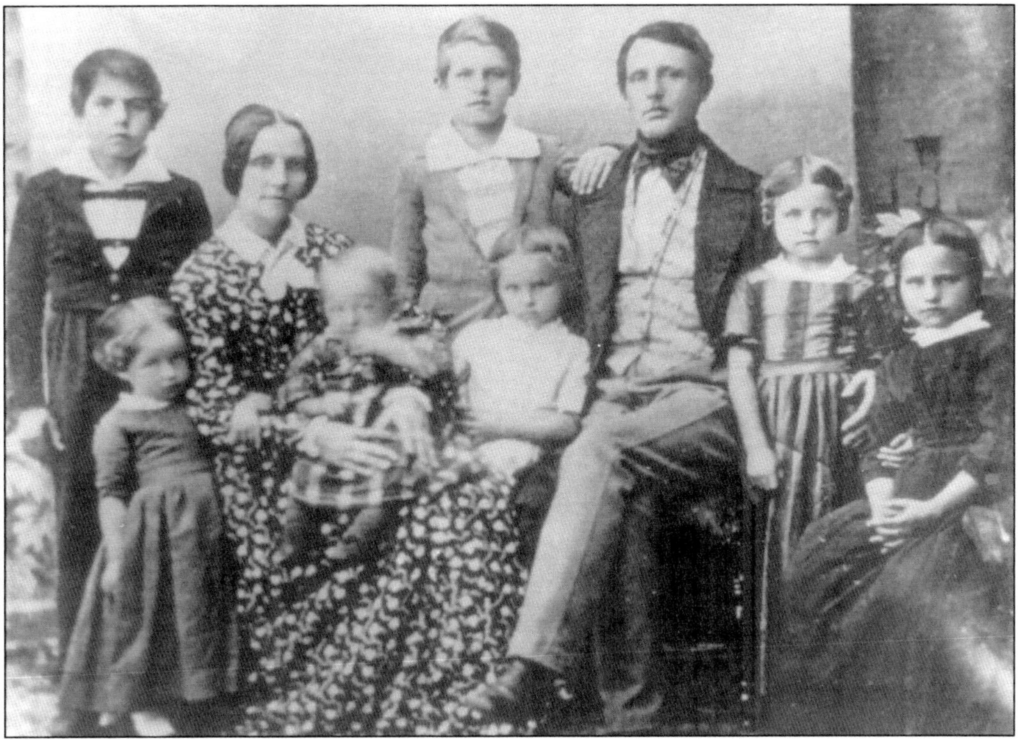

Caesar Eckhardt and his family arrived in Yorktown in 1849 and moved into his brother Charles's house while Charles was on a trip to Central America, where he died in 1852. Caesar took over the C. Eckhardt mercantile store. This 1847 photograph shows Caesar Eckhardt's family. From left to right are William, Mary (Gohmert), Louise Fischer Eckhardt, Herman Paul, Robert Christian, Johanna (Fechner), Caesar Eckhardt, Emily (Schmelzer), and Louise (von Roeder).

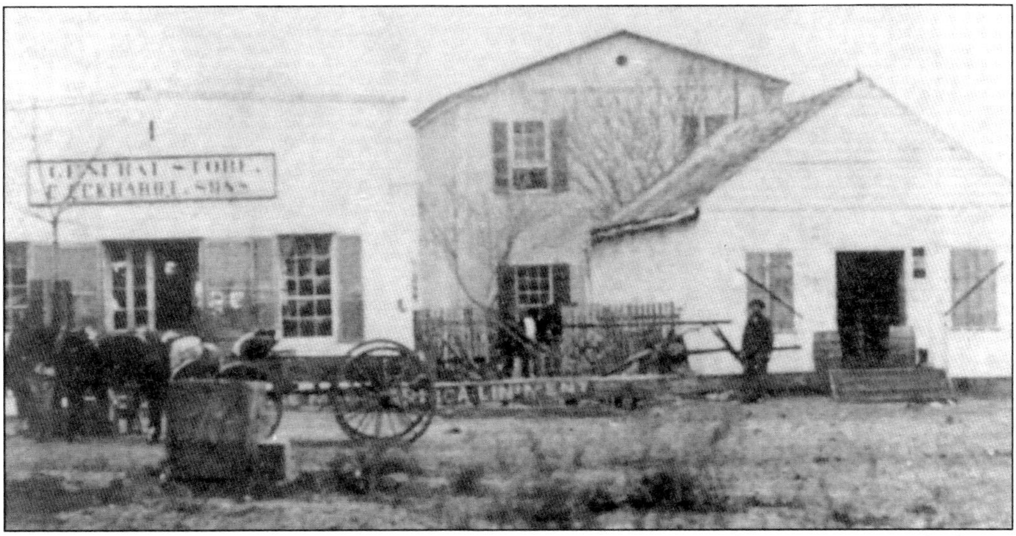

The first C. Eckhardt store was a 6-by-10-foot tent. Then in 1850 a log structure was built. By 1871, Eckhardt built a new store with 24-inch walls of sandstone, steel, and plaster. The building has iron shutters and doors. After Caesar Eckhardt's death in 1868, his widow and sons, Robert and William, continued the mercantile store giving it life for 50 years.

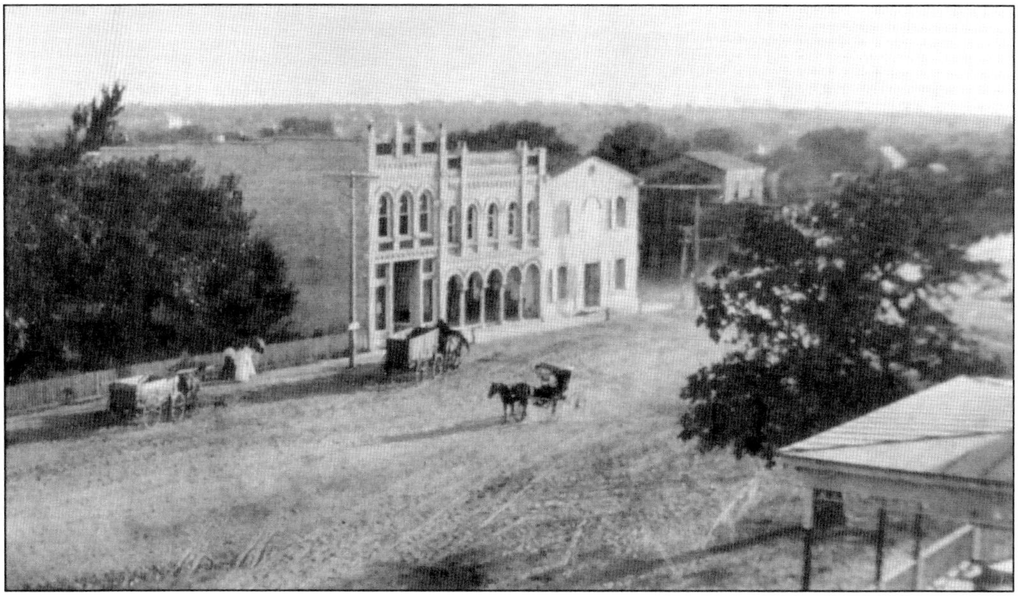

In 1871, C. Eckhardt and Sons mercantile store was flourishing, so on the corner of Main and Eckhardt Streets, a new building was constructed. The adjoining building was completed in 1876 with its arches being made of brick fortified with cast iron. The second story was added later with brick walls. The third building on the left is the Eckhardt Bank building. This bird's-eye view of Main Street shows the pedestrian and buggy traffic near the C. Eckhardt and Sons store and bank.

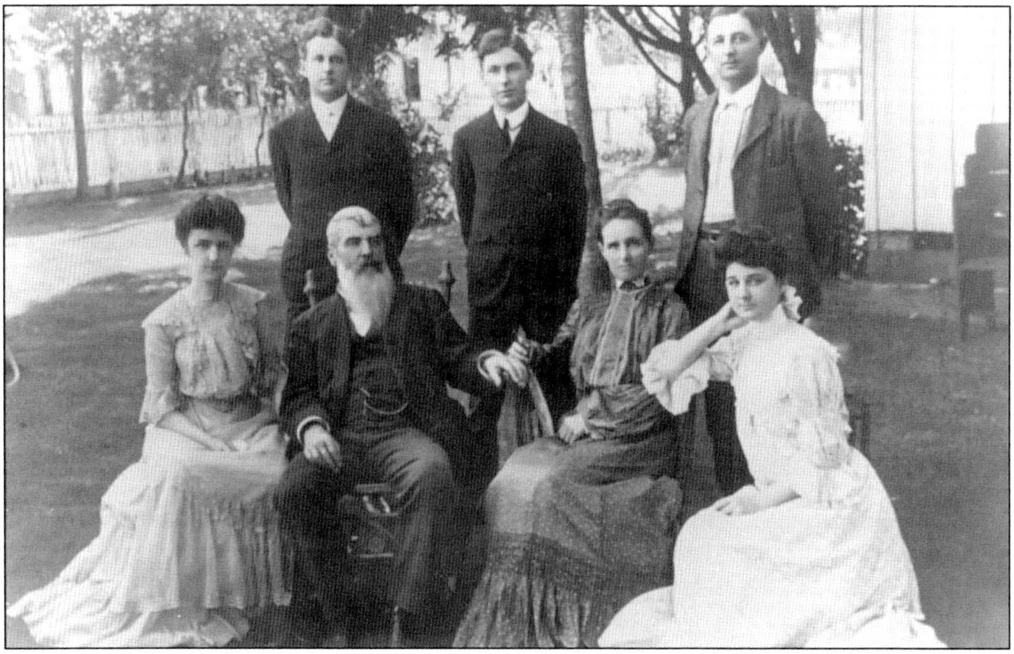

In the late 1800s, Rudolph Kleberg served as city attorney of Yorktown and later as county judge of DeWitt County. In 1898, Judge Kleberg wrote a history of Yorktown to commemorate its first 50 years of existence. The Kleberg family are, from left to right, (seated) daughter Lula, Rudolph, wife Matilda Eckhardt Kleberg, and daughter Matilda; (standing) sons August, Alfred, and Caesar.

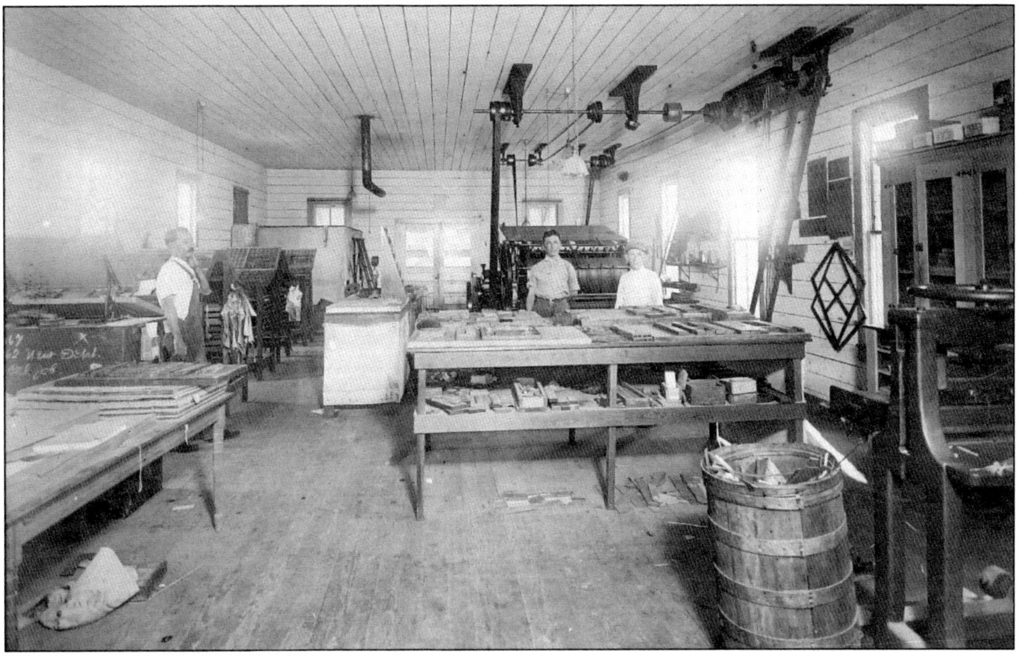

Yorktown Weekly News was taken over in 1895 by James Walton Blanton. By 1902, the *Yorktown Weekly News* was bought by William Hausmann. The inside of the newspaper building shows that things were all business, not for leisure. The linotype machine aided in the printing of the newspaper. (Courtesy Robert Muschalek.)

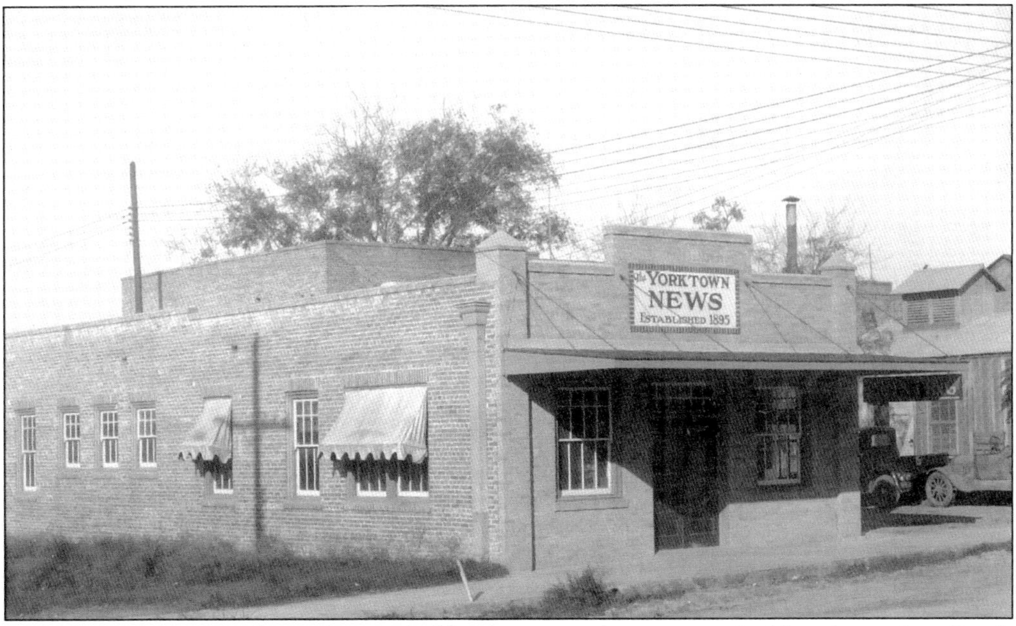

On February 27, 1913, the *Yorktown Weekly News* moved into a new building located on South Church Street. The contractor for the building was H. R. Gohlke. Owners of the newspaper were G. R. Beckham in 1915, Glenn Orville Beckham in 1951, Fred and Jo Pieper in 1955, and Lee Roy and Jo Ann Griffin in 1966. The Griffins retired and sold the business in 1997 to a Texas newspaper group. (Courtesy Robert Muschalek.)

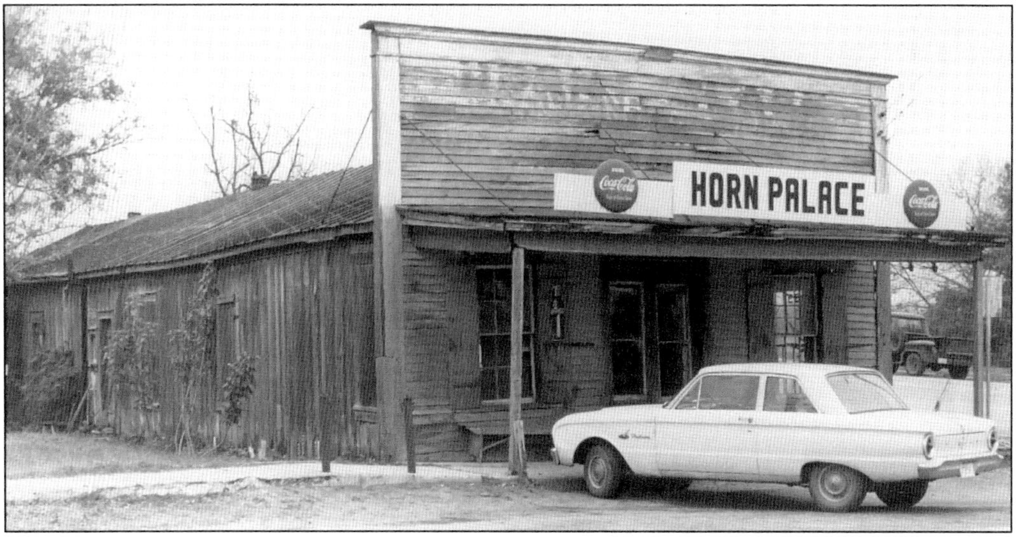

The Horn Palace was converted from a blacksmith shop into a beer hall by Joe Neumayer in 1895. Neumayer came from Germany and worked as a carpenter. He decided he could make more money selling beer to support his family of five children. During Prohibition (1918–1933), Neumayer and his son Charlie operated the bar selling "near beer," a substitute beverage.

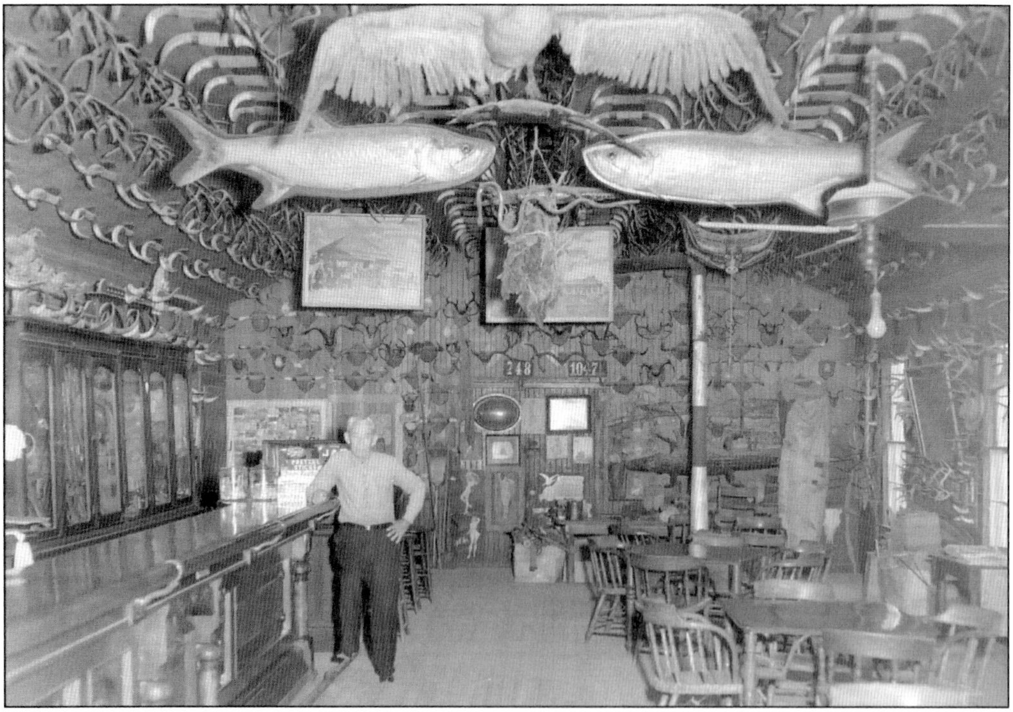

The inside of the Horn Palace was unique. Soon after opening, Joe Neumayer began lining the walls and ceiling with more than 1,000 sets of horns from deer, elk, moose, goat, and steers. Also covering the walls and ceiling were arrowhead collections, pipe collections, antique guns and ammunition, armadillos, moonshine jugs, stuffed birds and cats, a beehive, fish, voodoo dolls, and a shark jaw. His son Charlie continued the operation until the interior memorabilia was sold to a man from San Antonio.

The child pictured here is Frances Metz with her grandmother, Elise Gerhardt Metz. Elise Metz's husband, Anton Metz, made saddles and harnesses. Her eight siblings helped settle Yorktown. Her nephew C. F. Gerhardt was the mayor in 1898, and her son Gus was elected city marshal in 1893. Gus and C. F. Gerhardt both served on the executive committee for Yorktown's 50th Anniversary Celebration. Elise Metz's brother Karl's murder remains unsolved. (Courtesy Frances Ann Koopmann.)

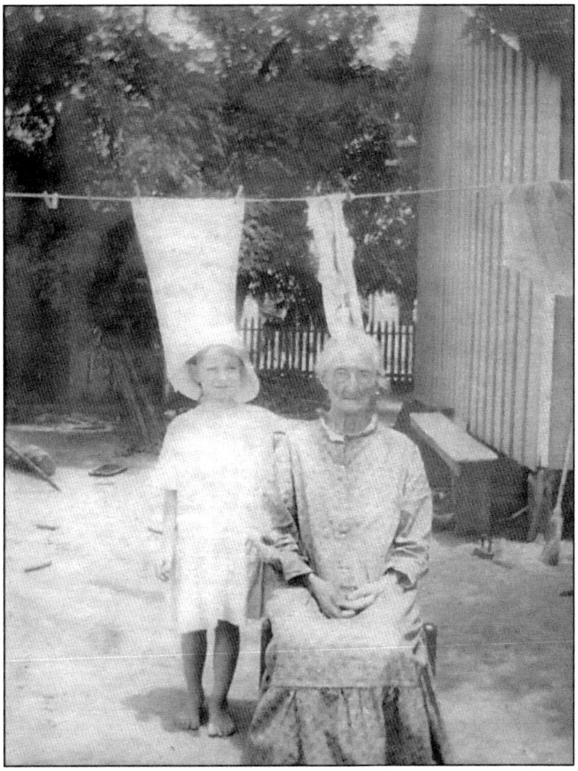

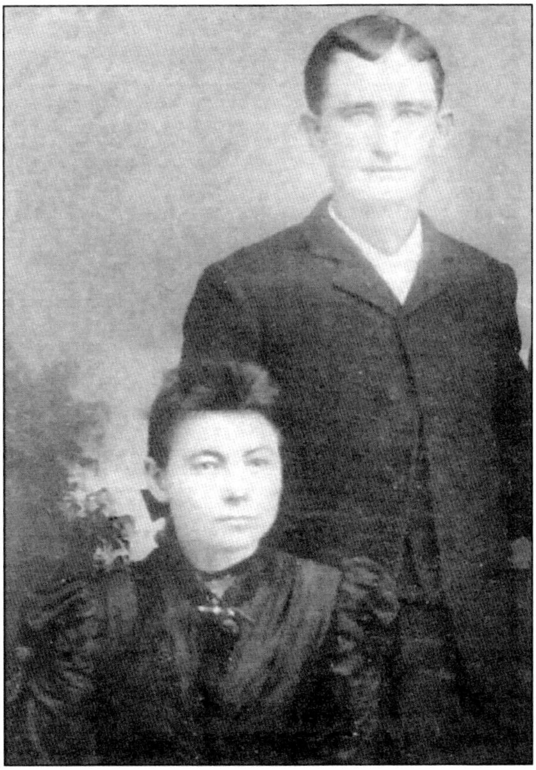

Reinhold and Lena Hoff Metz were first generation descendants of Yorktown pioneer families. Lena Metz's father Carl Hoff owned a grist windmill business. Her brother J. W. Hoff was elected mayor in 1893. Reinhold Metz's uncle Peter Metz built the first house in town for Charles Eckhardt. Reinhold Metz bought his father Anton Metz's saddle business in October 1893, for $400, and later in life Reinhold was a public weigher. (Courtesy Frances Ann Koopmann.)

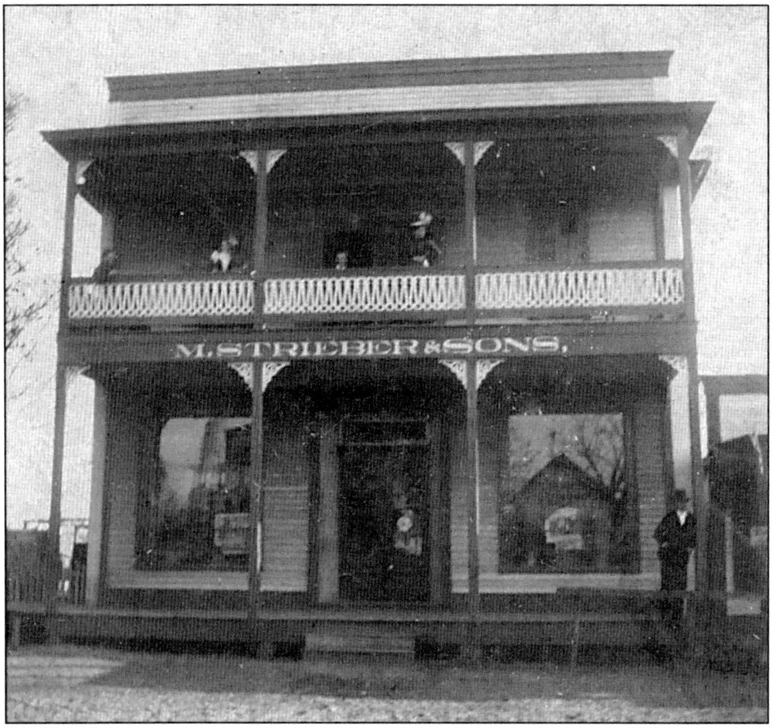

M. Strieber and Sons was a dry goods store opened in 1893. Notice that the sidewalks are not concrete but made of wooden planks. The planks were in vogue at that time. The gingerbread trim on the storefront added to its aesthetic beauty. (Courtesy Robert Muschalek.)

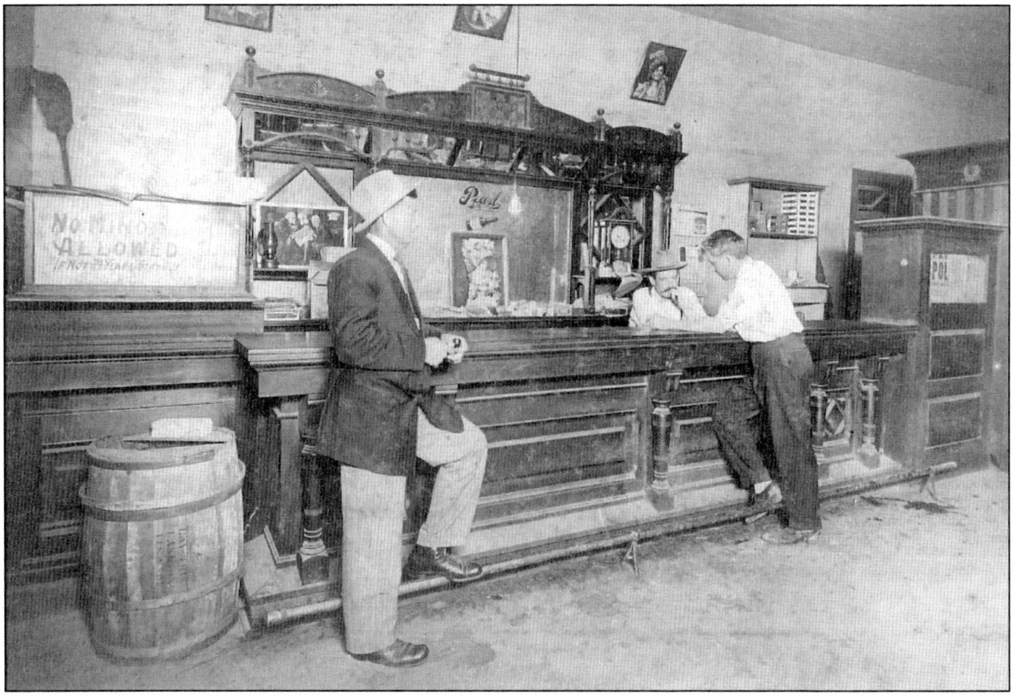

Two gentlemen lean on the bar of the Atlantic Saloon talking to the saloonkeeper. The Atlantic Saloon opened in 1890 and was one of 13 saloons in operation in Yorktown in 1898. On the bar mirror is an advertisement for Pearl Beer. The sign above the barrel reads, "No Minors Allowed/ If Not 21 Years, Stay Out." (Courtesy Robert Muschalek.)

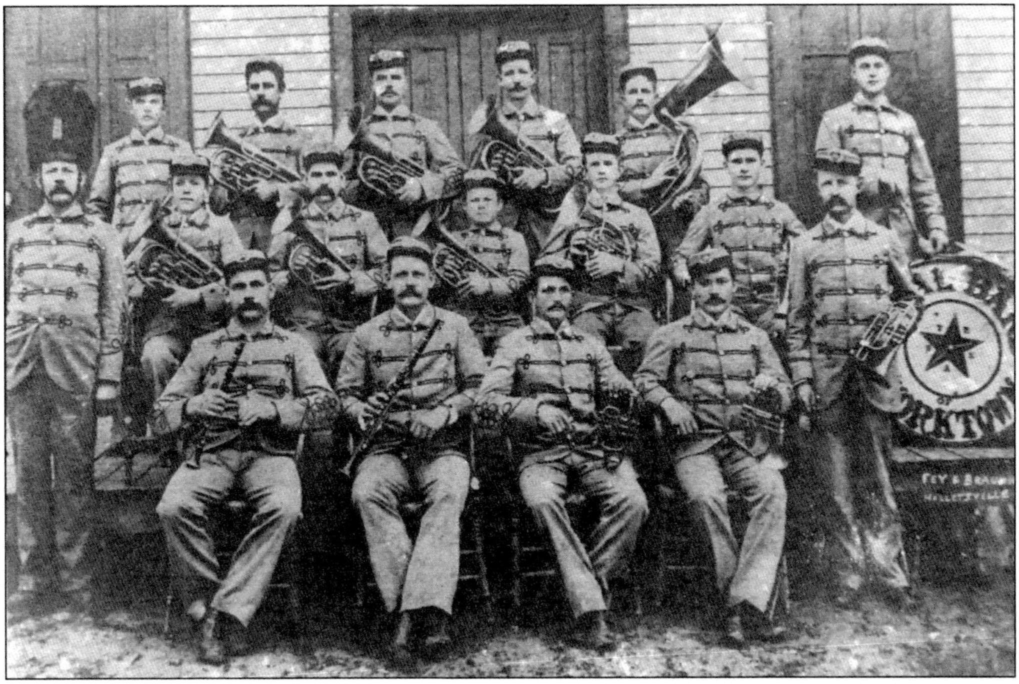

The Ideal Band was formed in the late 1890s and played at various celebrations in neighboring towns and at parties in Yorktown. They won a band competition in Hallettsville on July 4, 1899. Members of the band in 1898 were Charles F. Gerhardt (drum major), Blas Kulawik, Gus Lenz, Thomas Bock, Otto Riedel, Charles L. Strieber, Emil Hohn, Alfred Zedler, Arthur B. Grun, John Letsch, Louis Grun, Andrew A. Strieber, Otto H. Riedel, Ferdinand Strieber, W. F. Strieber, Berthold C. Gohmert, Gustav Schultz, G. A. Wanier, William Mueller, Otto Kraege, and Henry Hohn.

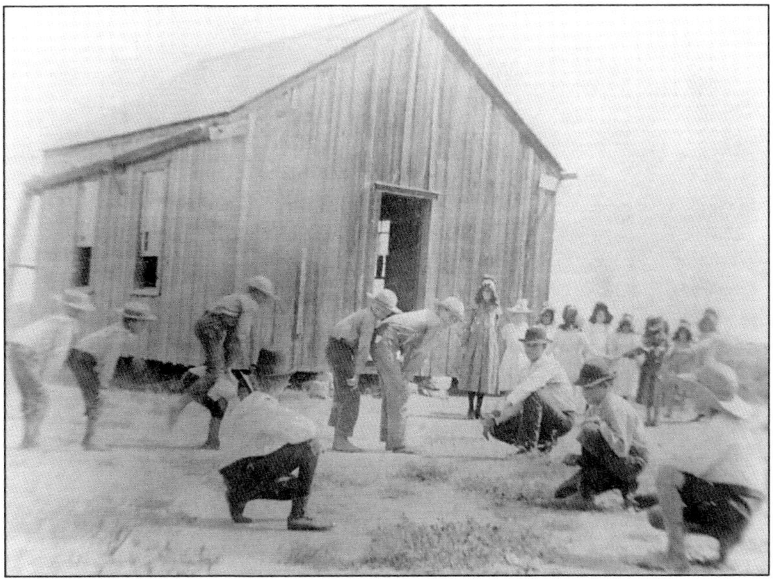

One group of boys plays leapfrog and another a game of marbles while the girls watch in the schoolyard of Yorktown's first stand-alone schoolhouse. It was built in 1855 at a cost of $324. O. Fuchs was the first teacher. One-room schoolhouses were popular in the towns and rural areas of the time.

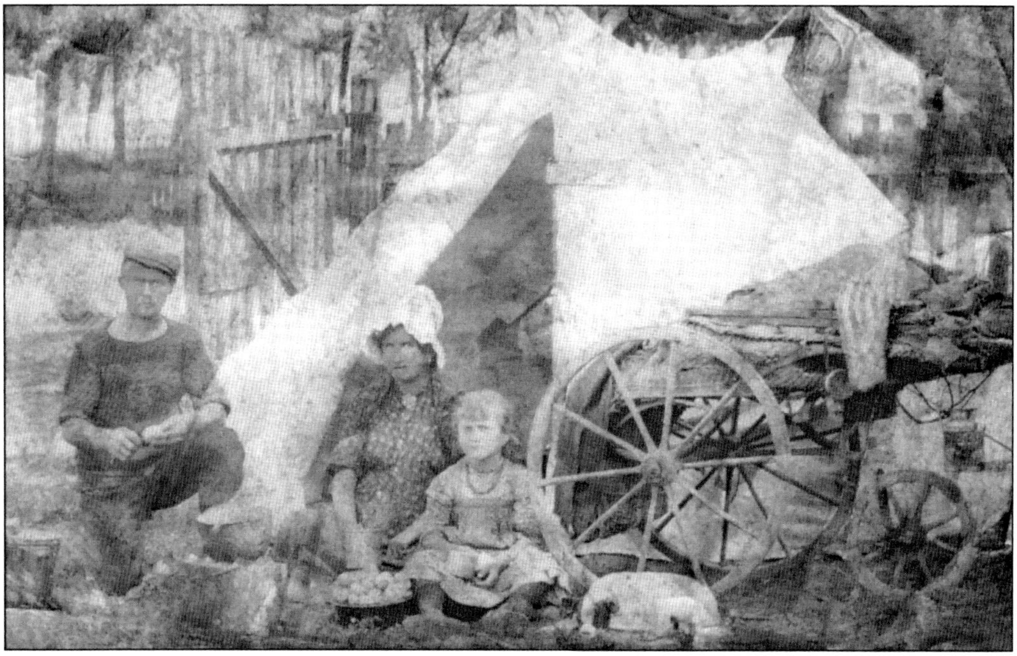

When an immigrant first moved into the area, he did not have a place to stay, so he and his family set up a tent and camped while he readied the land and built a house. Here the parents are peeling potatoes for their next meal while their daughter and dog sit nearby.

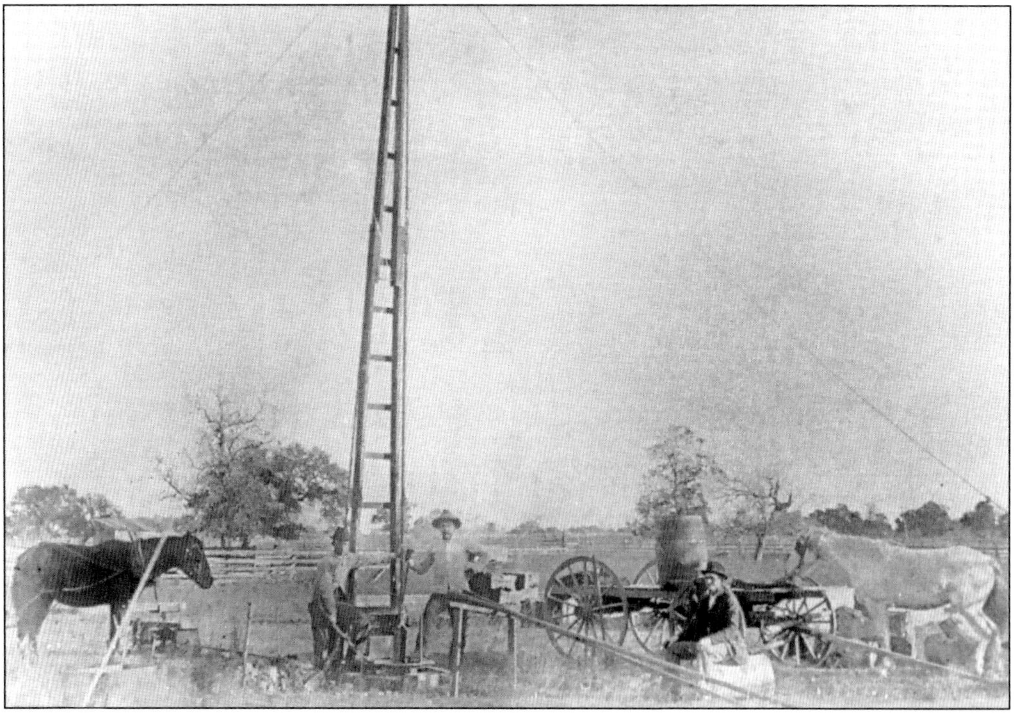

It took a lot of hard work and sweat to drill with this wooden drilling rig. The men and their horses are patiently getting the work done. This rig is very simple compared to the motorized rigs of today.

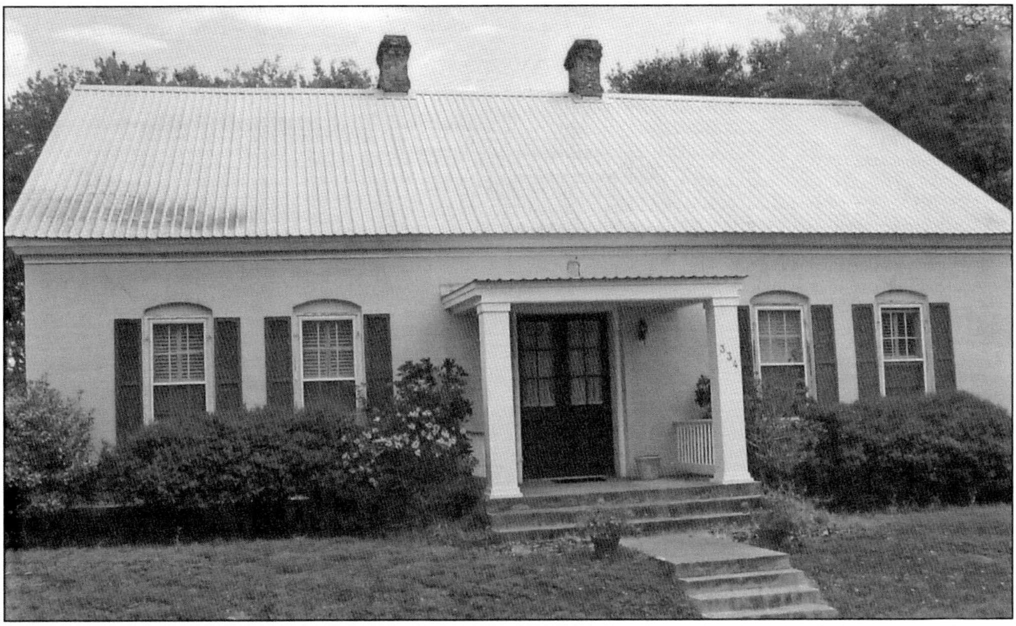

The Gohmert-Gohlke house, located at 334 Hoppe Street near the left bank of Coleto Creek, was the first house in town built of stone. It was built between 1866 and 1870 by Robert Paul Gohmert. The Georgian-style house was built with stones brought by ox cart from 15 miles north of Yorktown. In 1884, the house was sold to F. Wilhelm Gohlke Sr. whose heirs resided there until 1973. In 1978, the house was purchased by Dennis and Susan Phillips. (Courtesy Betty Ladner.)

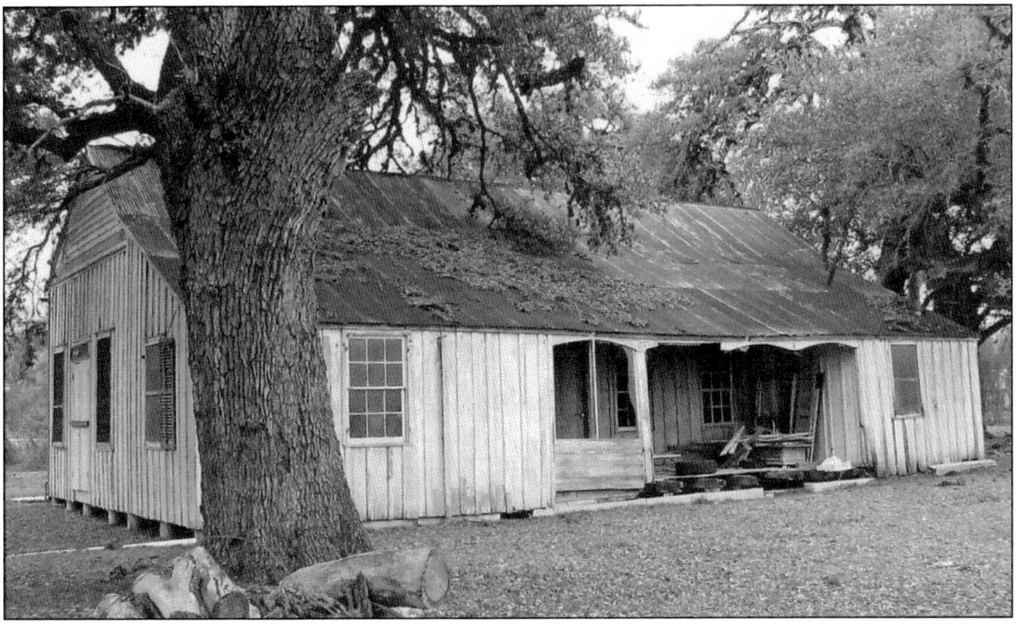

This townhouse was built in 1866 in what was later known as Upper Yorktown. It was built for Dr. William Cornick along the Indianola road for his wife Mary Labaitte Cornick. They had four children, William Jr., Mary, Adaline, and Agnes. The road brought Dr. Cornick many patients, as did the Texas Rangers. Dr. Cornick died October 20, 1871, and was buried in the Upper Yorktown (Friar) Cemetery. (Courtesy Betty Ladner.)

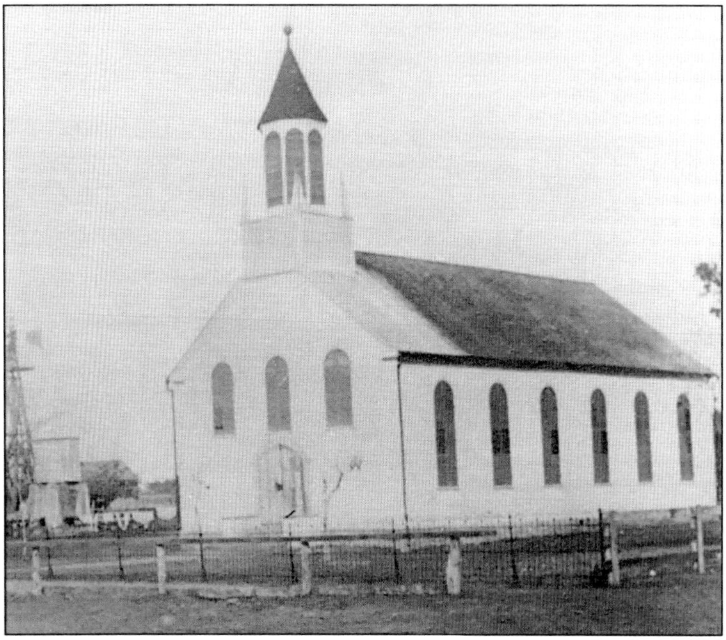

At first, the Lutherans met with opposition from a portion of the townspeople who did not want a church in the town proper. However, a group of Lutherans led by C. W. Nau, A. Sauermilch, M. Thiele, C. C. Stephan, and C. Dahlmann erected a church that was consecrated October 13, 1872, with Reverend Lettermann becoming its pastor. The wooden structure was 30 by 60 feet in diameter. In 1907 it was enlarged by 35 feet.

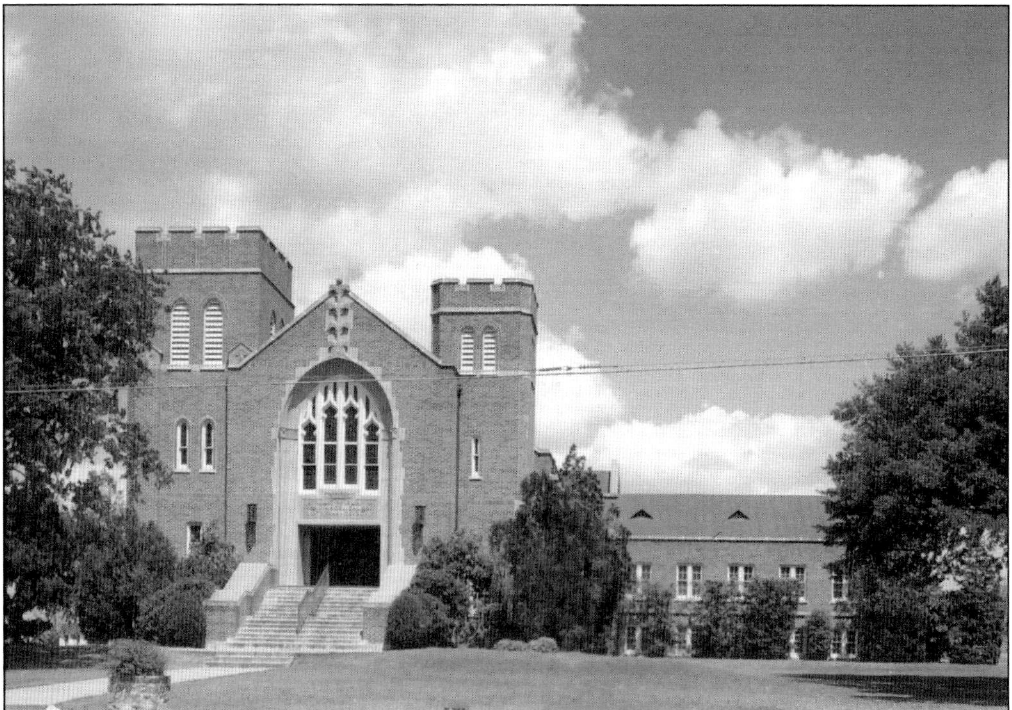

As the congregation grew, a large gothic red brick church was built. St. Paul Lutheran Church was dedicated May 31, 1931. A red brick parsonage was built in 1927, and an educational building was added in 1958. The church celebrated its 125th anniversary April 20, 1997. A massive oak tree on its front lawn is nearly 200 years old.

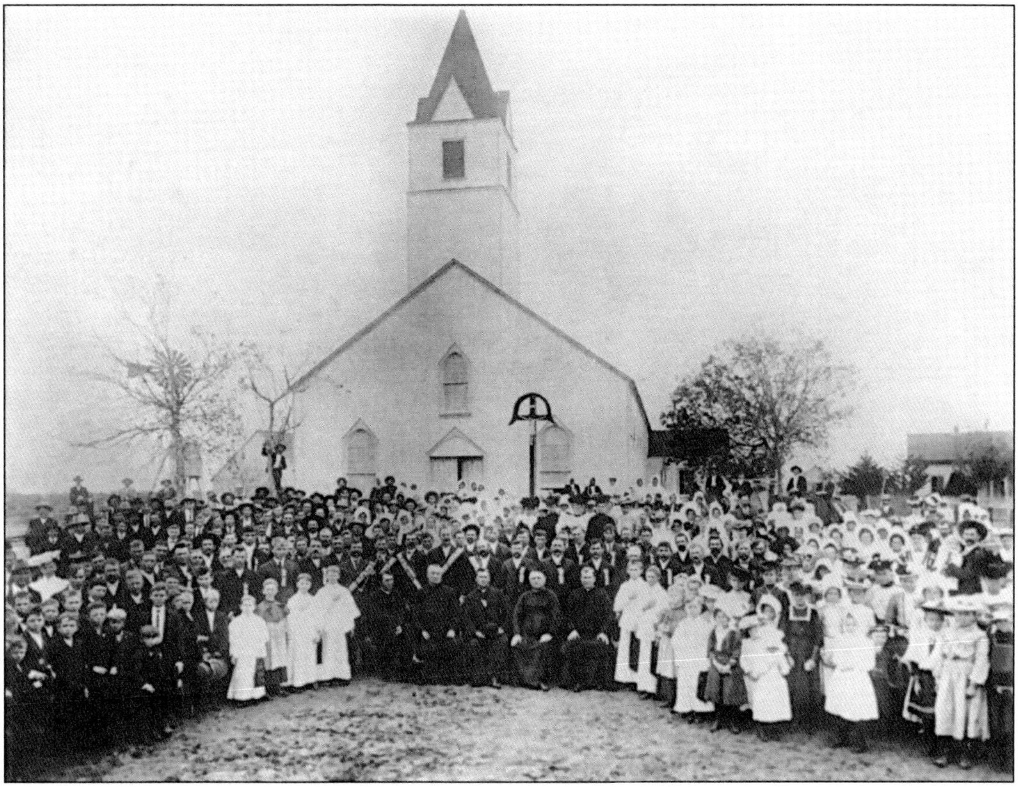

The congregation stands outside St. Mary's Catholic Church of the Immaculate Conception. It was built in 1868. In 1897, Fr. Thomas Moczygemba founded the congregation, consisting of 100 Polish members, 35 Bohemians, and a few Germans. The building was destroyed by fire April 7, 1914.

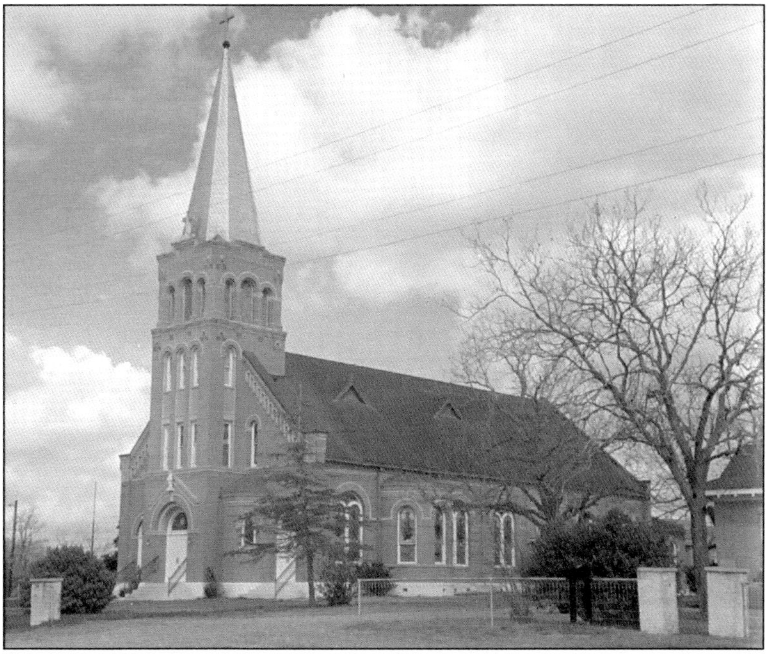

Holy Cross Catholic Church, a red brick building, was blessed on September 14, 1915. In 1947, a new Holy Cross School opened to replace the one built in 1870. In 1983, the school was converted into a Catholic Activity Center.

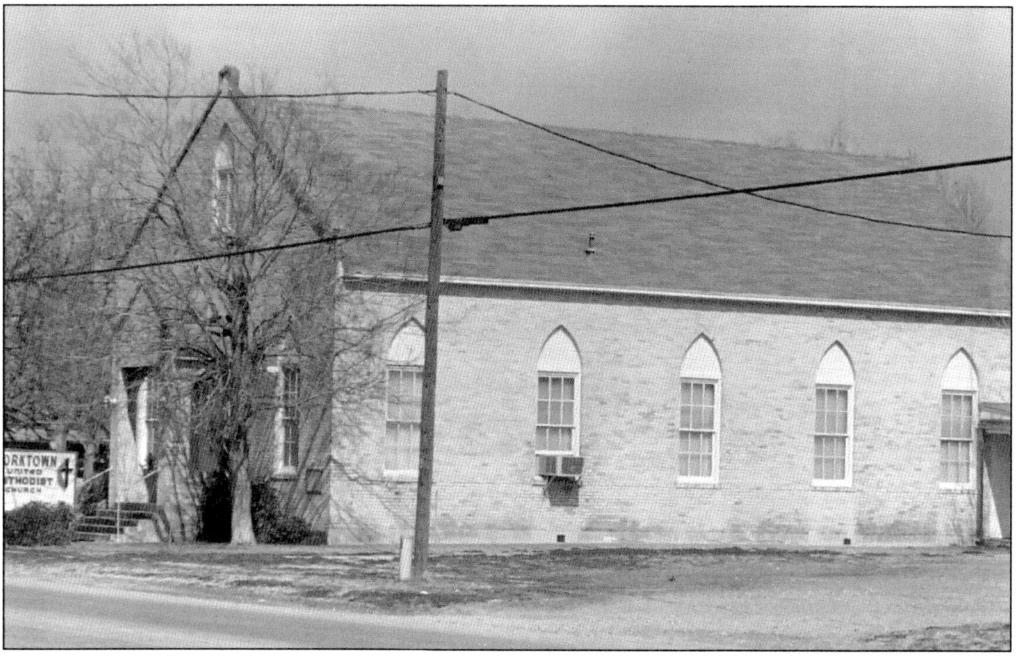

In 1854, a Methodist congregation met in private homes, but a brick church was eventually erected in 1929 with H. R. Gohlke as contractor. In 1956, the United Methodist Church built an educational building with a new fellowship hall added in 1982.

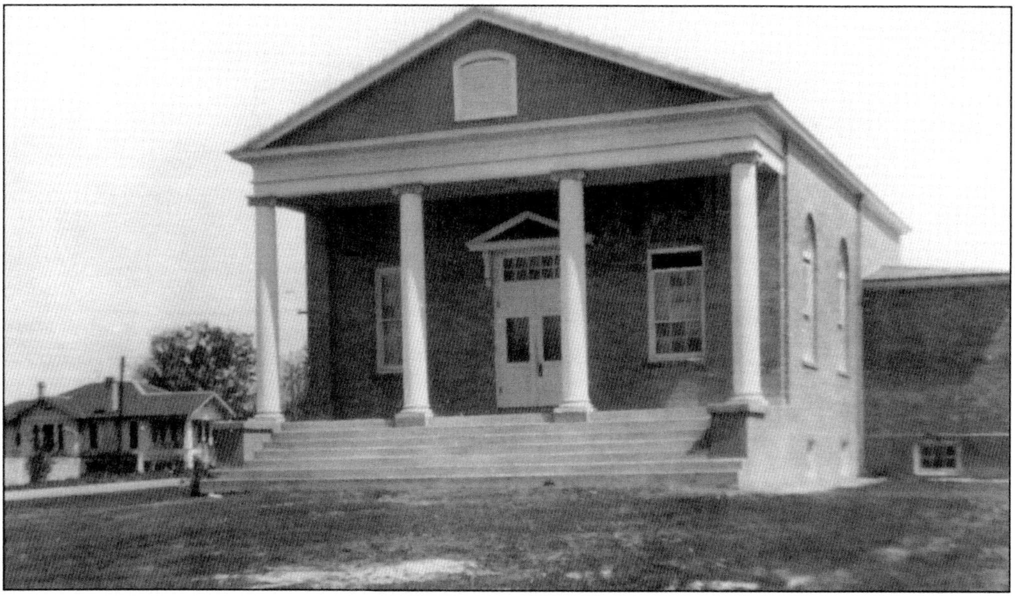

The Presbyterian Church formally began in 1896, meeting on the lower floor of the Masonic Lodge. The first church was a small frame building located on Third Street in 1897. The present Presbyterian Church was built by contractor H. R. Gohlke on land donated by Mr. and Mrs. John Alford of Topeka, Kansas. It held its first service September 13, 1925. The Alfords also donated pulpit furniture, pews, and a bell. In 1935, J. G. Kerlick built the bell tower in memory of his son J. G. Kerlick Jr. The stained glass windows were added in 1953, and in 1957 an educational building was built.

Two

Yorktown After 1900

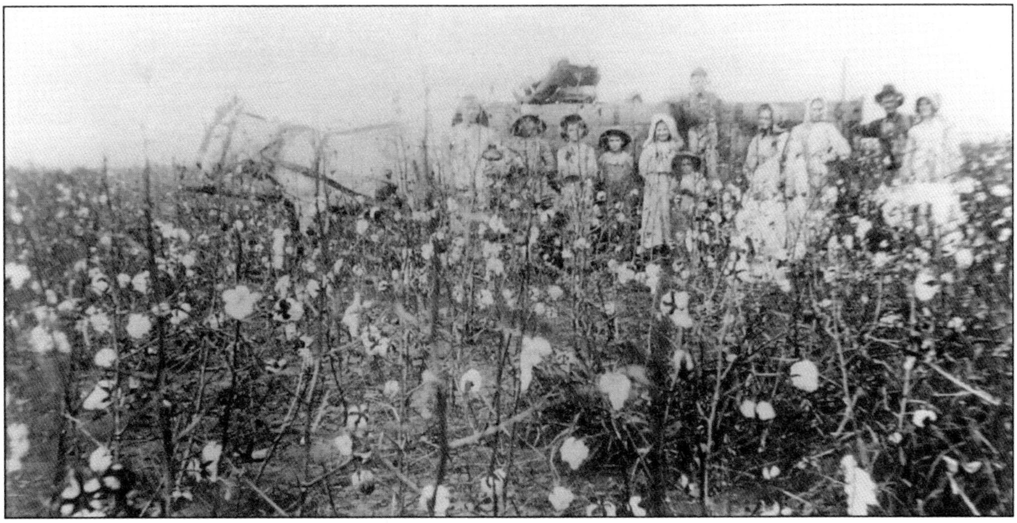

Cotton was king as a major cash crop in the early 1900s. Yorktown shipped as many as 15,000 bales of cotton a year. Every member of the family helped with the cotton picking, from the parents to the children. The child too young to pick either played in the shade under the wagon or rode on the bottom end of the mother's cotton sack.

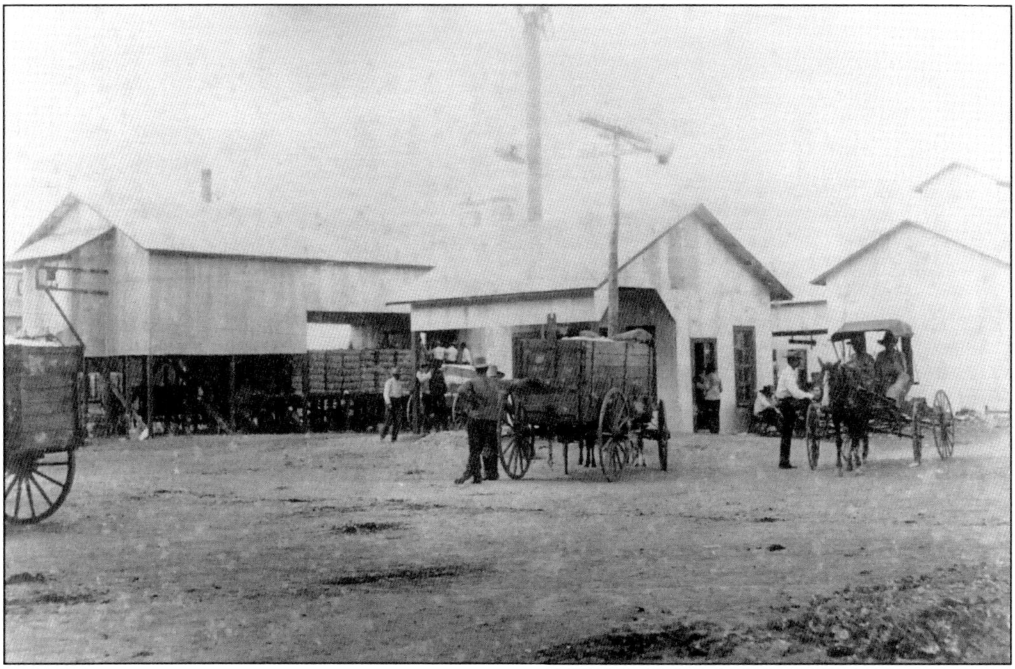

It seems to be a busy day at the Gras Gin. It was one of the leading cotton centers in DeWitt County. While waiting for their turns to unload cotton, men would discuss their crops and the weather.

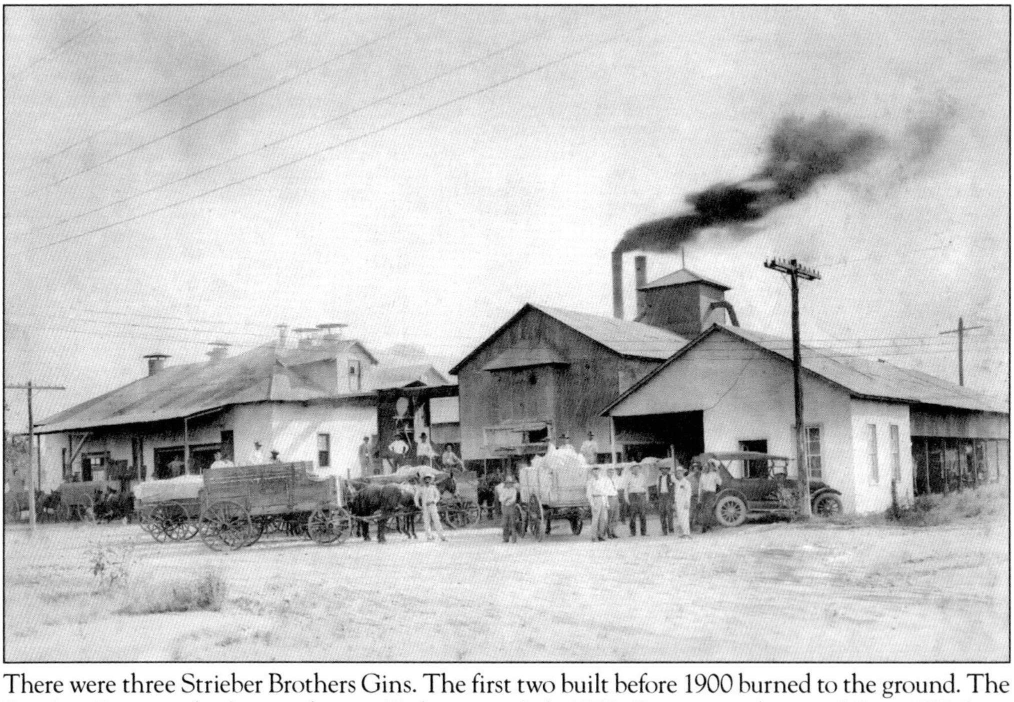

There were three Strieber Brothers Gins. The first two built before 1900 burned to the ground. The Strieber Gin was the last to close in Yorktown in July 1970. Cotton production fell in 1959 from a high in 1930 of 47,816 bales to 4,256 bales. The Jerry Strieber family sold the building to Geary and Judy Taylor who ran Taylor's Farm Supply until 1998. Following two other owners, the gin closed in 2002. The building was sold again and dismantled in 2009. (Courtesy Bea McKinney.)

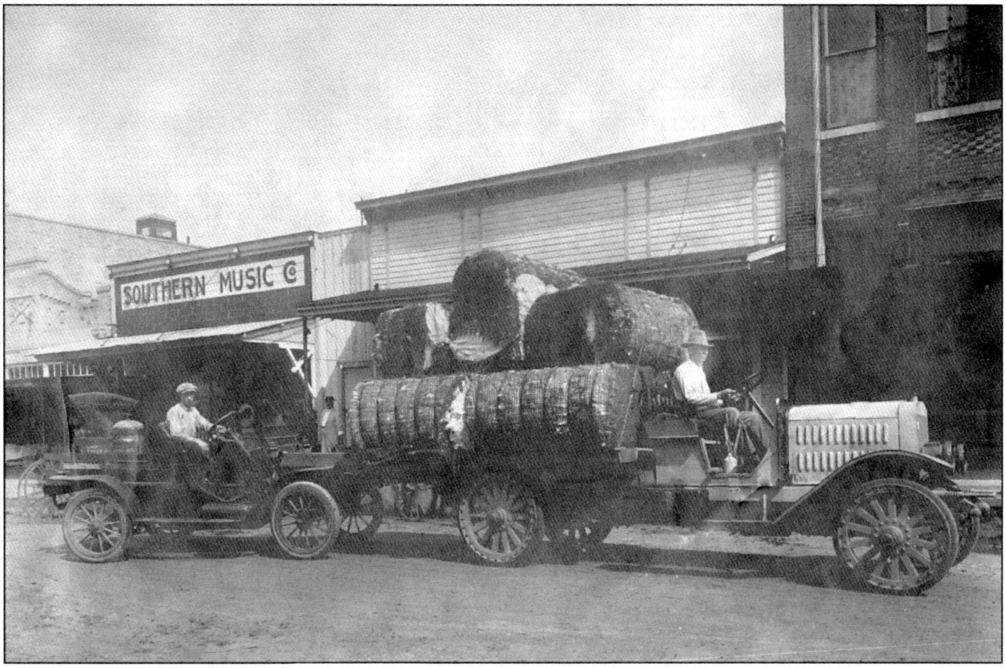

H. A. Mayer is driving a truck loaded with cotton bales. The solid tires deliver a rough ride, but there is no worry about having a flat. Standing on the sidewalk next to the Southern Music Company is R. G. Jersig. (Courtesy Robert Muschalek.)

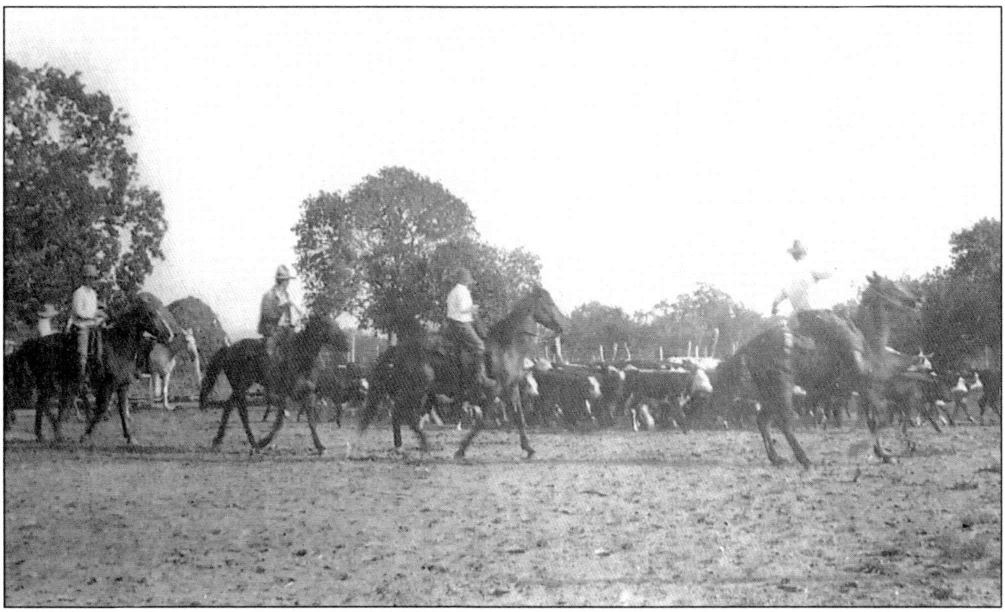

Cattle were an important part of the agricultural economy in the area. The cattle were used as food and as a means of income when taken to market. Here the cowboys are herding the cattle toward the dipping vat on the Menn ranch. Often neighbors would help each other and also bring their cattle over to be dipped to rid them of flies. The rider in the middle wearing a white shirt is Ella Menn. The other riders are Adolph Menn, Fred Menn, Lee Alves, and Gerhardt Henze. (Courtesy Beverly Bruns.)

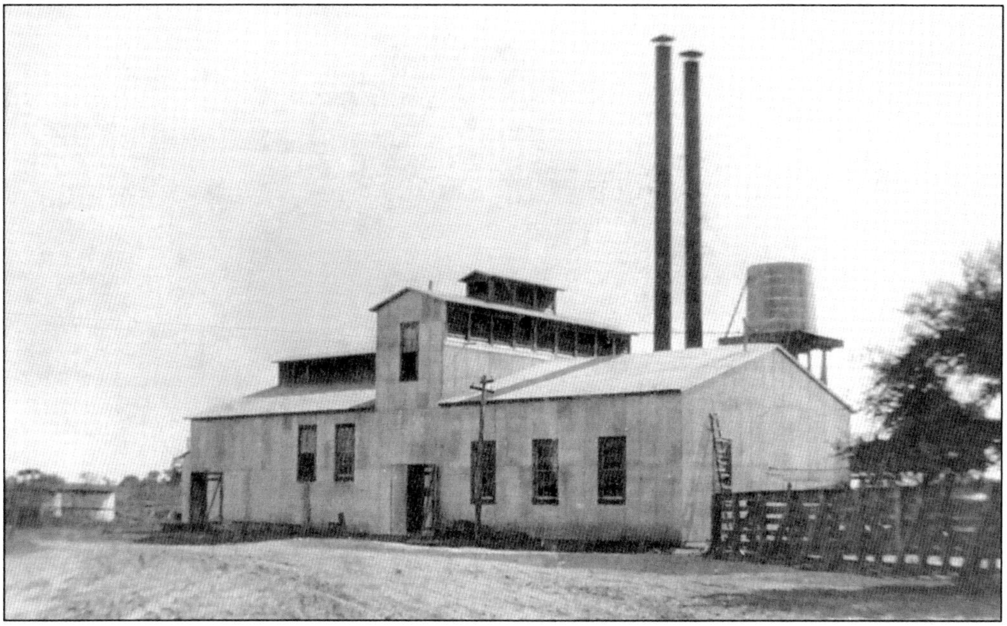

The first electricity provided by the Light Plant in this 1908 photograph was used to power lights in the business section of Yorktown. Richard Eckhardt was instrumental in acquiring the plant. In 1924, after several ownership changes, the business was sold to Central Power and Light.

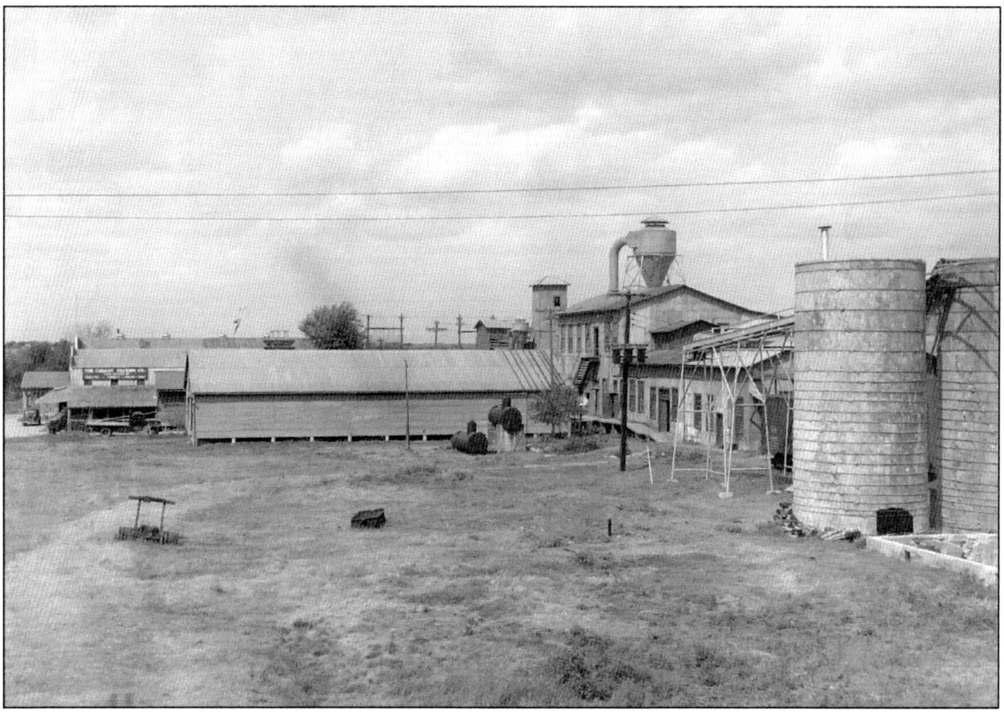

This industrial site located at First and Eckhardt Streets included the Cudahay Packing Company, which was a hatchery and feed store, the Cotton Oil Mill, the Peanut Oil Mill, and a turkey slaughtering plant. The Cotton Oil Mill was organized by William Eckhardt, president and manager. With the help of John George Kerlick, it became an important business in the area.

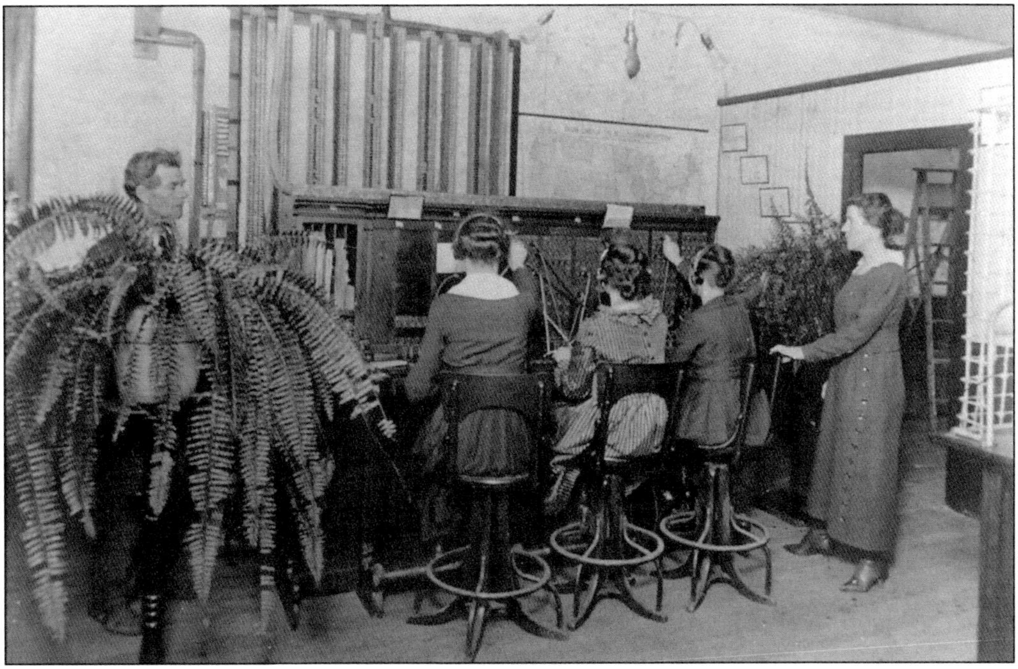

The telephone office was located on the second floor of the building on the southeast corner of East Main and Riedel Streets. Here operators are using the switchboard to connect telephone patrons in the 1920s. Elsie Poetter is standing on the right. The Eureka Telephone Company and J. A. Moore of San Antonio provided the first telephone service in Yorktown to A. W. Elmore's barbershop. In 1912, the company was sold to Southwestern Bell Telephone Company.

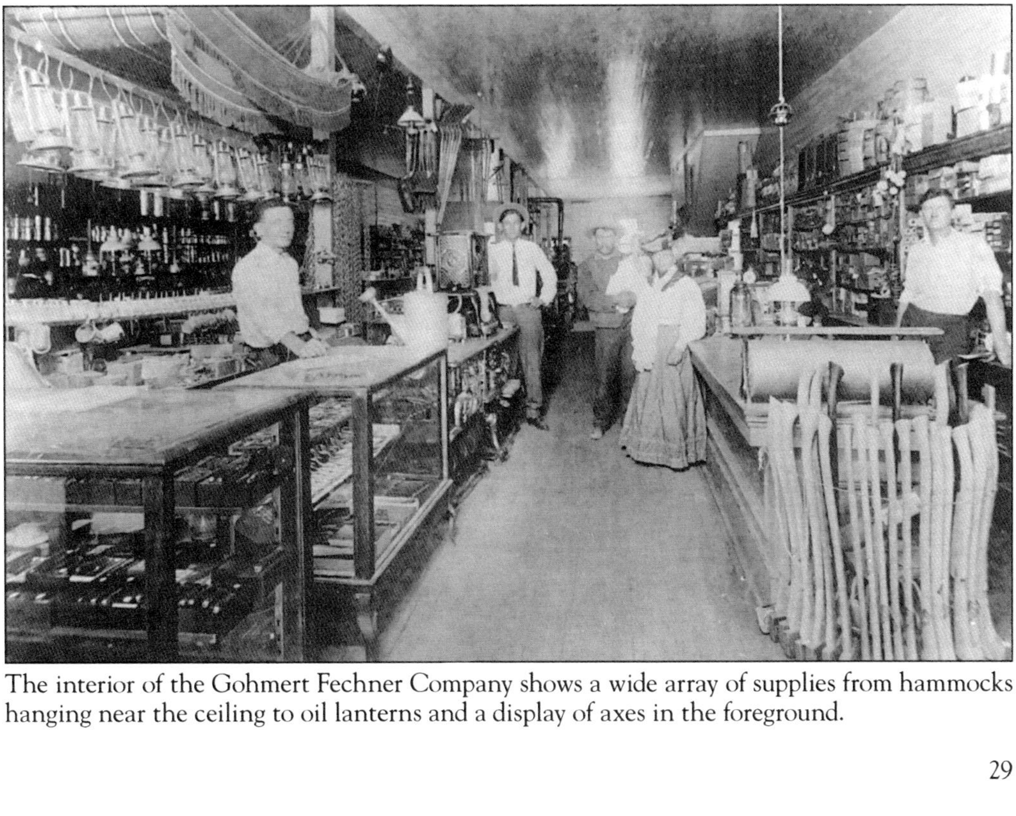

The interior of the Gohmert Fechner Company shows a wide array of supplies from hammocks hanging near the ceiling to oil lanterns and a display of axes in the foreground.

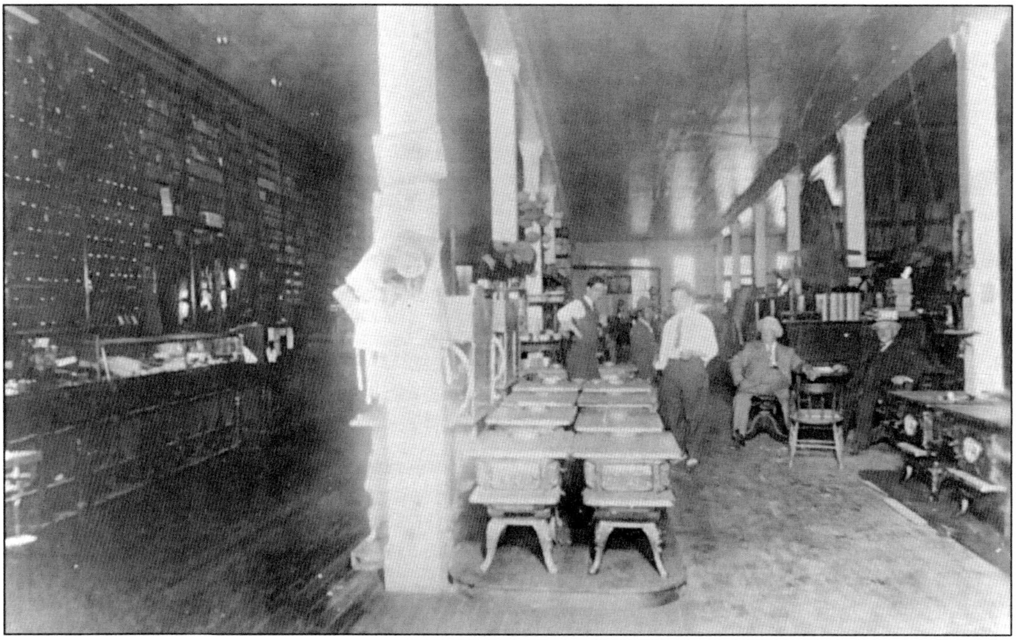

Customers are sitting in chairs at the right side of the store while others are milling around in the Bond George Hardware Company. The store featured wood-burning stoves and, on the left, a wall of boxes filled with hardware. Wood-burning stoves were a popular means of heating a home and were also used in cooking.

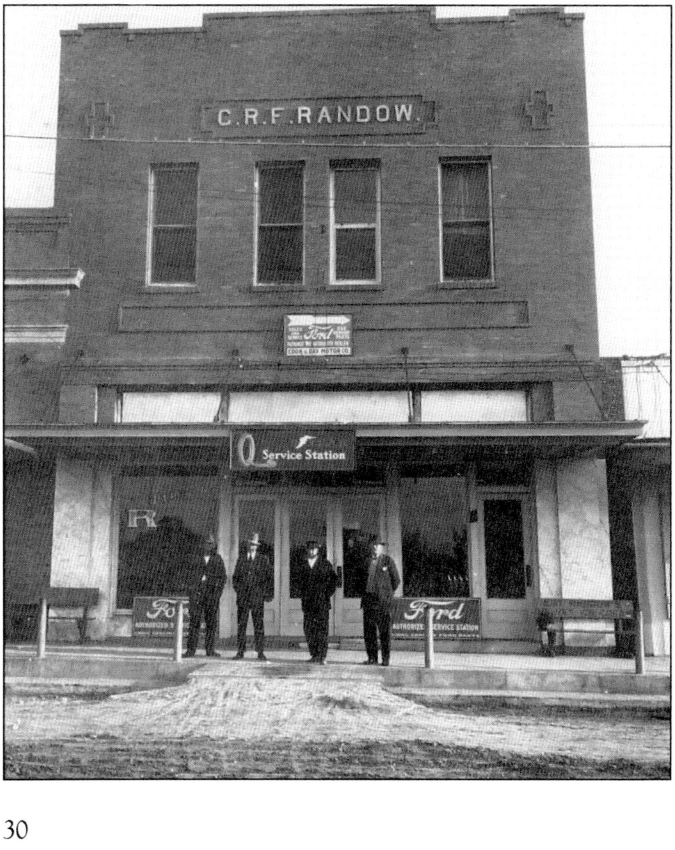

The C. R. F. Randow building housed the Cook and Day Motor Company, which was an authorized Ford sales and service station. Genuine Ford parts were used in their repairs. (Courtesy Linda Hurta.)

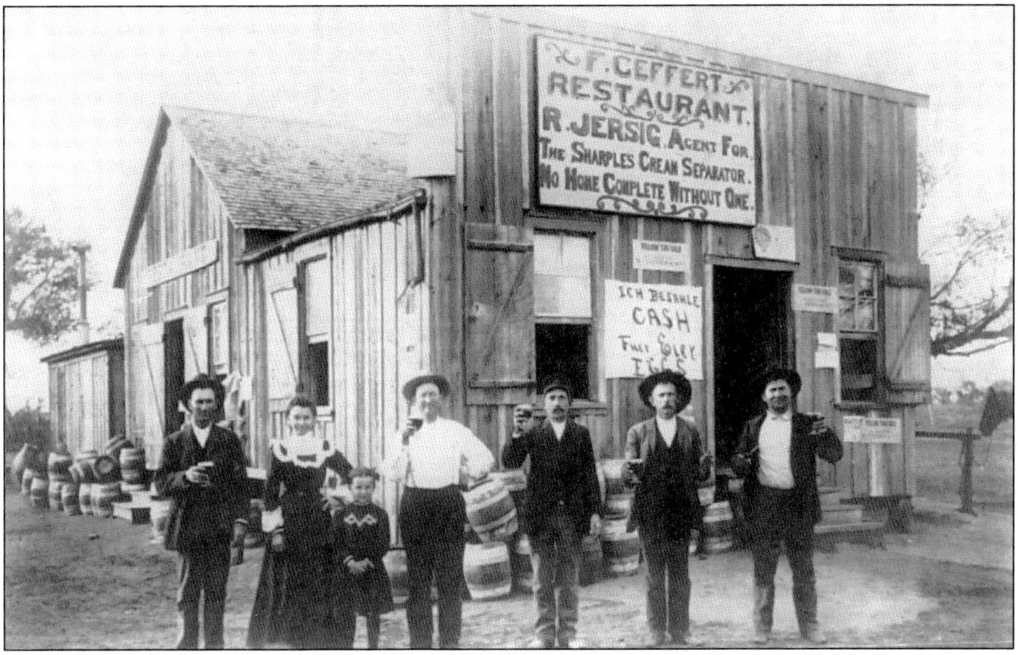

The men outside the F. Geffert Restaurant are making a toast with mugs of beer. Notice the kegs lining the outside of the building. A sign on the building advertises R. Jersig as an agent for the Sharples Cream Separator. "No home complete without one." (Courtesy Linda Hurta.)

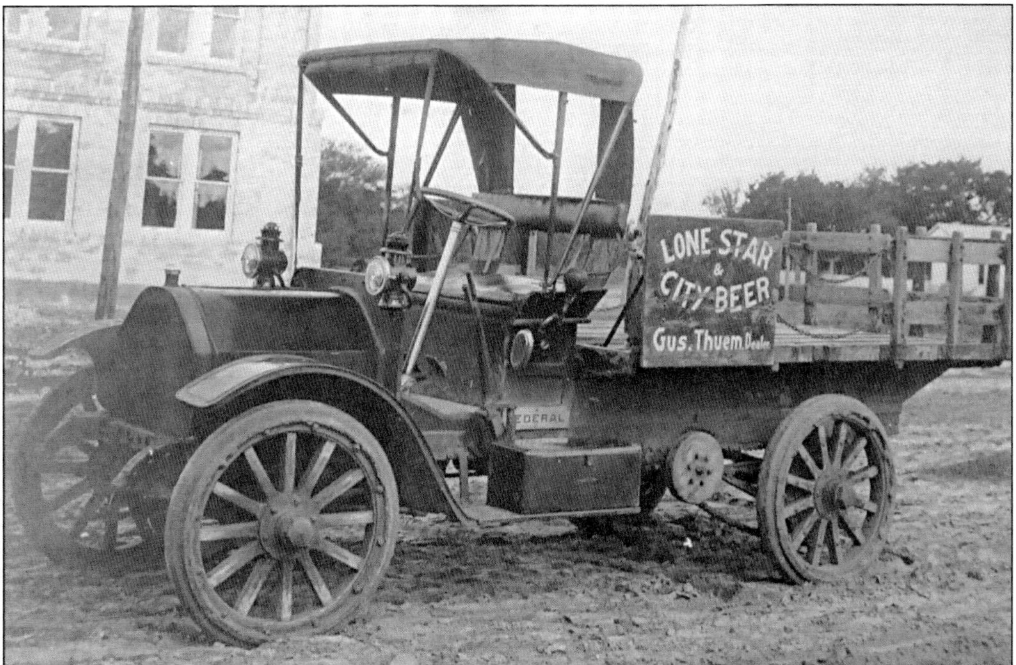

Gus Thuem drove this hard-wheeled truck to deliver beer for his Lone Star and City Beer distributorship. Notice the chain drive on the rear axle and the light lamps high on the cab of the truck. (Courtesy Linda Hurta.)

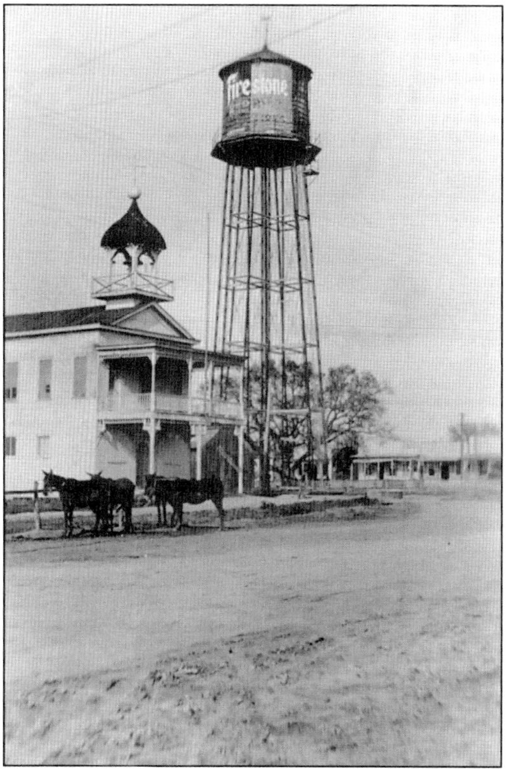

A volunteer fire department was organized in 1901, with a fire hall built in 1902. The hall was a two-story frame building with a cupola used as a bell tower. The first fire chief was Gus Nau. Next to the fire hall was the town's water tower. In 1919, the tower was painted to advertise Firestone. A new brick fire station was built in 1951, and a jaws of life was purchased in 1996.

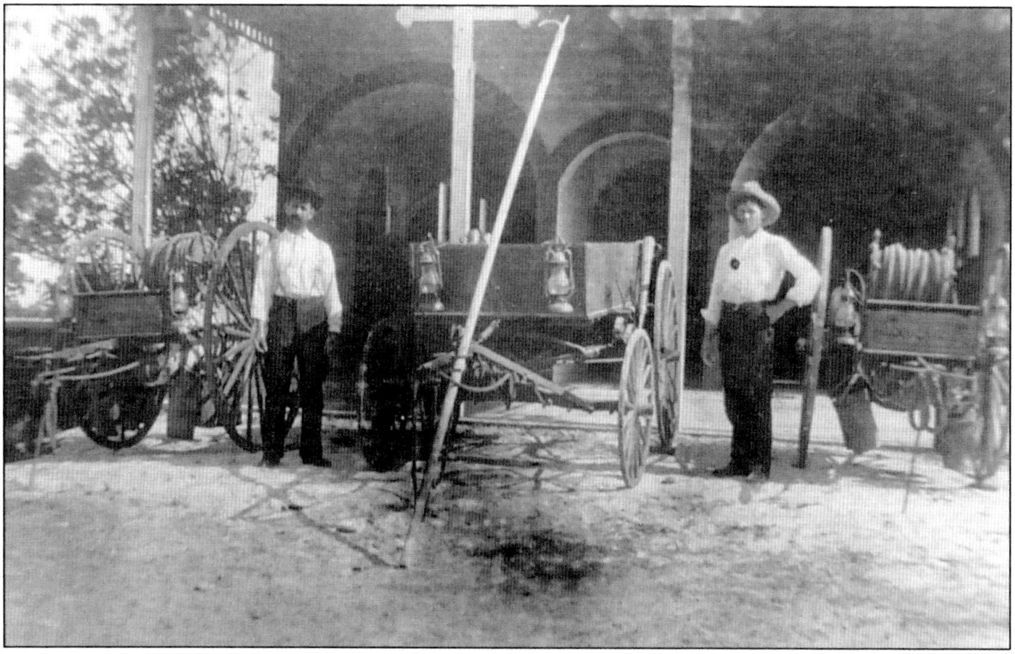

In front of the open doors of the fire hall are three fire wagons. The two outside wagons with the hoses are called pumper wagons and were used to pump water onto the fire. The wagons are propelled down the street by manpower, but occasionally someone would hitch his horse to the wagons to get to a fire quicker.

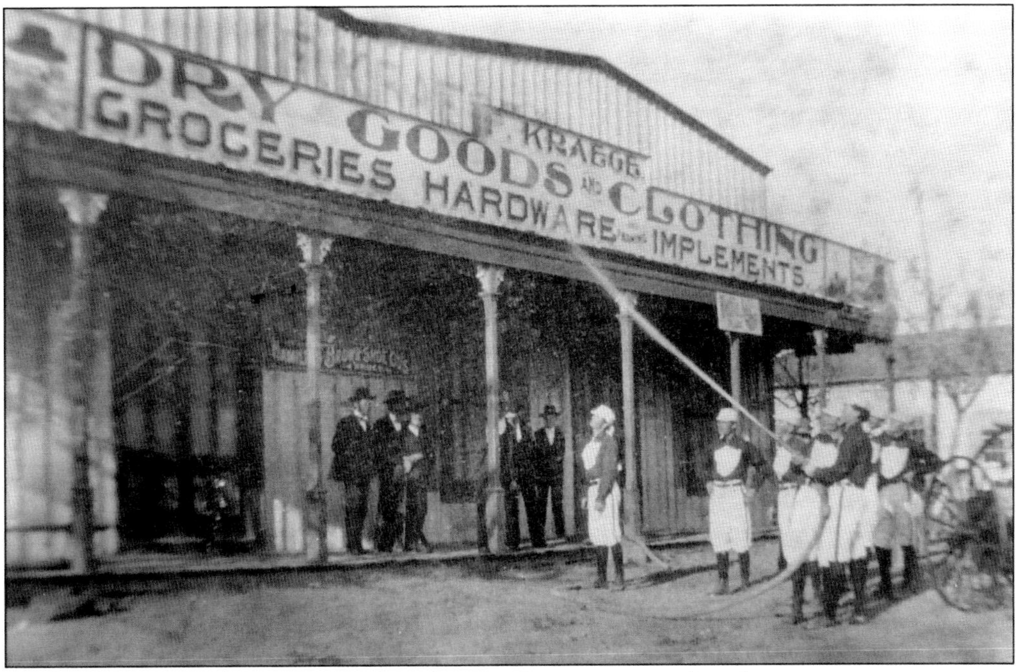

Members of the fire department in their dress uniforms are using their fire wagon pumper to spray clean the sign above the F. Kraege Store, featuring dry goods, clothing, groceries, hardware, and implements. In a form of competition, the firemen competed with fire companies in area towns running with the fire wagons to see who could get to a fire first.

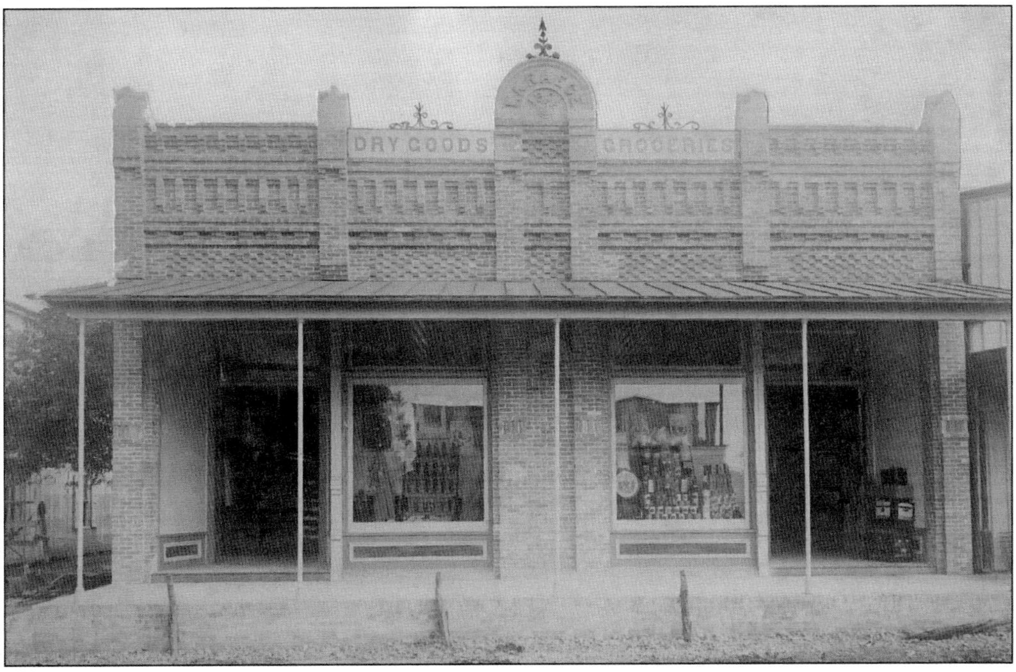

In 1901, the F. Kraege Store was built out of bricks with a concrete and brick porch next door to the old store. One side of the building featured dry goods and the other had groceries. Notice the three posts standing in front of the porch for customers to tie horses. (Courtesy Robert Muschalek.)

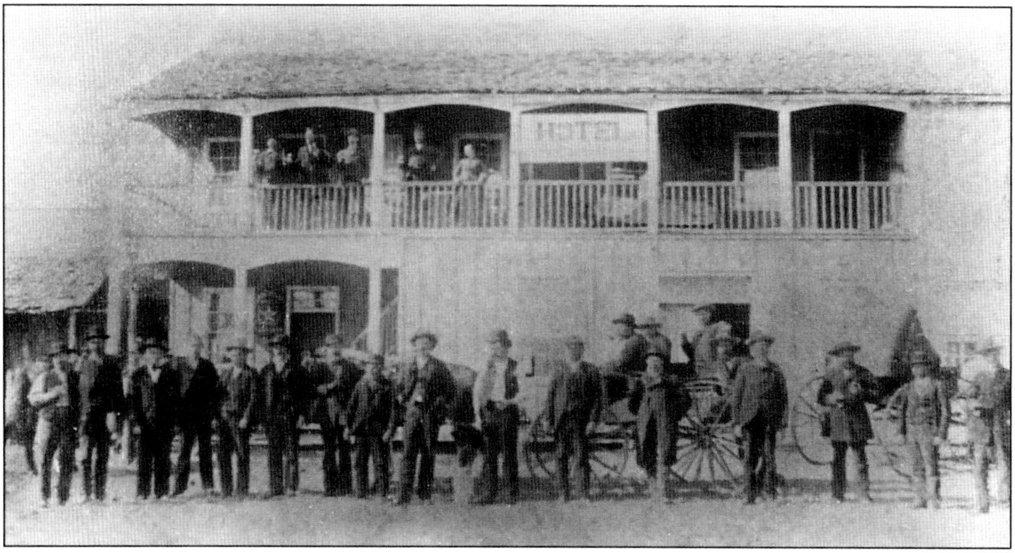

Many citizens are pictured standing outside the Duerr Hotel. The men are, from left to right, William Duerr, Adolph Noster, Louis Schumacher, William Zuch, Milam Harper, Hy. Borchers, Ludwig Zuch, Henry Poetter, Carl Strieber, William Thuem, Fred Gips, Joe Neumayer Sr., August Riedesel Sr., William Lude, Carl Bade, and Otto Mathis. In the buggy are Carl Bluhm, Robert Zuch, Ernest Zuch, and August Riedesel Jr.

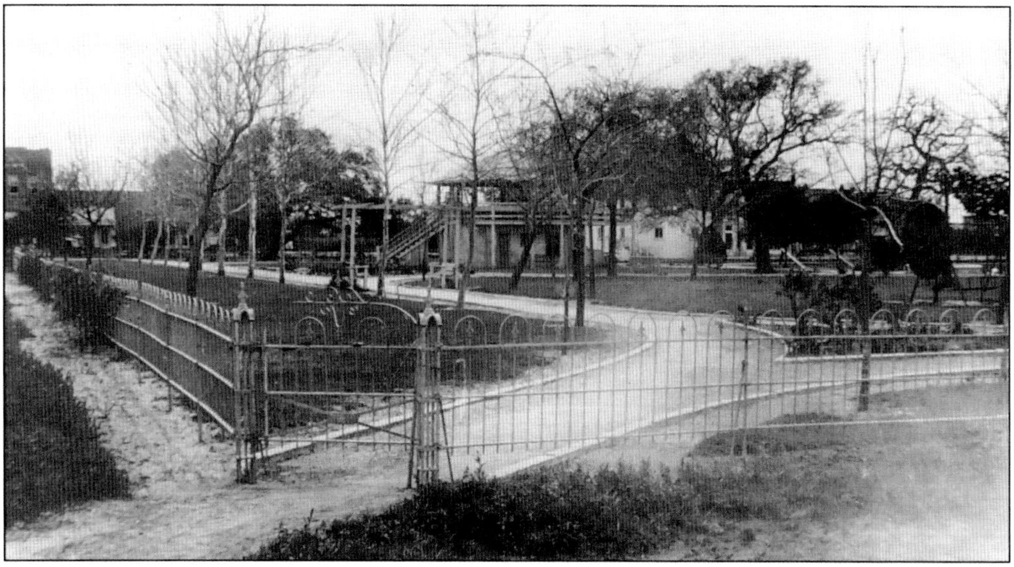

In the early 1900s, the city park of Yorktown was surrounded by a decorative metal fence. Notice the neat brick-edged walkways and the bandstand along the left walkway. The park contained flowerbeds, a gazebo, merry-go-rounds, a slide, and a two-seat Ferris wheel that is still in the park almost a century later.

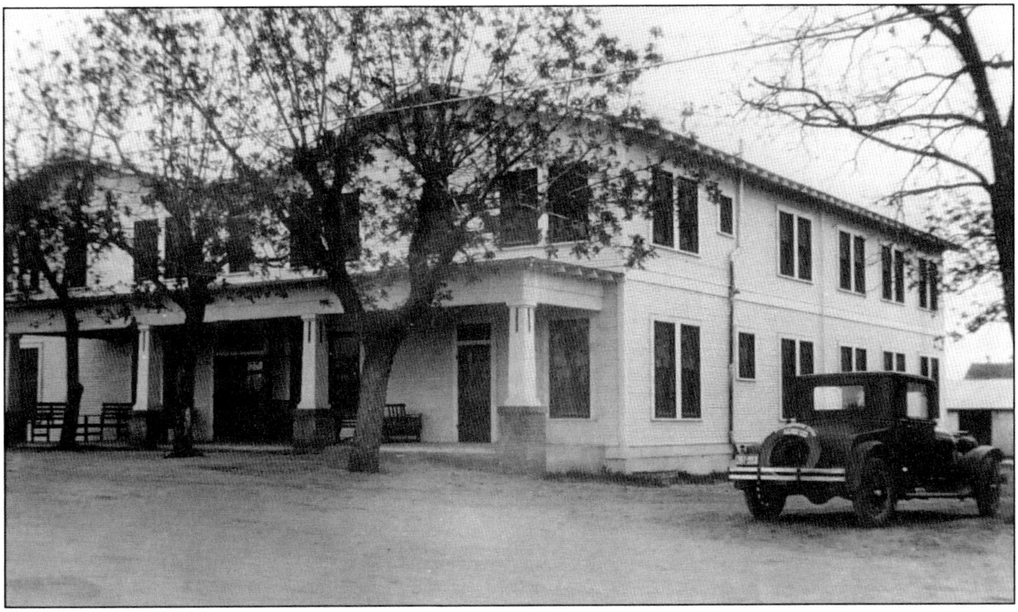

The Smith Hotel was located on the west side of the Coleto Creek along Main Street. It was owned and operated by Frank and Elsa Jacob Smith. This hotel was recognized as the first hotel in the South Texas area to have running water in each guest room.

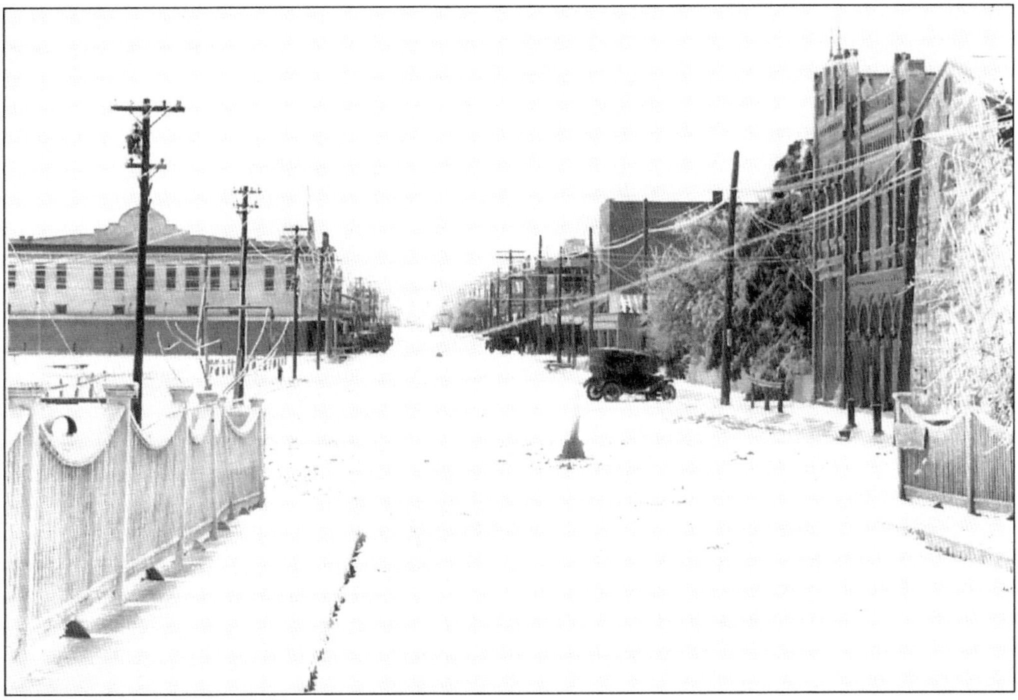

Snow is a rare occurrence in Yorktown, happening approximately every 10 to 15 years. Looking east from the wooden bridge and railing built in 1904 by Reinhold Jacob, one can see a snow-covered Main Street with ice covering the tree branches to the right of the bridge. This photograph was taken in the mid-1920s. (Courtesy Arlene Schroeder.)

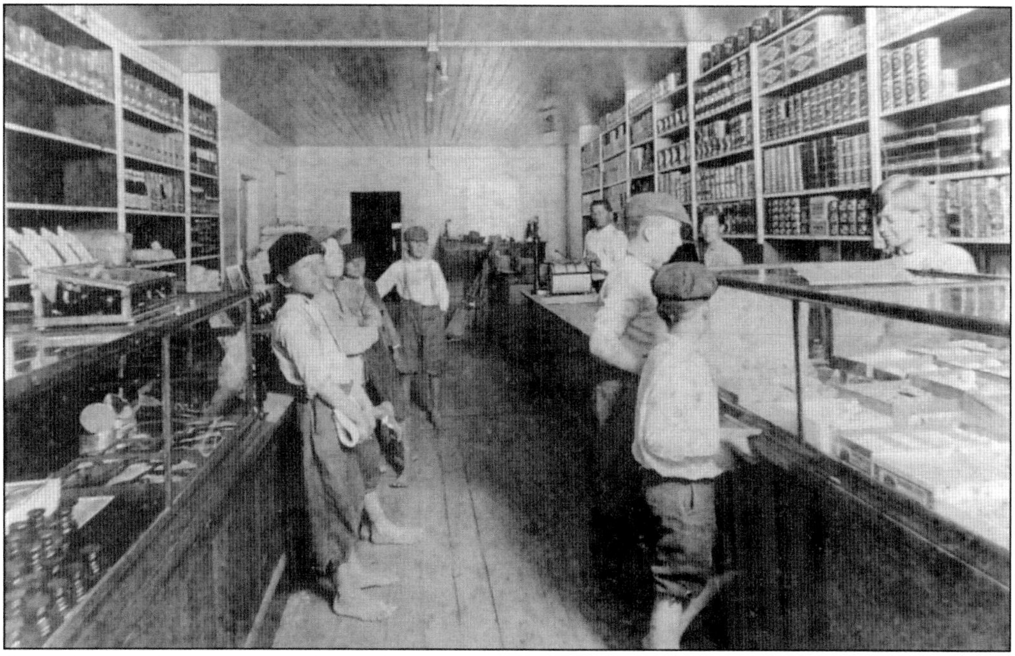

Several young boys attended the Eicholtz Store's first day of business on March 10, 1911. It looks like the young man waiting on the two boys is about the same age.

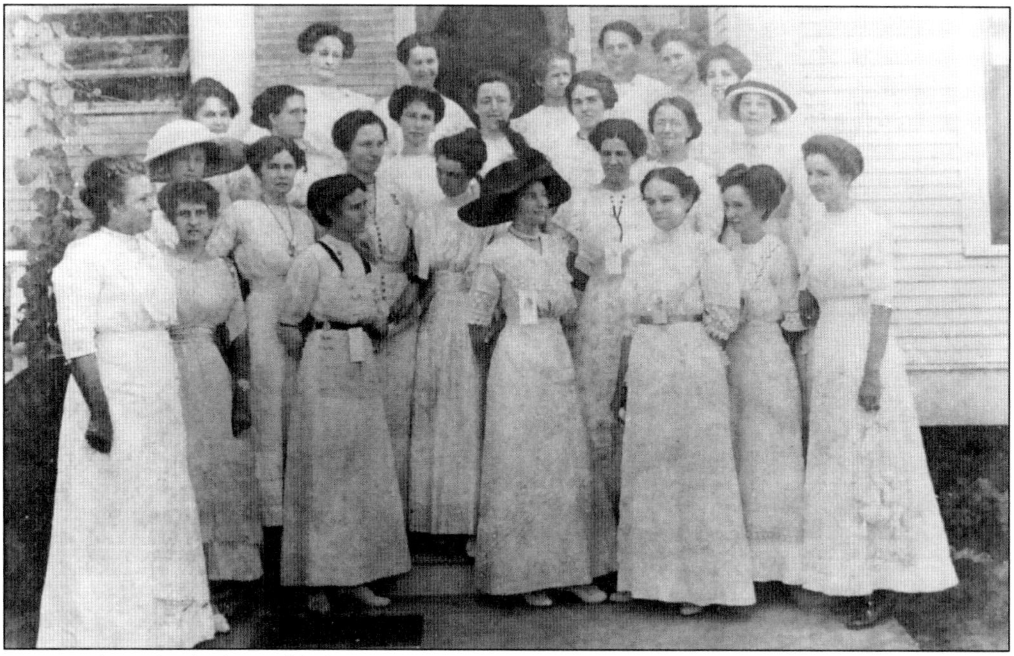

In 1912, these finely dressed ladies were guests at a card party at the home of Mrs. J. W. Westhoff Sr. From left to right are (first row) Helen Hoff, Hermine Fechner, Bertha Kraege, Jane Gohmert, Ella Vierick, and Jane Thuem; (second row) Fritchen Schuhart, Lilly Davies, Emmie Randow, Ada Ladner, and Emily Young; (third row) Hilda Ehlers, Alice Neumayer, Ida Metz, Etchen Kraege, Ida Gohmert, and Lou Westhoff; (fourth row) Nettie Metz, Josie Strieber, Lena Strieber, Marie Strieber, and Lillian Allen.

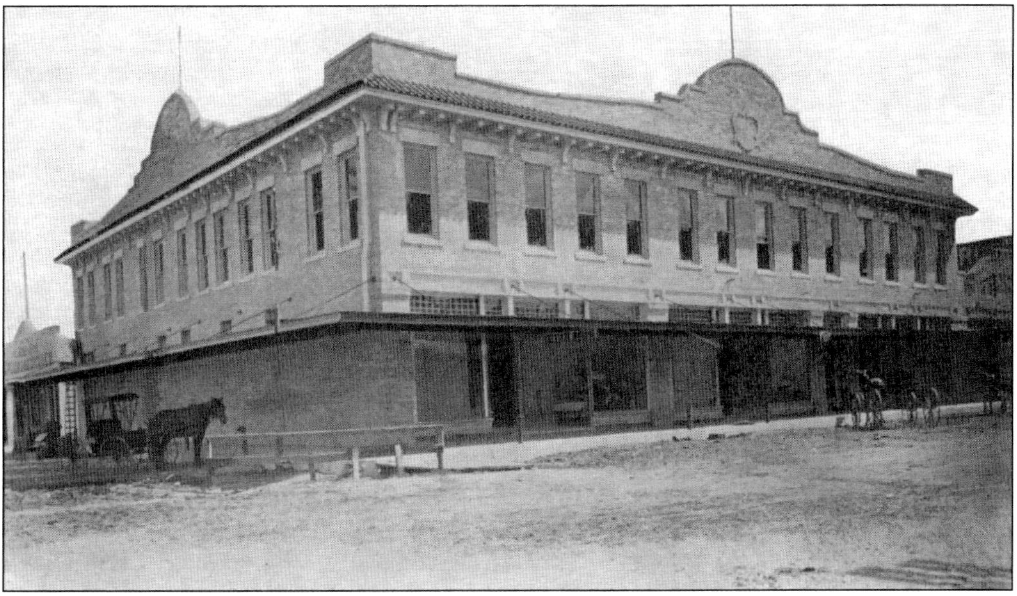

The Riedel Building was located on the corner of Main and Riedel Streets. It began as a dry goods, grocery, and hardware store by Carl Nau and Mr. Bauer. Nau was a chemist and pharmacist, so he opened a prescription and patent medicine department. M. F. Riedel took over the pharmacy and renamed it M. Riedel and Sons. It remained in the family until the 1980s when it was sold to Melvin and Brenda Podsim. It closed in 1989. (Courtesy Robert Muschalek.)

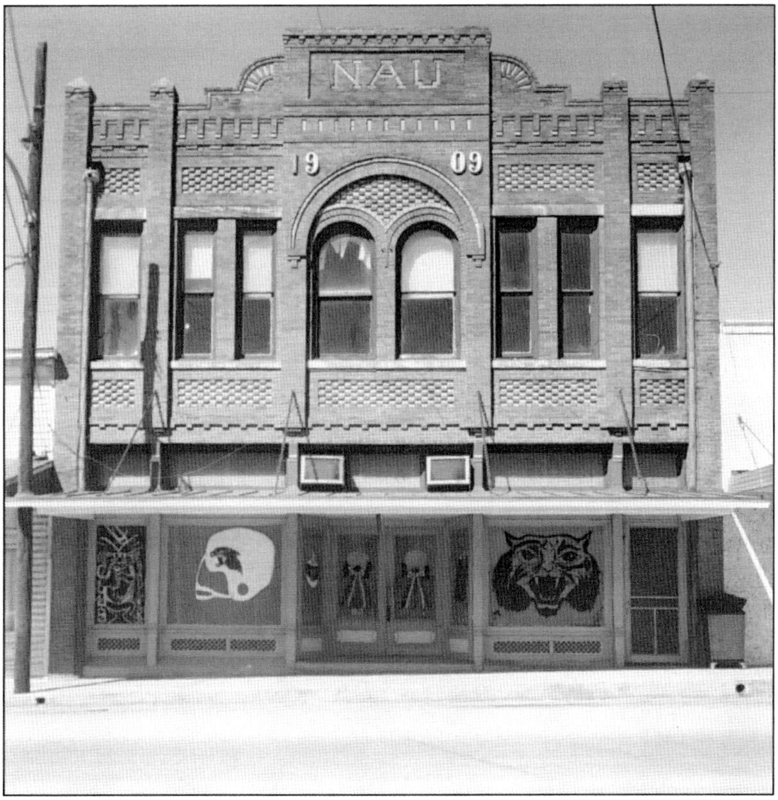

The Nau Building was built in 1909. Here in the mid-1900s the store promoted Homecoming Week as students painted the windows of the store to boost school spirit during football season. On each door is a homecoming corsage of mums and ribbons. (Courtesy Robert Muschalek.)

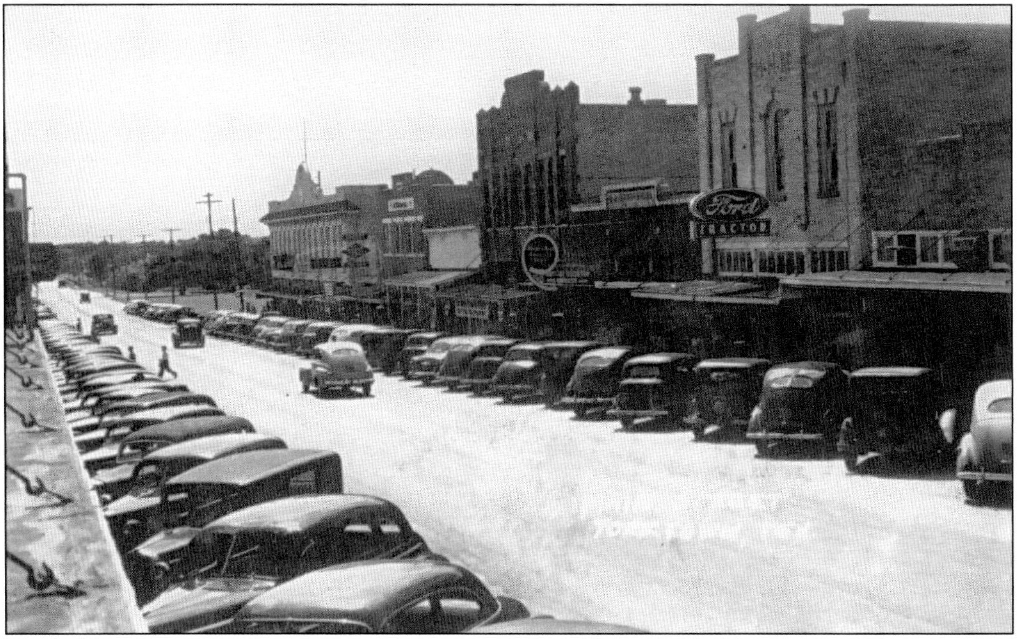

Pictured is a bird's-eye view of Main Street around 1940. Business seems to be good with all the parking spaces filled with cars.

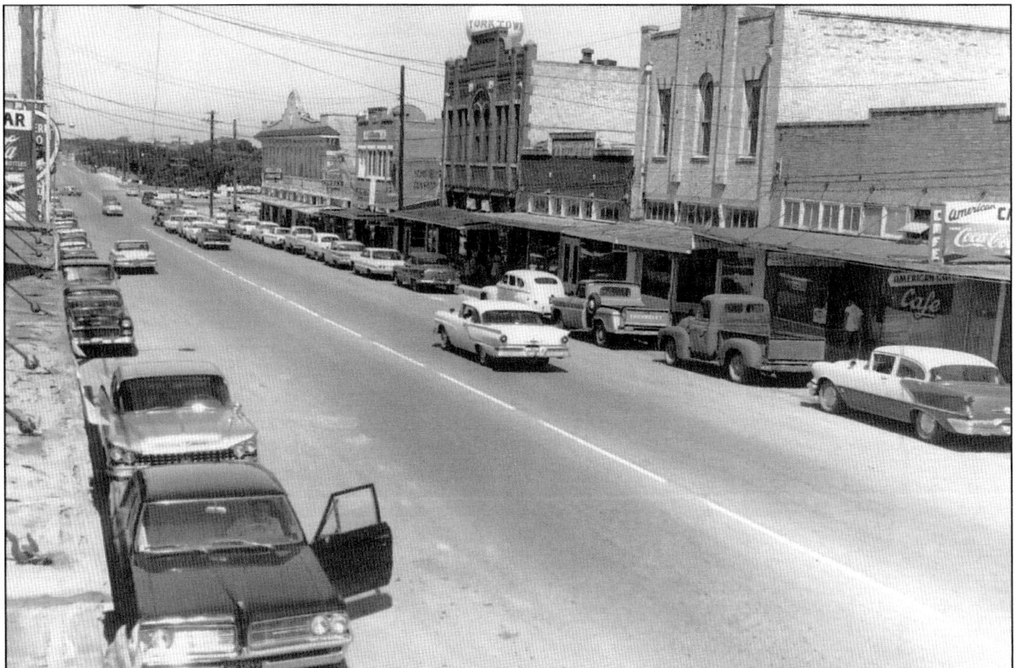

This is the same bird's-eye view as the picture above but approximately 20 years later. Notice the vehicles are parked parallel to the street, because the length of the cars has increased, thus parking diagonally would leave little room to drive safely on the street.

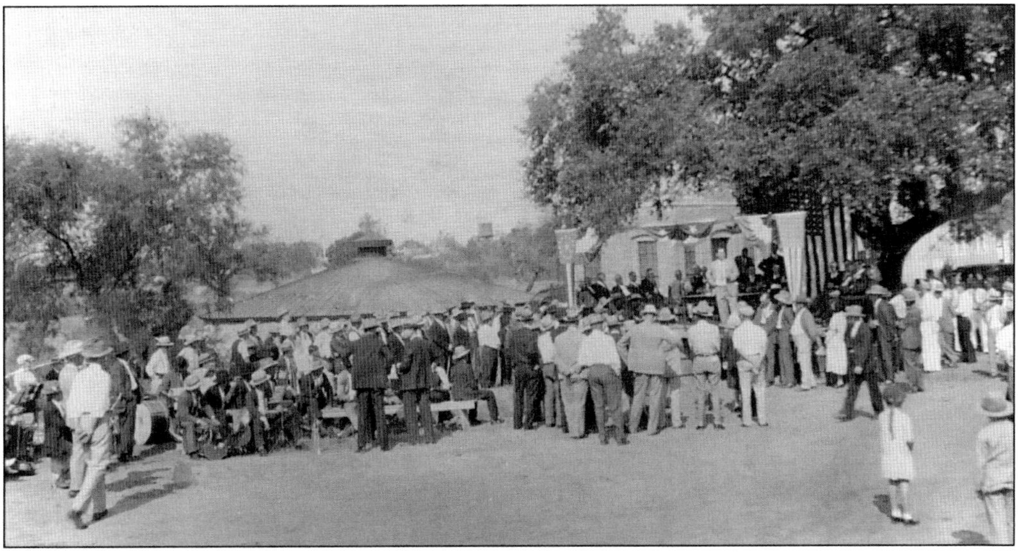

A political rally draws a large crowd. The politician on the stage is making campaign promises to help rally the crowd to support him. Band members are resting on the left side of the crowd.

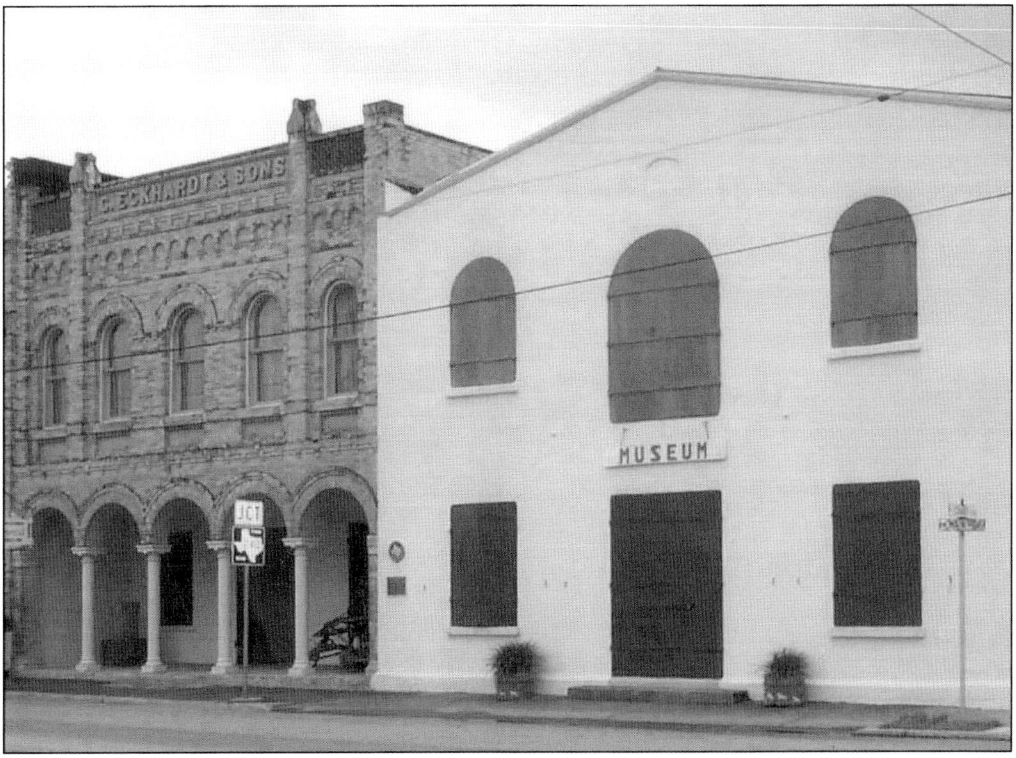

The Yorktown Historical Museum was dedicated April 2, 1978. Newly elected officers were Eugenia Studer, president; Frances von Roeder, vice president; Margarite Strieber, recording secretary; Elvie Beken, corresponding secretary; and John Koopmann and Rosa Lou Skinner, directors. Caroline Blain was the outgoing co-chairman of the organization. In 1976, the C. Eckhardt and Sons Building, which houses the museum, was listed on the Register of Historic Buildings and has received the Texas Historical Medallion.

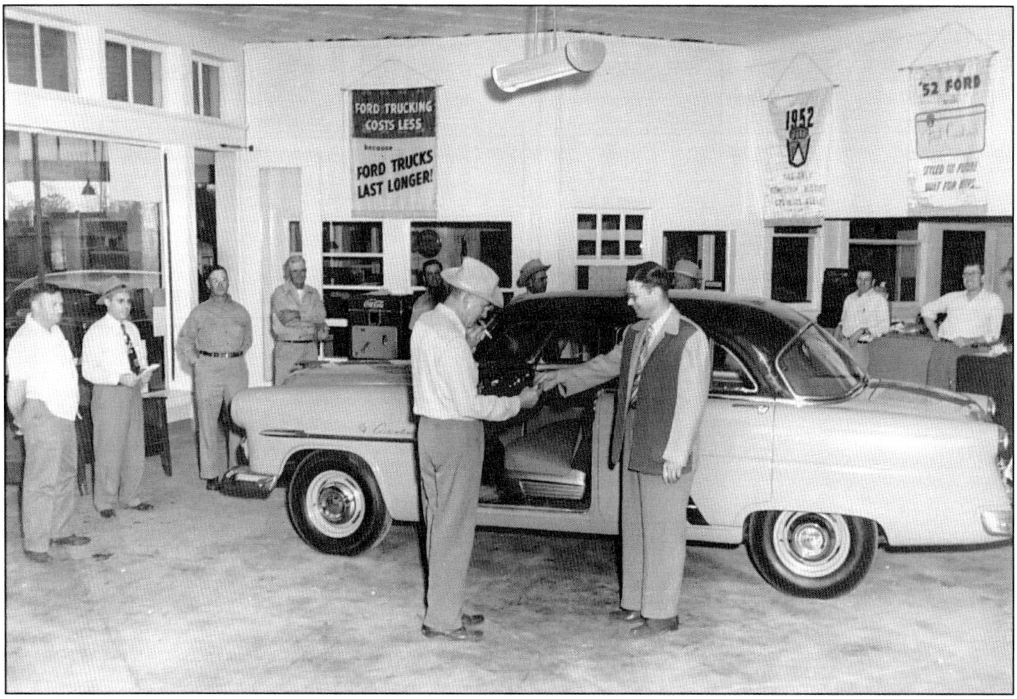

In October 1951, Theodore "Ted" Koopmann handed the keys to a 1952 Ford to its new owner. Koopmann was the owner of DeWitt Motor Company, selling Fords. The building is located at the corner of Riedel and Fourth Streets. Standing on the left are Henry Koopmann and Alvin Croom in the hat. Marcellus Weischwill is on the far right. (Courtesy Linda Hurta.)

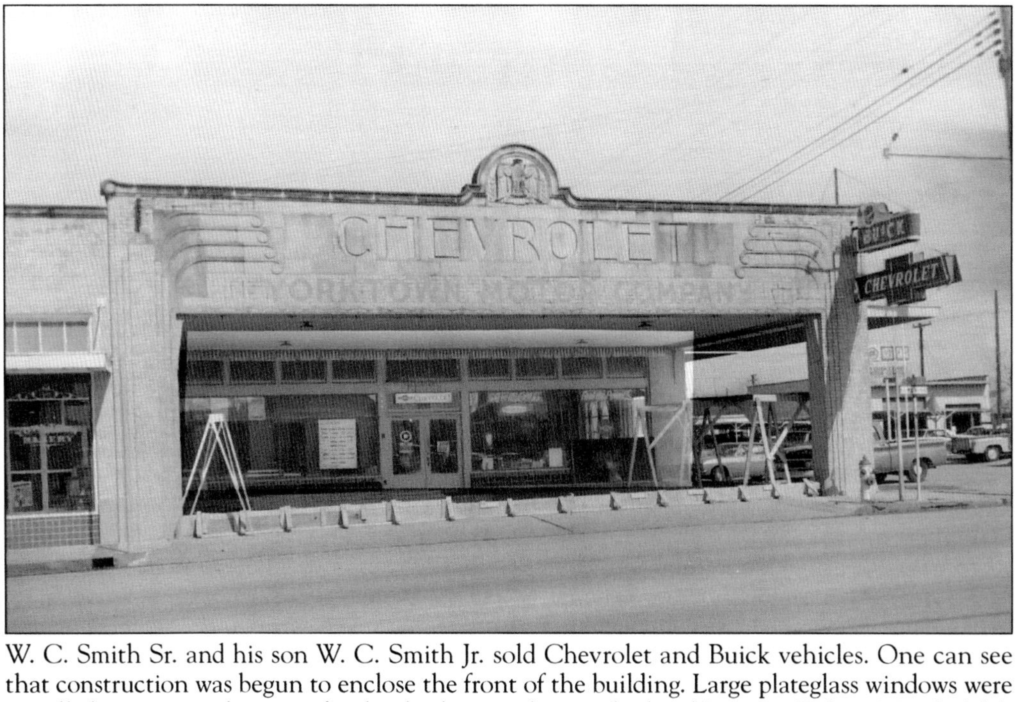

W. C. Smith Sr. and his son W. C. Smith Jr. sold Chevrolet and Buick vehicles. One can see that construction was begun to enclose the front of the building. Large plateglass windows were installed to create a showcase for the displaying of new vehicles. (Courtesy Robert Muschalek.)

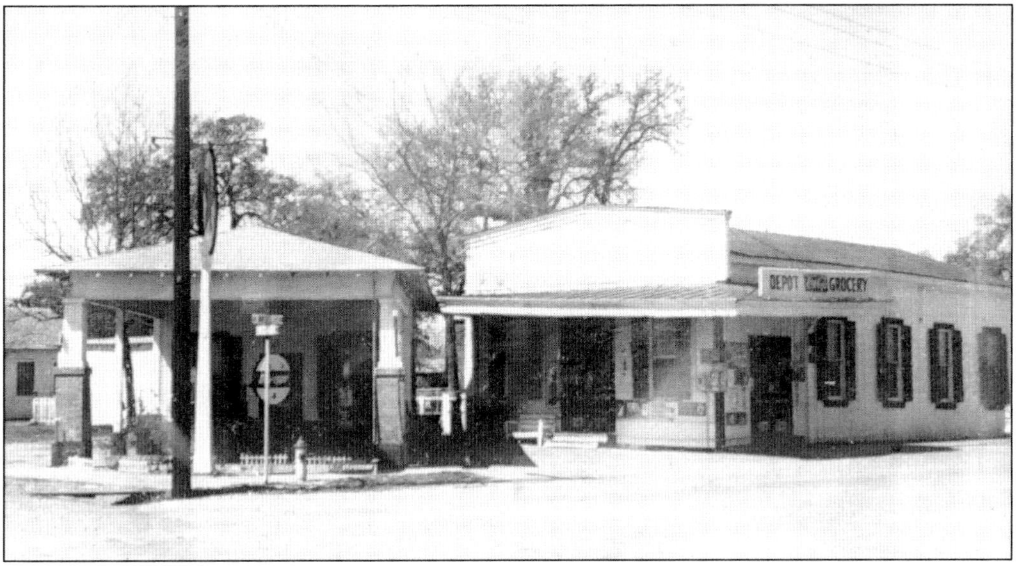

The Depot Grocery and Service Station on Riedel Street was owned and operated by Alonzo Otto and Mary Stepanski Luedicke for 28 years. Over time, they opened a small bar in the gas station area and served food at lunch for workers on that side of town. The Luedickes bought the store from Alton Martin in the 1950s. Five years after Alonzo's death in 1974, his wife worked out an agreement with Joe Baros who then took over the building. (Courtesy Cathy Wilems.)

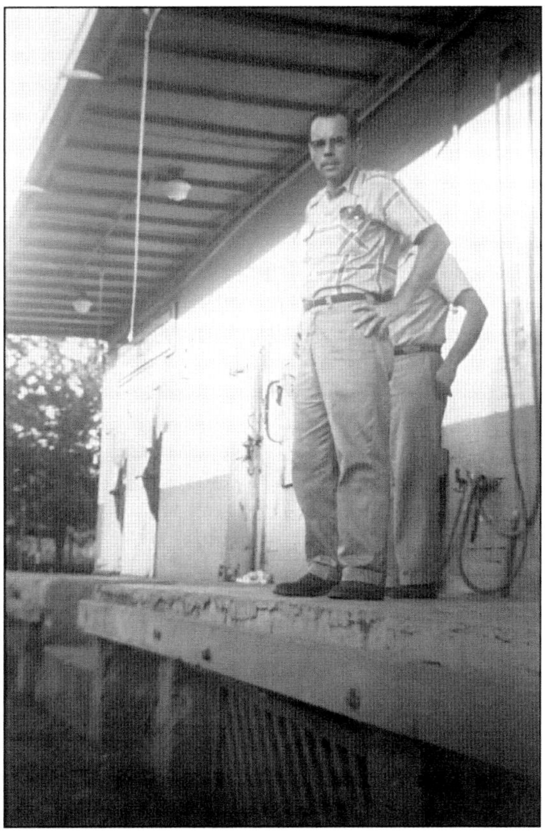

Anton "Tony" Heil bought the Yorktown Ice Plant and Frozen Food Locker building in 1958. He sold block ice for two to three years before stopping because of increasing health code requirements. He slaughtered and butchered animals for customers and rented out frozen food lockers. After 20 years, he sold the building to William "Bill" Smolik for his barbecue business. He in turn sold it to A. W. Podsim and Sons. In 2010, Timothy Deason bought the building and is renovating it. (Courtesy Jay Heil.)

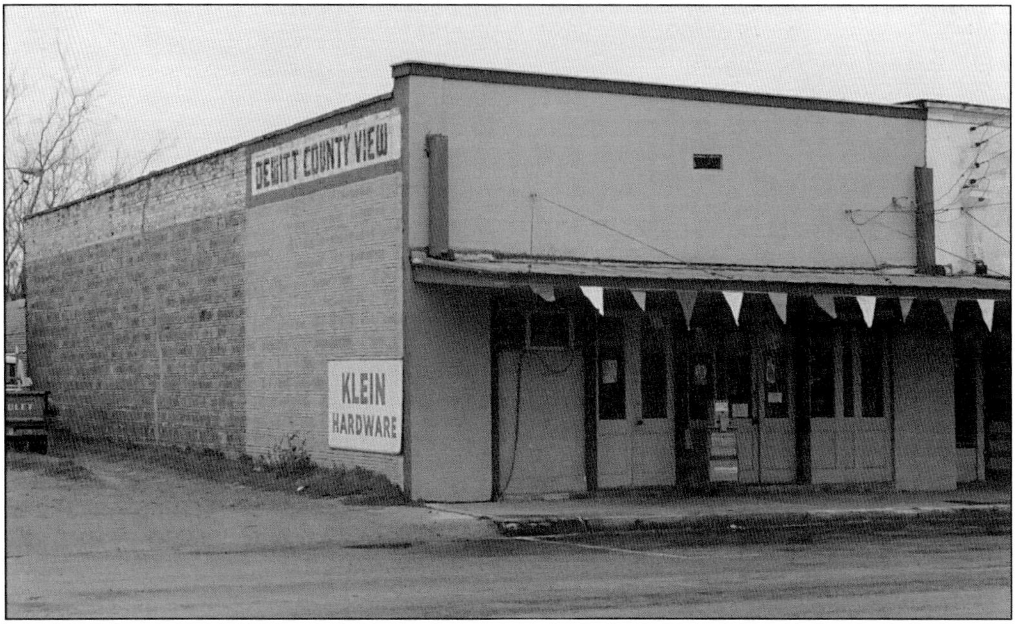

The *Nordheim View* moved to Yorktown in June 1951, and was renamed the *DeWitt County View*. The newspaper was run by Jane Morisse in Nordheim and her brother Paul A. Schmidt in Yorktown. It was sold to John and Mary Ann Janacek on January 1, 1970. It became the first offset newspaper in DeWitt County. In 1997, the Janaceks sold the paper to a Texas newspaper group who merged the *Yorktown News* and *DeWitt County View* to become *The Yorktown News-View* with Glenn Rea of Cuero and Bruce Morisse of Angleton in charge.

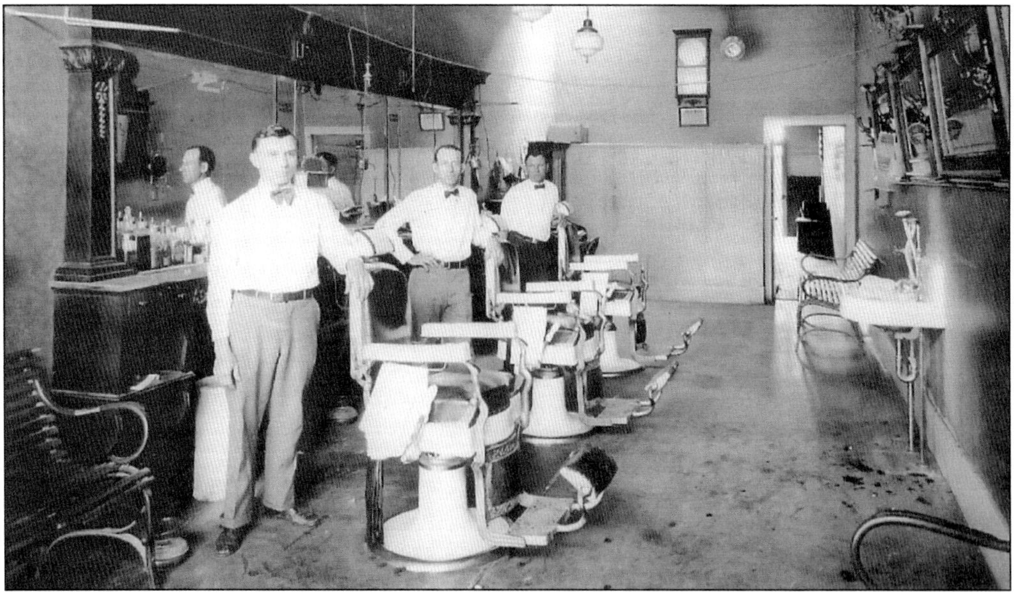

The Smith Barbershop on Main Street had three chairs lined up to eliminate the wait time for a haircut. The barbers in bow ties are Tommy Danysh, Bert Parks, and L. Frank. Today Douglas Audilet owns and operates the Main Barbershop and Shoe Repair. He bought the Best Barbershop from Freddie Turner in 1967. In the back room, Audilet repairs boots and shoes. (Courtesy Arlene Schroeder.)

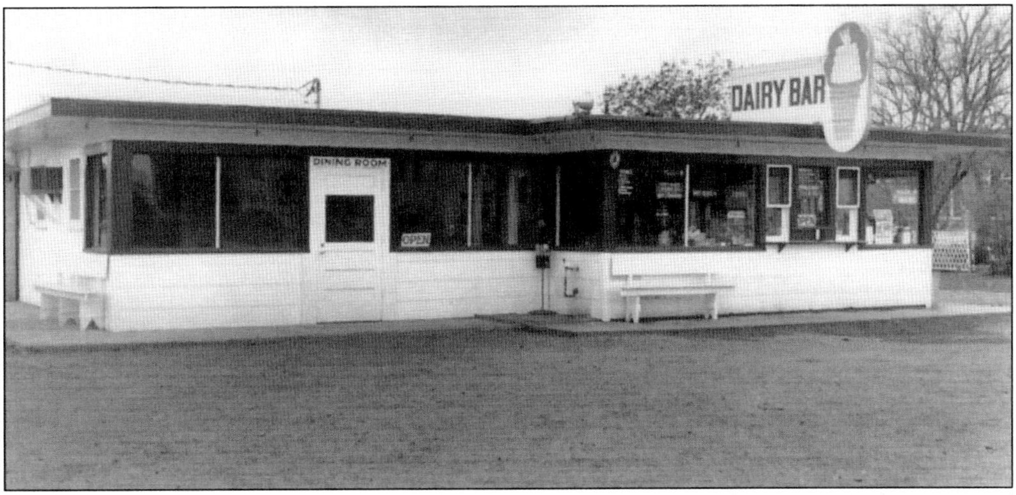

The Dairy Bar owned by Arlon "Shrimp" and Clydelle Jacob Schroeder was opened in 1954 and remained a popular eatery in Yorktown until its closure in 1992. It was located near the high school on Main Street. A dining room was added a few years after opening to accommodate customers ordering their hamburgers, onion rings, and other treats. Their three children, Stuart, Arlene, and Norma, grew up in the Dairy Bar. (Courtesy Clydelle Schroeder.)

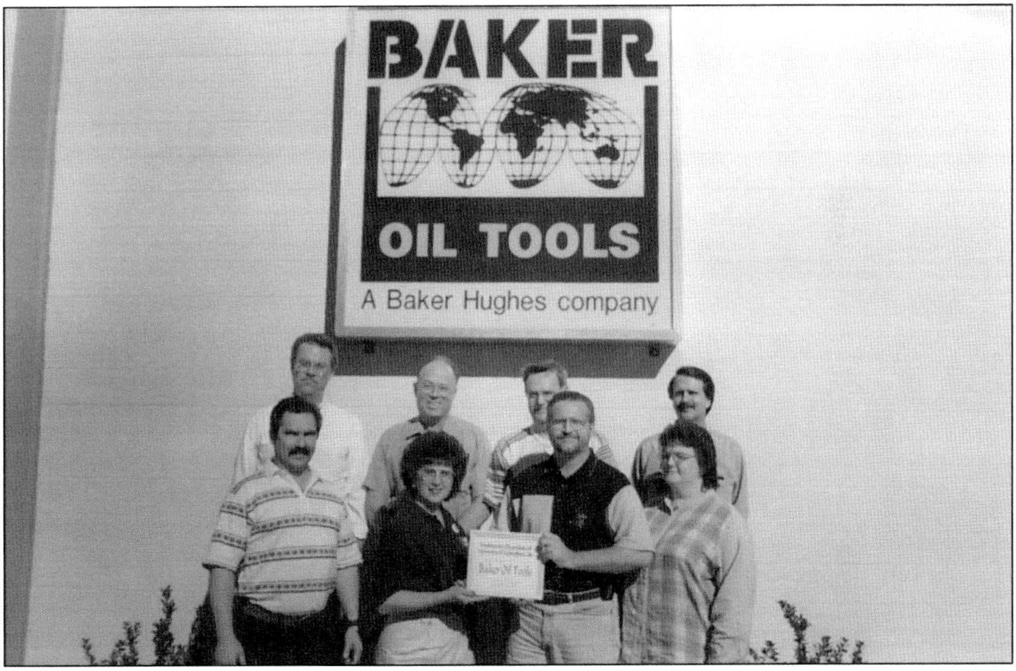

Representing the Chamber of Commerce, Lorene Migura presented Richard Finney of Baker Oil Tools with a new business certificate. Baker Oil Tools purchased Elder Oil Tools in 1991. Present are (first row) Bob Goodman, Lorene Migura, Richard Finney, and Pam Stehle; (second row) John Godby, Glen Schulte, Wilbur Kenne, and James Henneke. Elder Oil Tools had been Yorktown's largest employer. In the 10 years from 1979 to 1989, Elder employed 100 people to manufacture and distribute packers, tools, and gas lift equipment for oil and gas well completions. Baker Oil Tools also manufactured products and equipment used in oil field drilling. In 2009, Baker sold out to Howco Oil Field Services.

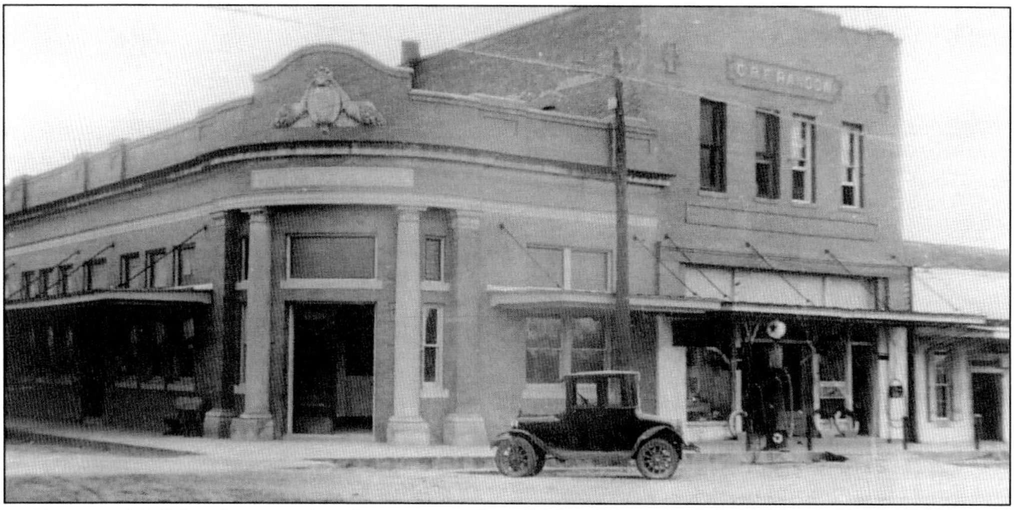

In October 1903, William Eckhardt and other family members opened the First National Bank. By 1913, the stock was sold to William Green and Philip Welhausen, and in 1914 the First National Bank opened in a new building at the southwest corner of Main and Riedel Streets. In 1927, E. B. Zincke took over and successfully saw the bank through the Depression. Lou Evan Gips became the bank president in 1975. Soon after, the bank was sold to Family Financial Institution, and the building was then used as the city hall and police station.

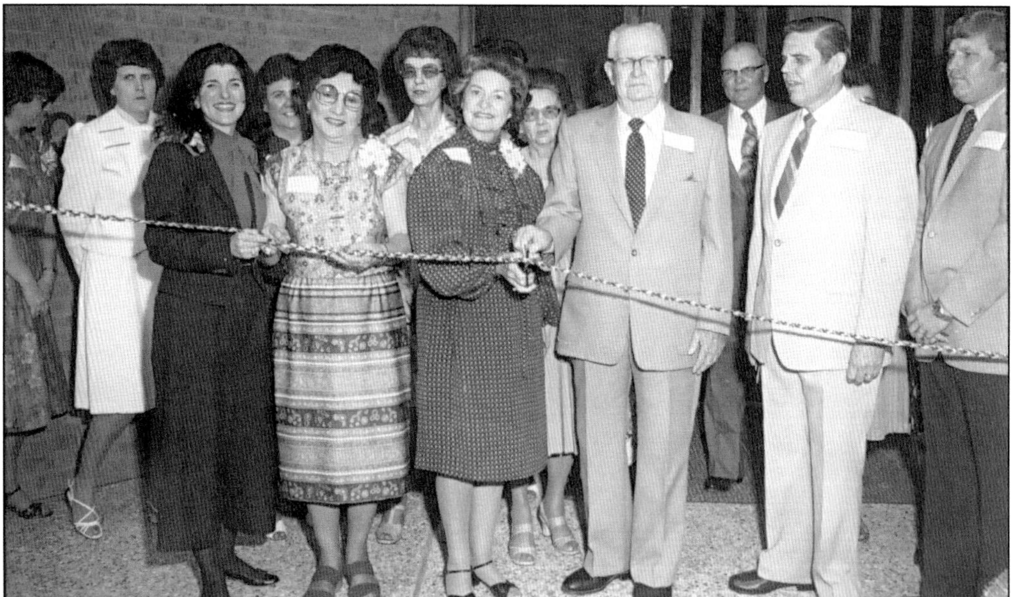

On March 21, 1982, the Family Financial Institution, represented by Lady Bird Johnson, wife of Pres. Lyndon Baines Johnson, was present at the grand opening ceremonies of the new building housing the First National Bank at the corner of Main and Gohmert Streets. Present at the ribbon-cutting ceremony were (first row) Luci Johnson Turpin, bank vice president Caroline Blain, Lady Bird Johnson, Mayor Collie Meyer, bank president Lou Gips, and bank vice president David Styra; (second row) unidentified, Jo Nell Gips, Sandra Heil, Elenora "Elly" Voelkel, Alice Meyer, and Gilbert Koopmann. In 1992, the bank was bought by Citizens Bank of Kilgore with David Styra as senior vice president/bank manager. (Courtesy Robert Muschalek.)

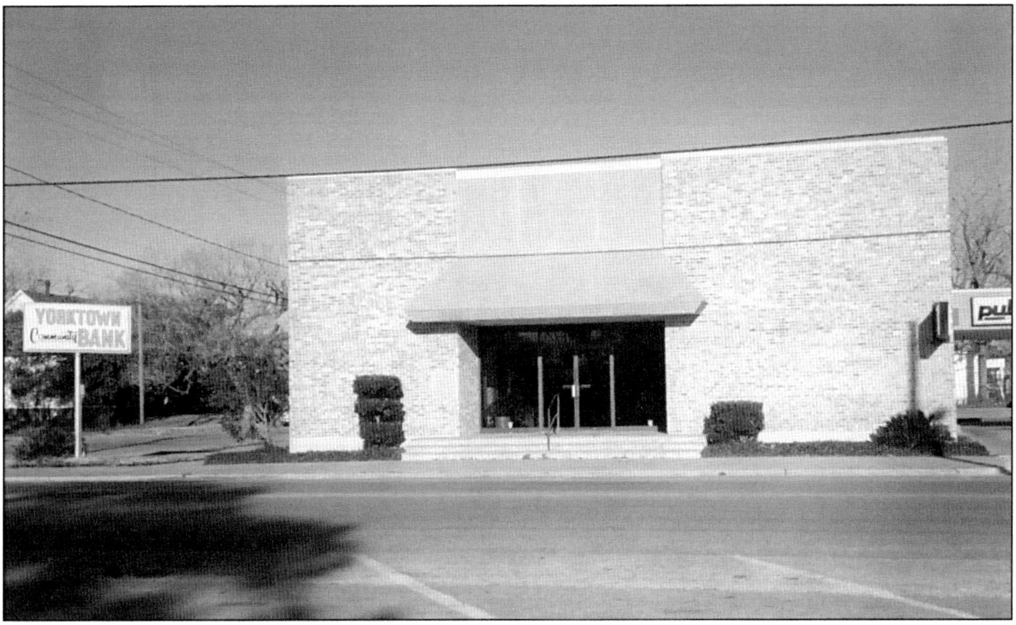

Yorktown Community Bank opened in a new building at the corner of Riedel and Fifth Streets dedicated on September 3, 1974. The bank received its charter in July 1964, and opened on February 1, 1965, with J. O. Frisbie as president. In 1989, James Burda became president. On October 15, 1994, the bank was taken over by the First National Bank of Beeville. Bobby Strieber became branch president on January 1, 2004.

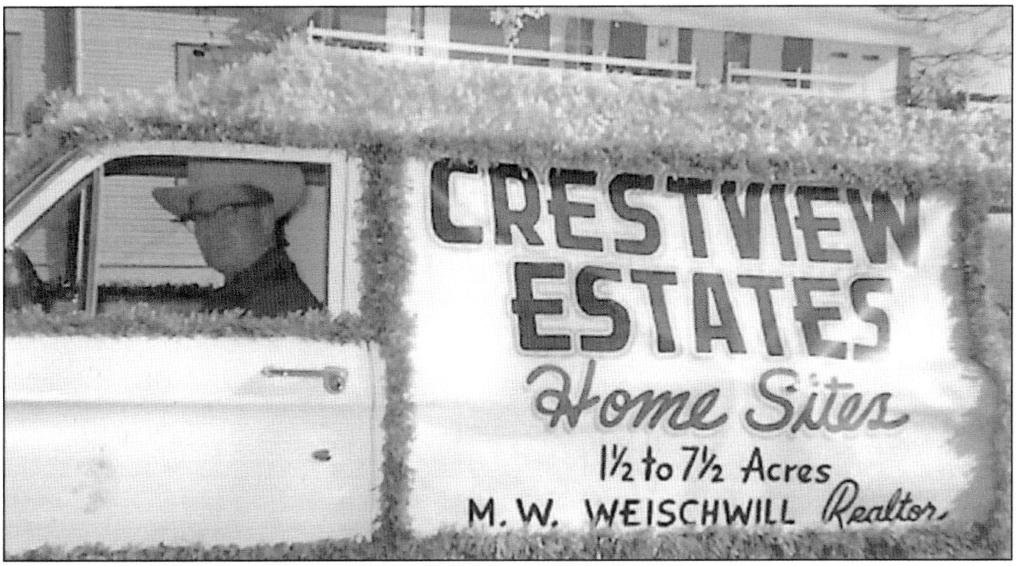

Marcellus W. Weischwill owned a real estate business but expanded into the development and building of two housing subdivisions on the outskirts of Yorktown. Here he is driving in the 1961 Western Days parade advertising the first of his subdivisions. In 1961, he bought 120 acres north of town from Edgar and Gus Grun and subdivided it into lots called "Crestview Estates." Then in 1970 he bought 300 acres from Herbert and Flora Rabke and 7 acres from Albert Grun on Highway 119 south of town and named it "Royal Oaks." There are many homes in both subdivisions. (Courtesy Mark Weischwill.)

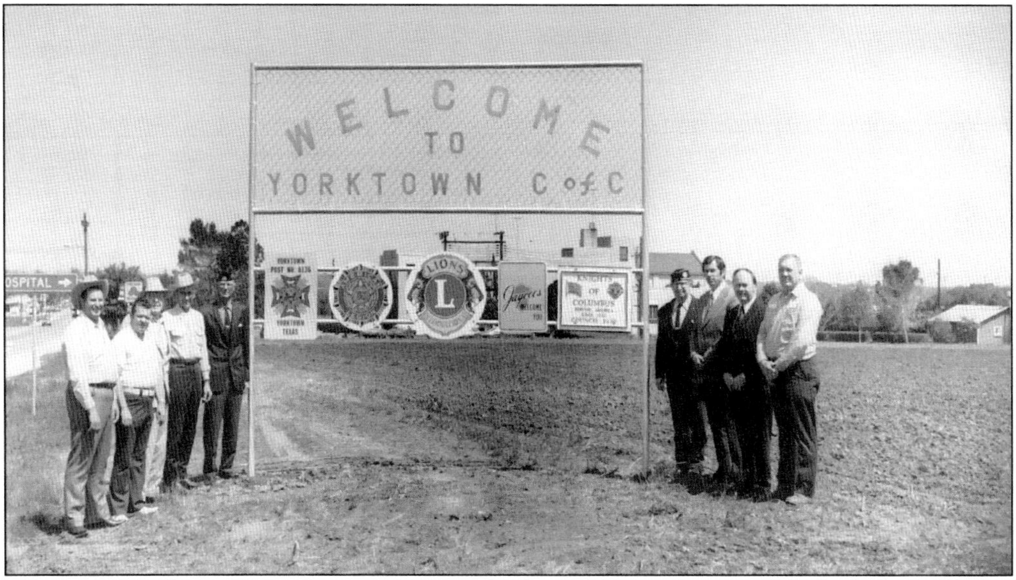

In the 1970s, various active organizations gathered to dedicate the new "Welcome to Yorktown" signs at the east and west entrances of town. Present for the dedication were, from left to right, Emil Geffert, chairman and designer; Lee Roy Griffin, city council; Mayor Albert Schwartz, City of Yorktown; Warren Schorlemer, president of Chamber of Commerce; Robert Afflerbach, Veterans of Foreign Wars; Charles Meyer, American Legion; Jimmy Burda, president of Jaycees; Felton Schroller, Lion's Club; and Arthur Goehring, Knights of Columbus. Emil Geffert and his son Larry Geffert built the signs.

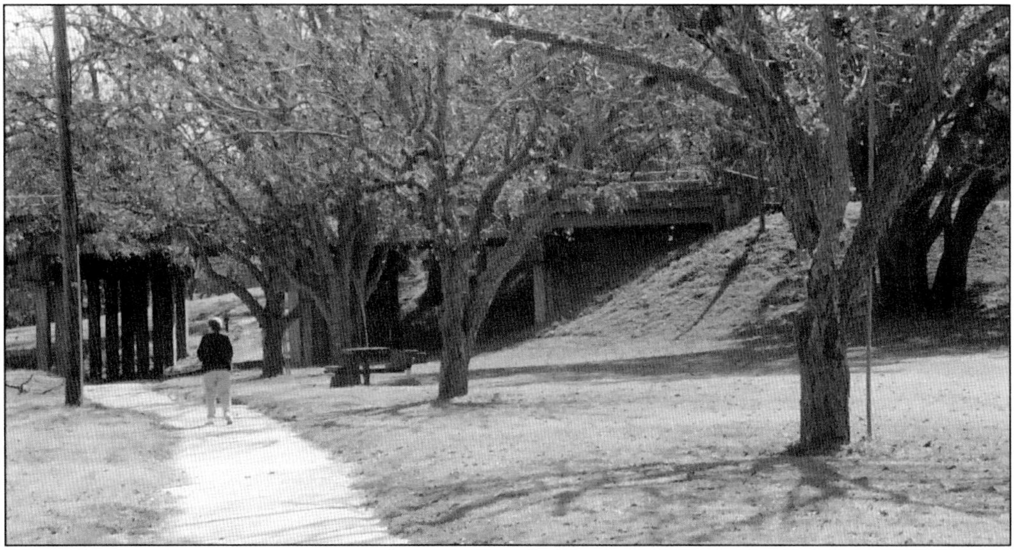

On January 26, 1996, the Coleto Creek Park was dedicated. This was a joint project between the city and the Texas Parks and Wildlife Department. The park area covers nearly 25 acres from below First Street to Fifth Street along the Coleto Creek. The park features a paved walking trail and picnic tables. During the spring, many wildflowers bloom along the trail. Ducks were donated to the creek project, and they swim peacefully on the water. During the Christmas season, the trees along the bridge and creek twinkle festively with lights provided by the Chamber of Commerce and valued citizens.

Three

Yorktown Hospitals and Schools

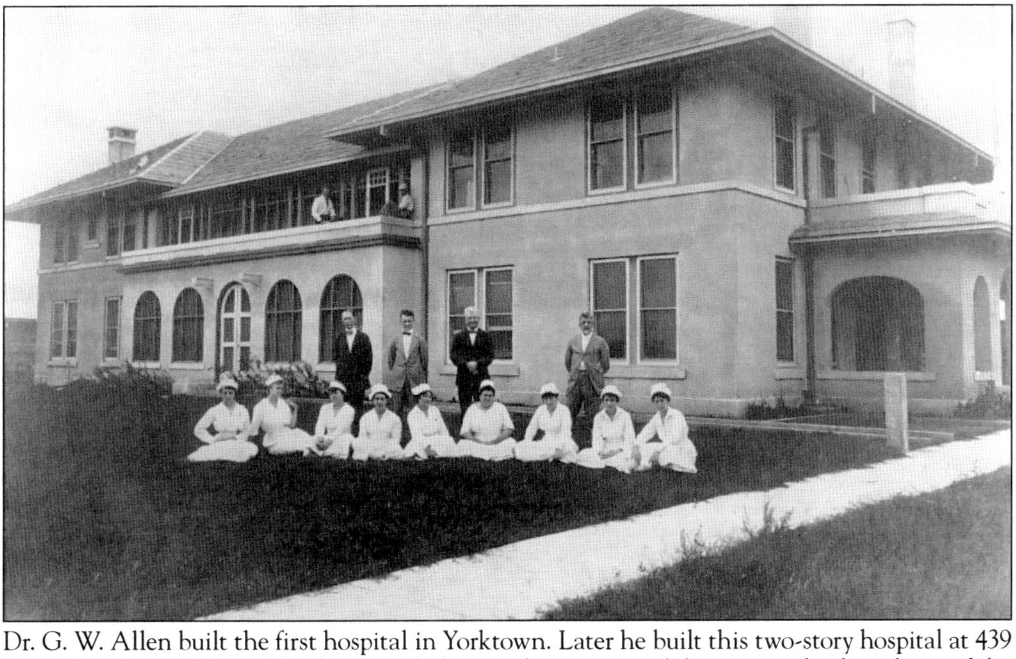

Dr. G. W. Allen built the first hospital in Yorktown. Later he built this two-story hospital at 439 East Main Street. This 1919 photograph depicts the nurses and doctors on the front lawn of the hospital. When the hospital closed, it became the DeDear Nursing Home. Then in the 1950s it was the Laster Nursing Home. In 1979, it opened as the Hygeia Health Retreat. Later purchased by John Golden, it was reopened as the Golden Days Villa, a nursing home that closed in 2009.

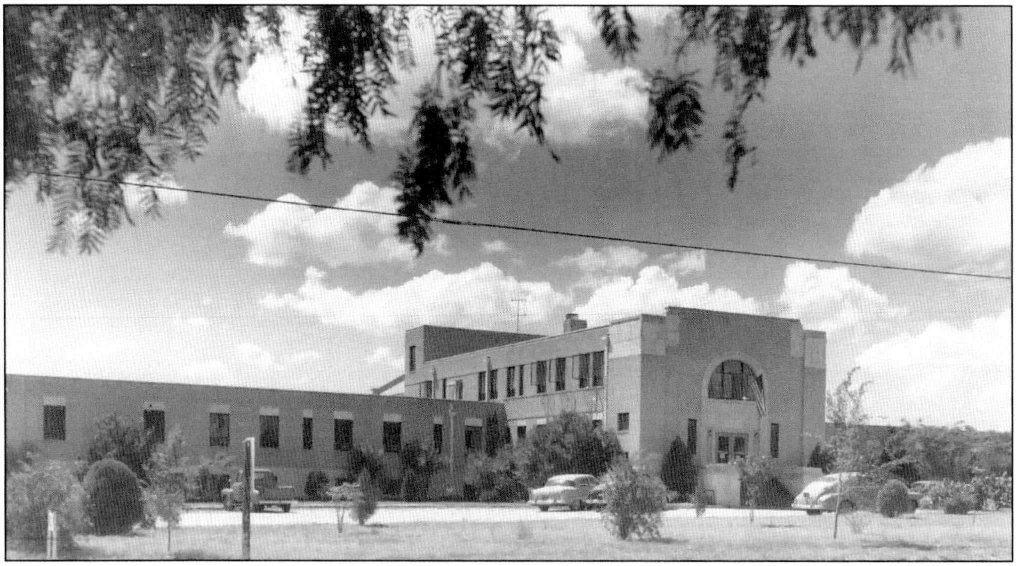

Yorktown Memorial Hospital was built for $500,000 and began operations on March 25, 1951, with a complete staff of technicians and nurses. Sister Mary Monica was the hospital administrator and the Felician Sisters helped operate the hospital. Physicians on staff were Dr. Leon W. Norwierski, Dr. G. W. Cross, Dr. John Barth, and Dr. Marvin Gohlke Sr., all of Yorktown; Dr. M. Rittiman of Runge; Dr. Elder of Nixon; and Dr. Dobbs, Dr. Ehlers, and Dr. Patterson of Cuero. The hospital closed November 30, 1986. On duty since 1983, Dr. Gordon Barth has his office in the Yorktown Medical Clinic on Riedel Street.

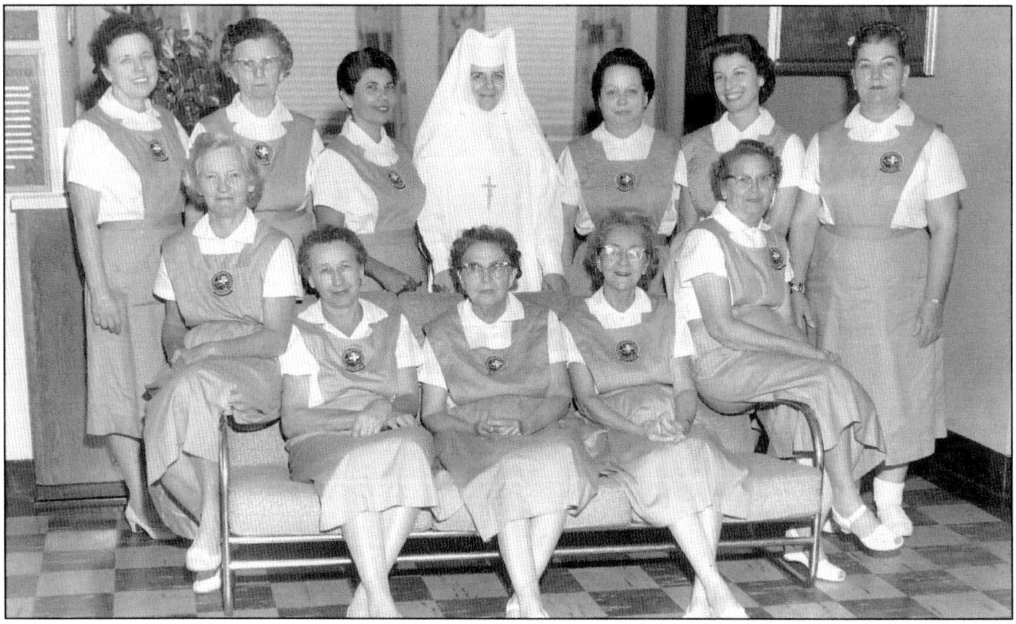

The Yorktown Memorial Hospital Guild signed their charter on April 15, 1959. Members on November 27, 1960, were (first row) Mrs. F. Styra Sr., Mrs. P. Jablonski, Mrs. O. W. Ehlers, Mrs. W. C. Smith Sr., and Mrs. J. W. Deborah; (second row) Mrs. Harry Gips, Mrs. Ervin Kozelski, Mrs. Jerry Champion, Sister Agnelis, Mrs. William Knandel Jr., Mrs. W. C. Smith Jr., and Mrs. P. Damauer.

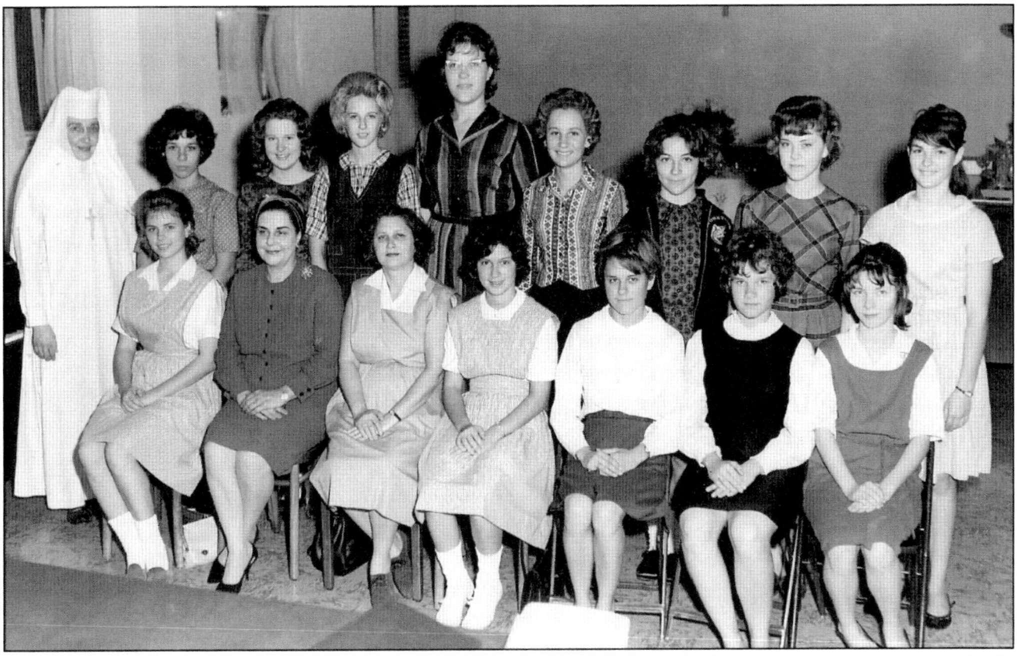

In 1964, a Candy Striper organization began with teenage girls volunteering their time to help throughout the hospital. Some worked in the kitchen, some in the laboratory, some in the office, and some visited and helped the patients. The 1964 group was composed of (first row) Kathy Wojtasczyk, unidentified, Mrs. Sammie Dishongh, Nancy Dishongh, Florence Hahn, Theresa Stratmann, and Shirley Plasczyk; (second row) Sister Jovella, Barbara Jaeger, Evelyn Stoever, Carla Lewis, Marilyn Jonischkies, Shirley Geffert, Arlette Tiemann, Janet Casparis, and Annie Plascyzk. Kathy and Nancy are wearing the striped pinafore of the Candy Stripers.

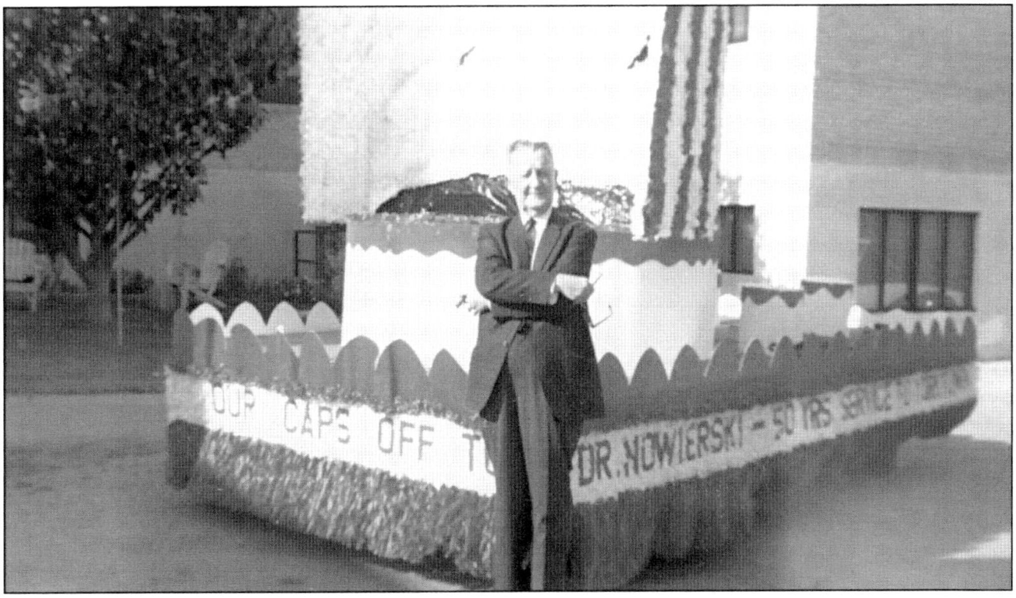

Dr. Leon Nowierski stands next to a Western Days float honoring his 50 years of medical service. His entire medical career was conducted from his office above the Kraege Drugstore. His father had his practice above the Riedel Drugstore.

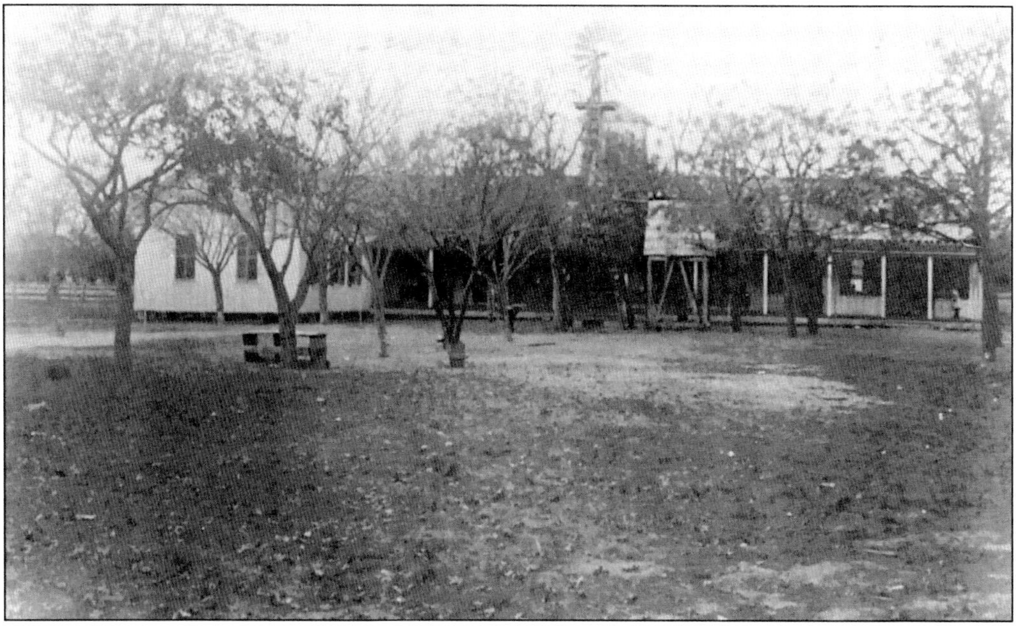

Yorktown's Normal School was the first public school established in 1878. It had four rooms and J. L. Boal was the principal. School lasted 10 months. The first four months it was a pay school with tuition rates from $1 to $2.50. When school became free on February 1, attendance increased by 25 percent. Latin was taught until 1924 when it was dropped, and Spanish was added.

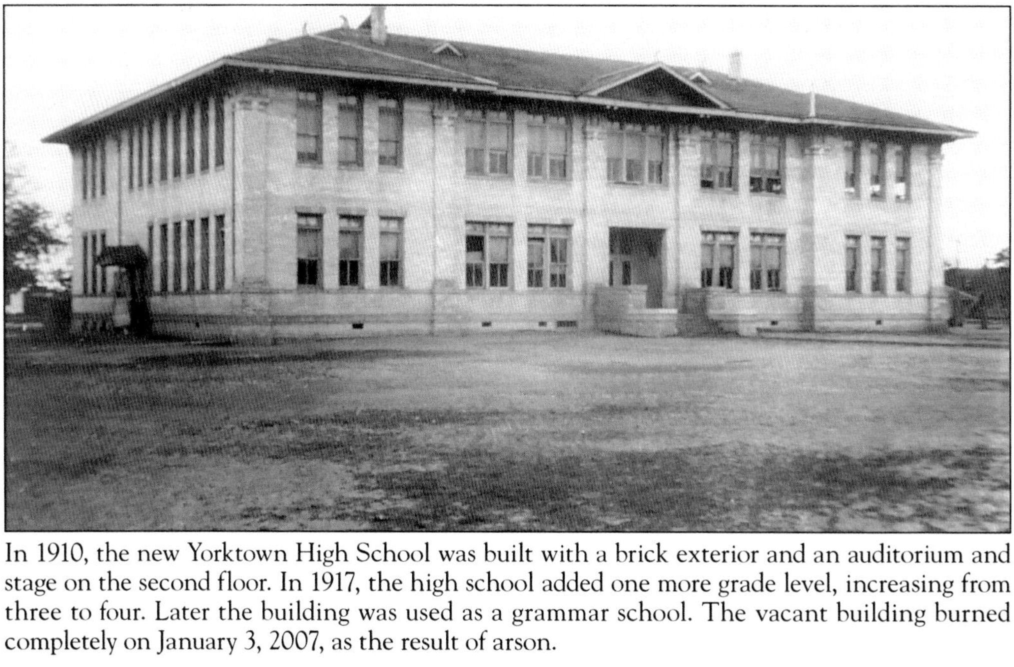

In 1910, the new Yorktown High School was built with a brick exterior and an auditorium and stage on the second floor. In 1917, the high school added one more grade level, increasing from three to four. Later the building was used as a grammar school. The vacant building burned completely on January 3, 2007, as the result of arson.

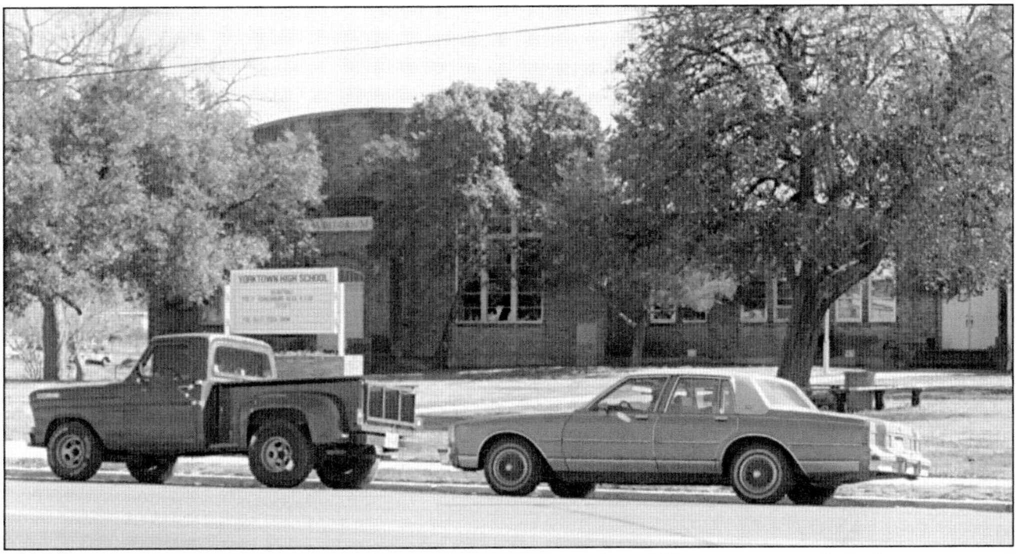

The present high school was built in 1929. As time went by, additions to it included a vocational agriculture building in 1940, and an auto mechanics shop and a playatorium for athletics in 1965. Also built was a homemaking cottage and a separate library. In 1985, a new science building was constructed and named in honor of Hubert L. Menn, a retired mathematics and science teacher, for his 37 years of service.

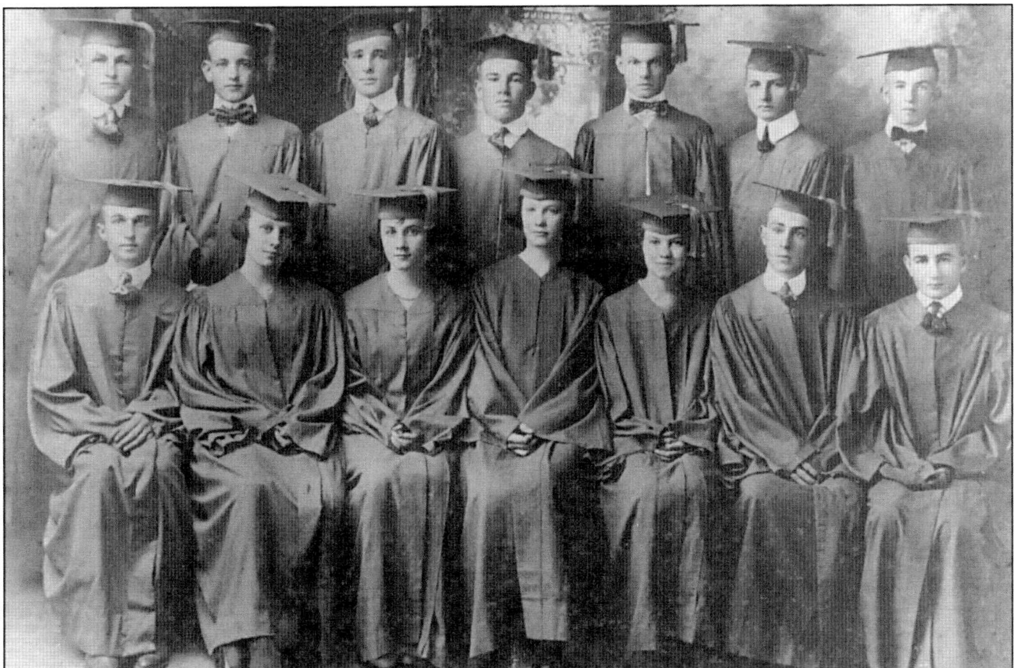

Yorktown High School's 1920 graduating class was the first class to wear caps and gowns. Class members were, from left to right, (first row) Orland Eckhardt, Julia Kolodzey, Antonette Wanier, salutatorian Marguerite Riedel, Johnnie Mae Evans, Manfred Gips, and Walter Hohn; (second row) Albert Leissner, Charles G. Hoff, Julius Metz, valedictorian Henry Grun, Albert Harper, Anslem Hohn, and Charles F. Hoff.

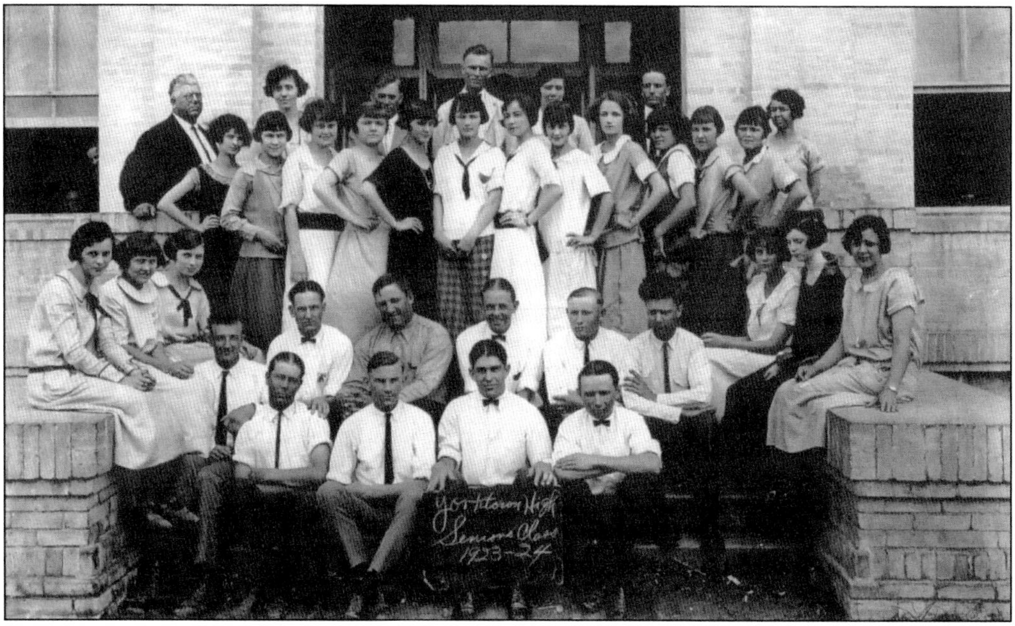

Lined up on the steps of Yorktown High School is the senior class of 1923–1924. The students are dressed in their "Sunday best." Seated in the first row holding the sign is Wilbert Poetter, and Alvin Sunday is seated in the second row, sixth from the left. In the third row, the seventh girl is Frances Lena Metz, and the ninth girl is Corinne Westphal. (Courtesy Frances Ann Koopmann.)

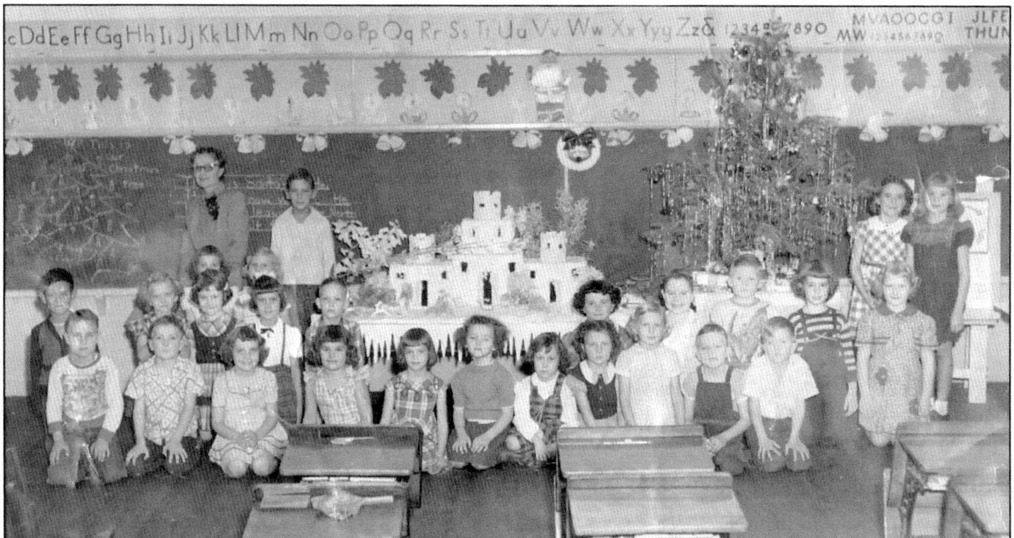

At Christmas each year Viola Demmer decorated her classroom with a Christmas tree and displayed a Christmas castle she made of boxes covered with the detergent Ivory Snow Flakes. Members of this 1951 first grade class were, from left to right, (first row) Don Simecek, John W. Schmidt, Deanna Morisse, Patty Blain, Joyce Martin, Linda Sinast, Jean Harp, Irene ?, Marian Wehe, Wally ?, and Clark Kerlick; (second row) Augustine ?, Beverly Kerlick, Ann Barrett, unidentified, Joe Meuret, Martha Kneifel, Victor Riske, Dennis Henze, Marlene Hoepkin, and Linda Lamprecht; (third row) Gladys Haak, Wanda Rabke, unidentified, and Carolyn Weise; (fourth row) Viola Demmer and unidentified. (Courtesy Beverly Bruns.)

Four

Yorktown Celebrations and Music

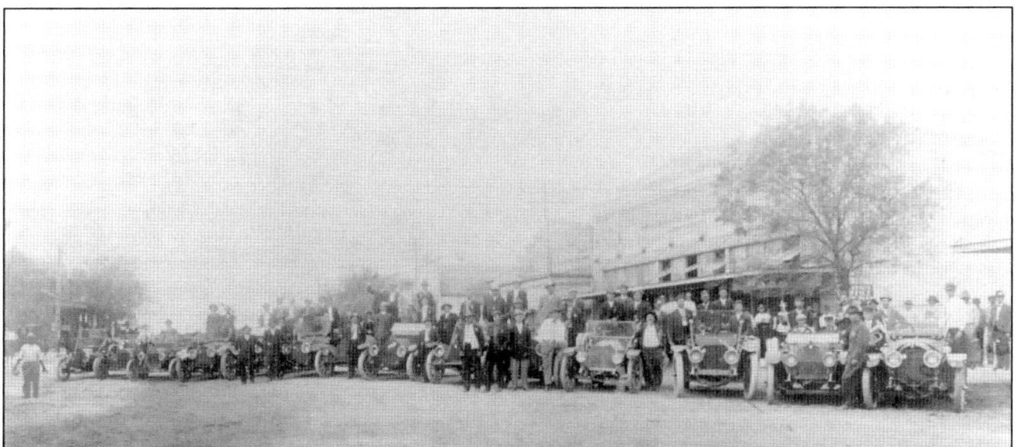

The Yorktown Commercial Club lined up their cars in front of the Neutzler and Osterloh buildings on Nordheim's Broadway Street to advertise the 1912 Yorktown Harvest Feast. The club was on a 125-mile advertising tour to towns in the area.

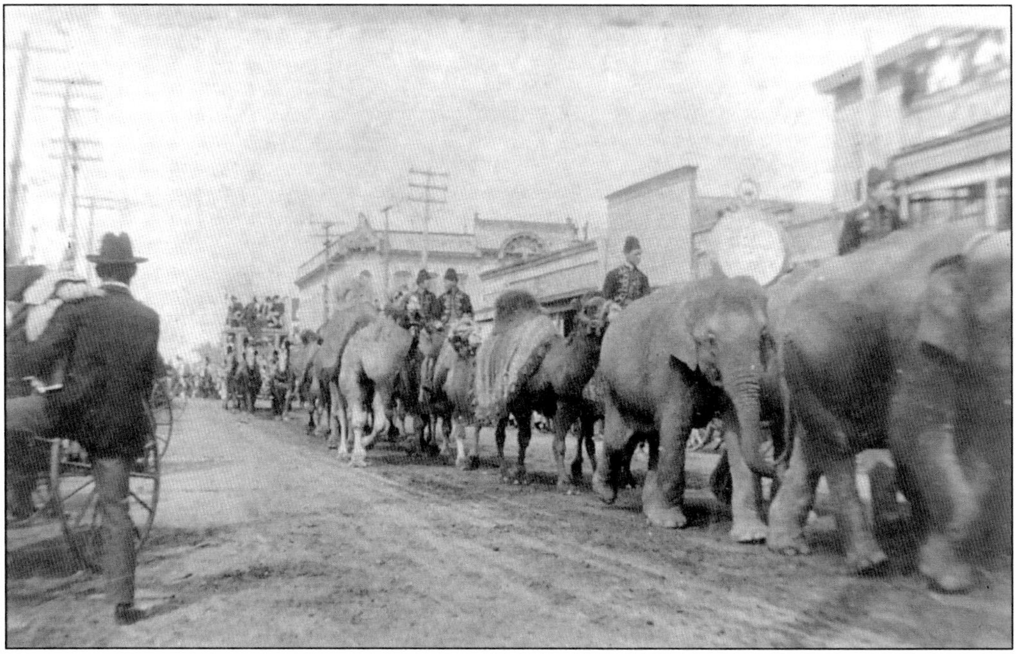

The circus came to town with elephants, camels, and horse-drawn circus wagons walking down the unpaved Main Street. The gentleman on the left is holding his young child for a better view of the parade.

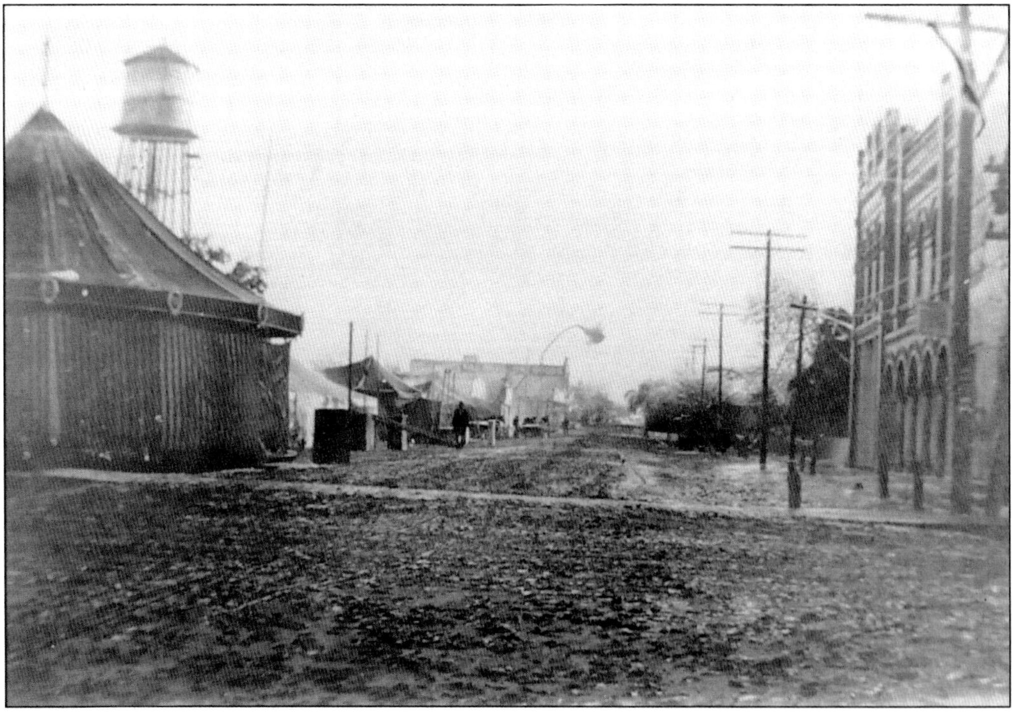

Carnival tents line Main Street across from the C. Eckhardt and Sons store in 1909. This signified that another celebration was in the making. Yorktown had many celebrations such as the Fall Fair in 1905 and a Mexican Fiesta in 1906, among many others through the years.

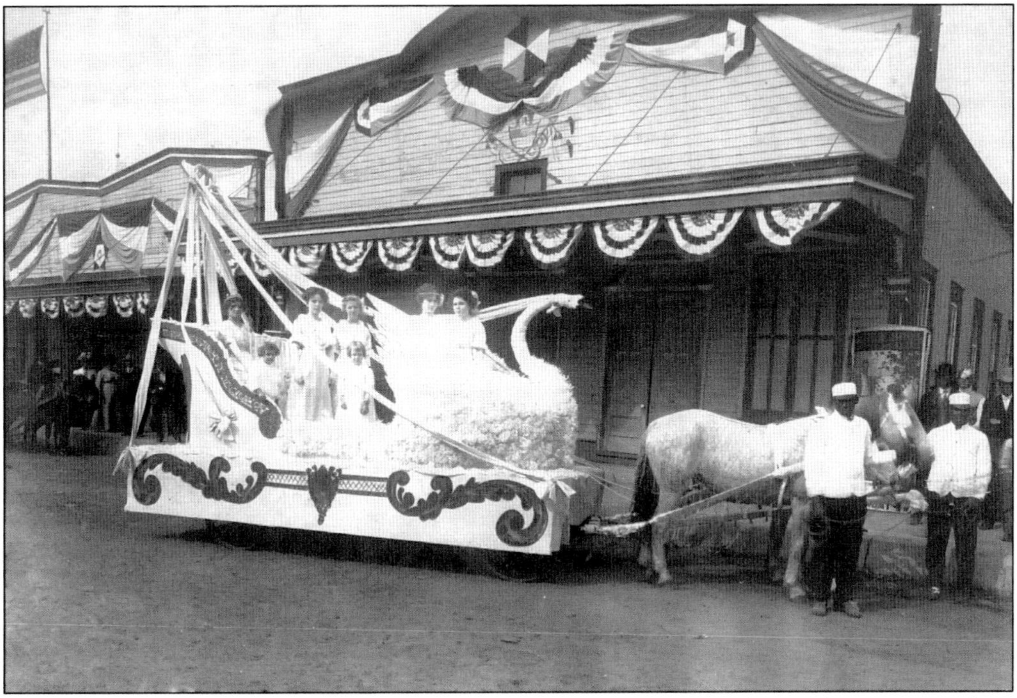

The 1912 Harvest Feast Queen's float features a large white swan. In the royalty court are, from left to right, Queen Annie Heinrich, Friedschen Thuem, Emma Braunig, Hilda Gips, and Isabella Metz. The two young girls are unidentified.

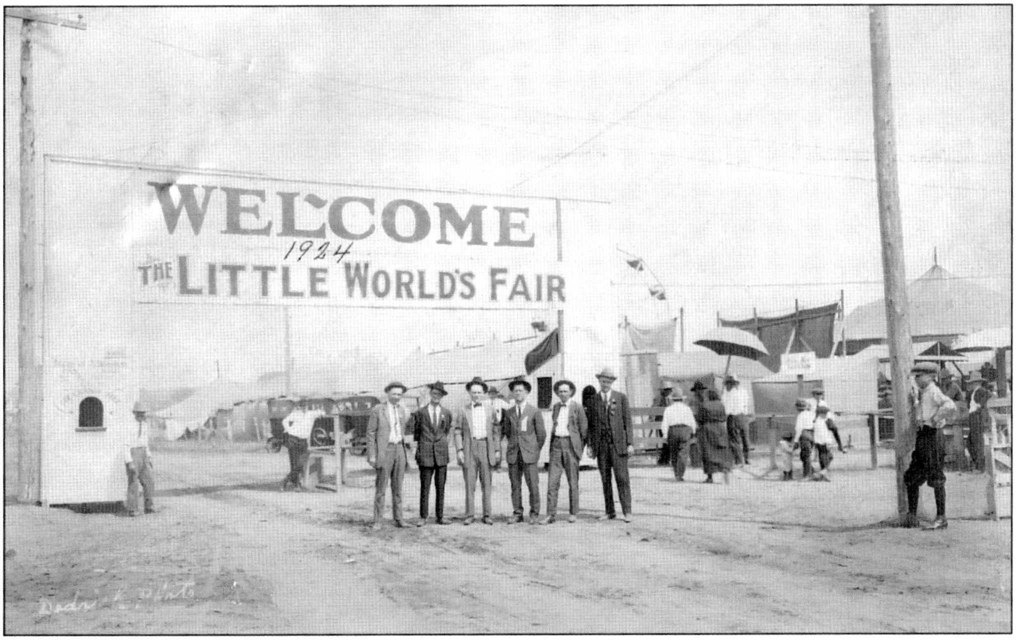

The Little World's Fair became one of the main celebrations in Yorktown for almost 30 years. The executive committee and grand chairman of the 1924 Little World's Fair are, from left to right, Paul A. Schmidt, E. G. Schiwetz, Walter Reifschlager, grand chairman Herman Mollenhauer, Ferd Kraege, and August Braunig.

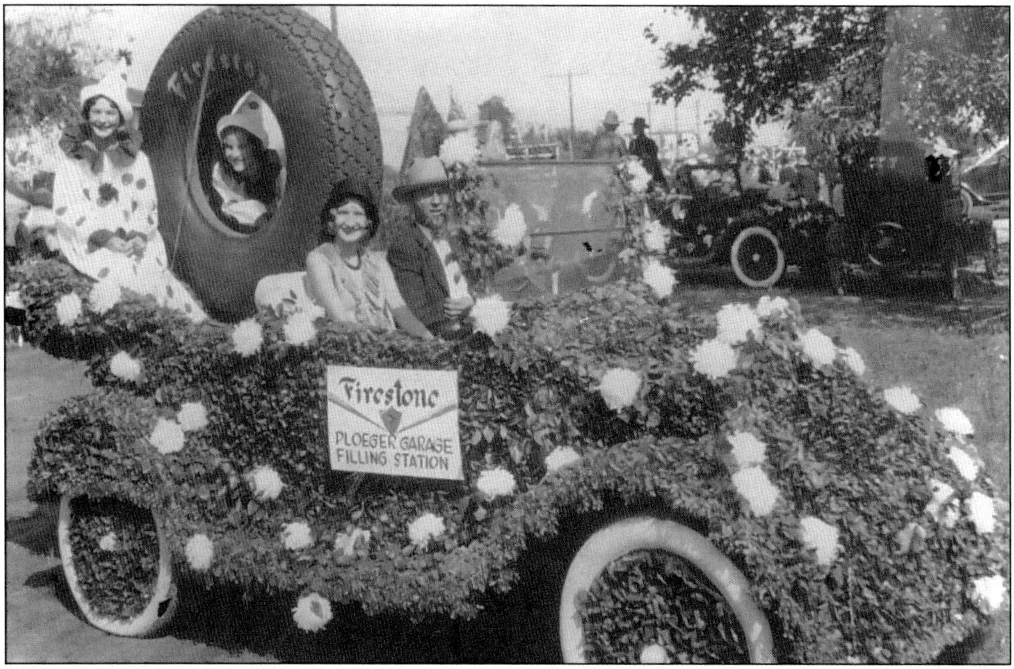

This flower-covered float is an example of how the citizens decorated their cars in the 1920s and 1930s for parades. Riding on the float are, from left to right, Fay Nuniez (back), Idell Strieber (in tire), Gordie Smith, and Richard Schultz advertising the Firestone Ploeger Garage Filling Station.

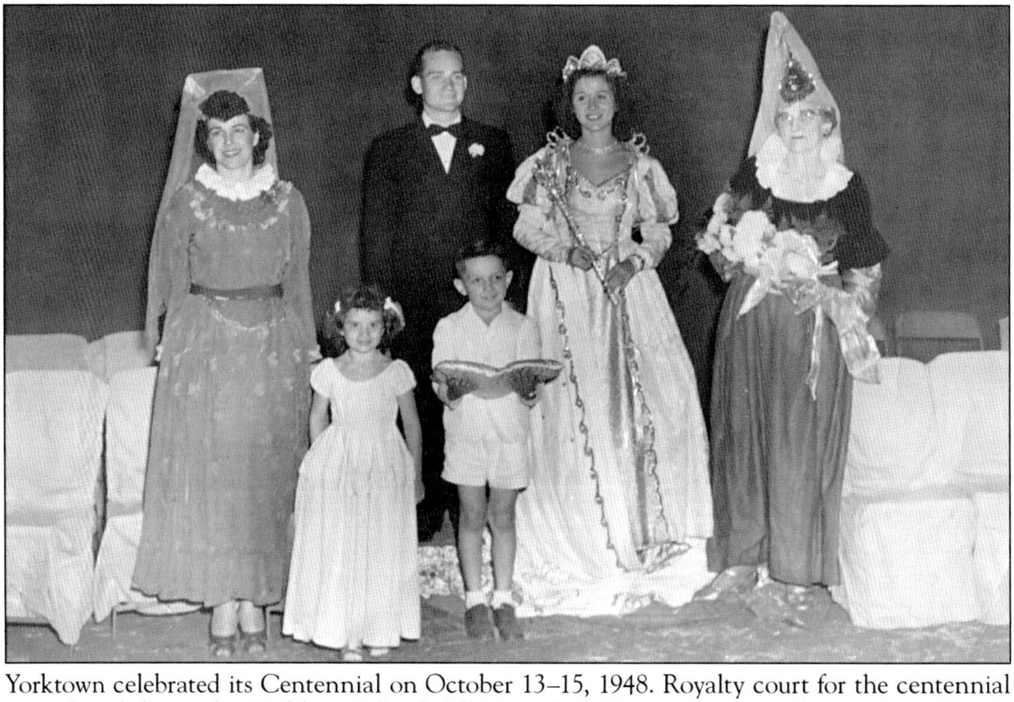

Yorktown celebrated its Centennial on October 13–15, 1948. Royalty court for the centennial were, from left to right, Kathleen Schwab, Jill Haun, Jack Harrison, escort John Simpson, Queen Dianne Poetter, and Mrs. F. F. (Matilda Korth) Schwab, queen of the town's Silver Jubilee in 1898, who served as Dowager Queen of the Centennial.

After the Little World's Fair closed in 1950, the M and M Rodeo Company, owned by Leslie and Cecil Mueller, organized parades of cowboys on horseback as advertisement for their rodeo on Smith Creek during the early 1950s. (Courtesy Andra Wisian.)

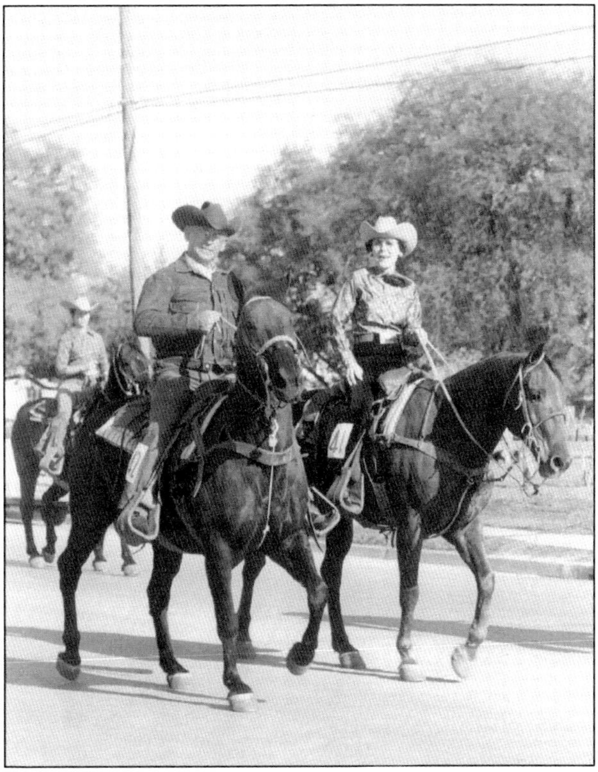

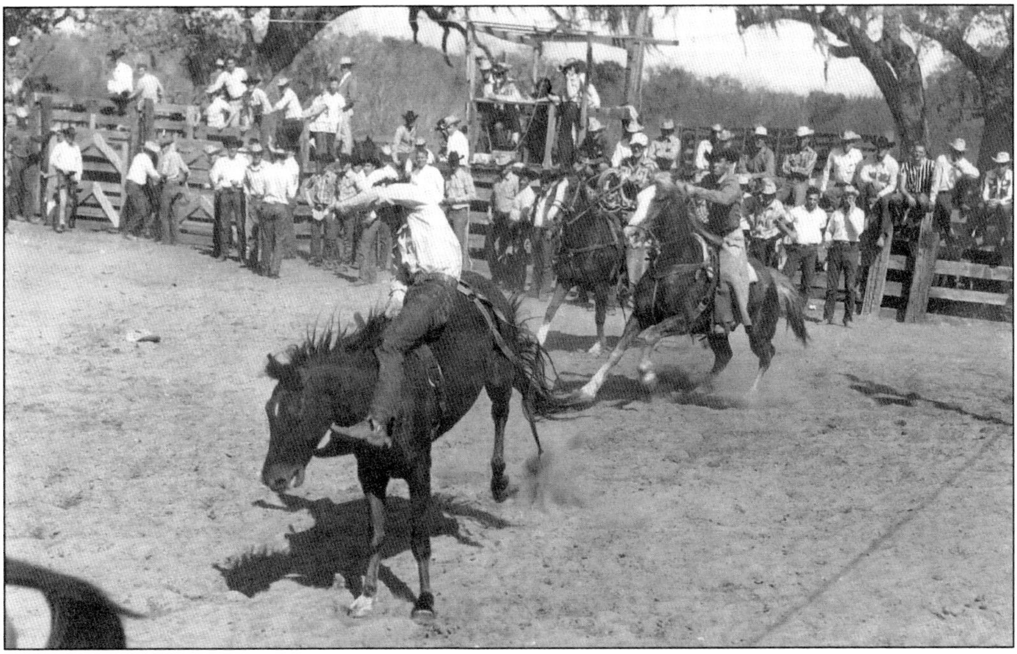

Western Days officially began in 1958 with the united efforts of Leslie Mueller and the Yorktown Chamber of Commerce. A rodeo and parade were planned with local and out-of-town floats and bands. Here Leslie Mueller's son Don (on right horse), as a pick-up man, prepares to rescue the bareback bronc rider at a 1958 rodeo. (Courtesy Andra Wisian.)

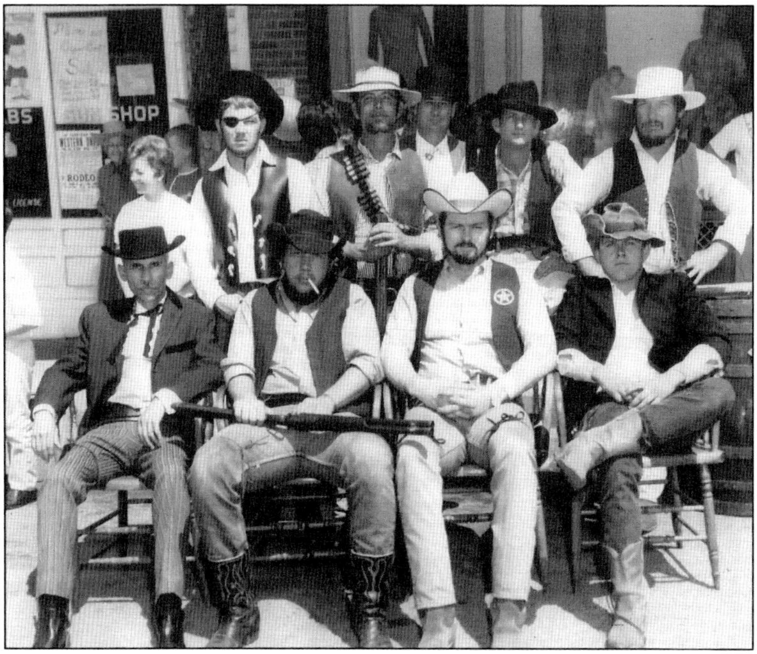

One of the main attractions before the Western Days parade commenced was a shootout between the Yorktown Gunslingers. In this particular gunslinger group the members are, from left to right, (first row) Jerry Champion, Felix Kolodziejczyk, John Ziese, and Glenn Jendrzey; (second row) Steve "Catfish" Nesbitt, Richard "Pug" Sparks, Carl Schwab, Bobby James Kubala, and Jerry Jaeger.

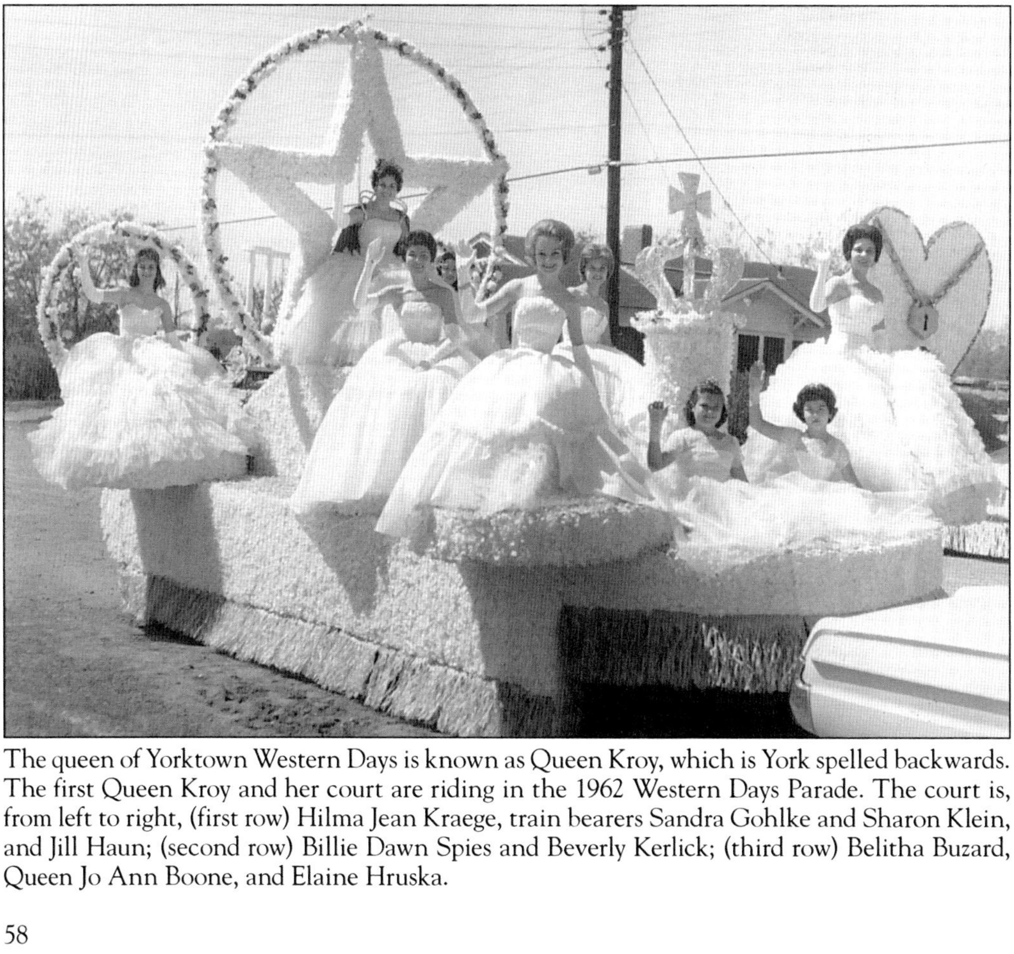

The queen of Yorktown Western Days is known as Queen Kroy, which is York spelled backwards. The first Queen Kroy and her court are riding in the 1962 Western Days Parade. The court is, from left to right, (first row) Hilma Jean Kraege, train bearers Sandra Gohlke and Sharon Klein, and Jill Haun; (second row) Billie Dawn Spies and Beverly Kerlick; (third row) Belitha Buzard, Queen Jo Ann Boone, and Elaine Hruska.

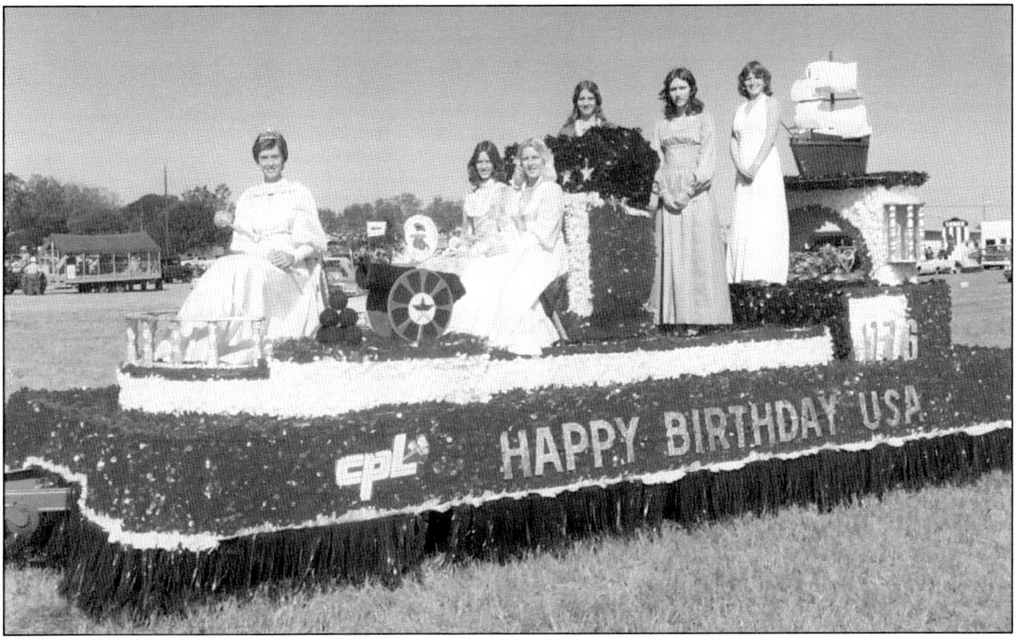

Yorktown celebrated the bicentennial birthday of the United States along with the rest of the country during 1976. Riding on the Central Power Light bicentennial float are Queen Kroy Twyla Hruska and her court. The court is, from left to right, (second row) Leah Burda and Andra Mueller; (third row) Diane Griffin and Susan Menking; (fourth row) Debbie Armer.

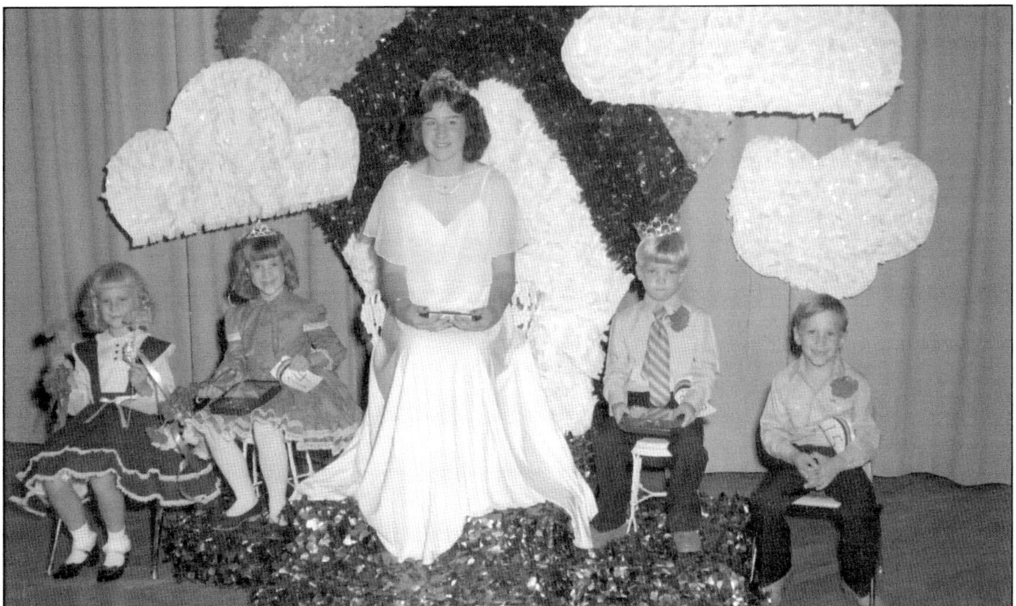

Queen Kroy XIX Julie Hays shares the stage with the Little Miss and Mister Yorktown winners in 1983. Here the winners are, from left to right, runner-up Lynn Marie Kenne, Little Miss Yorktown Brittany Podsim, Queen Julie Hays, Little Mister Yorktown Jason Spies, and Little Mister runner-up Jarred Karnei. The Little Miss and Mister court usually rode a float in the children's parade held the Friday afternoon of Western Days.

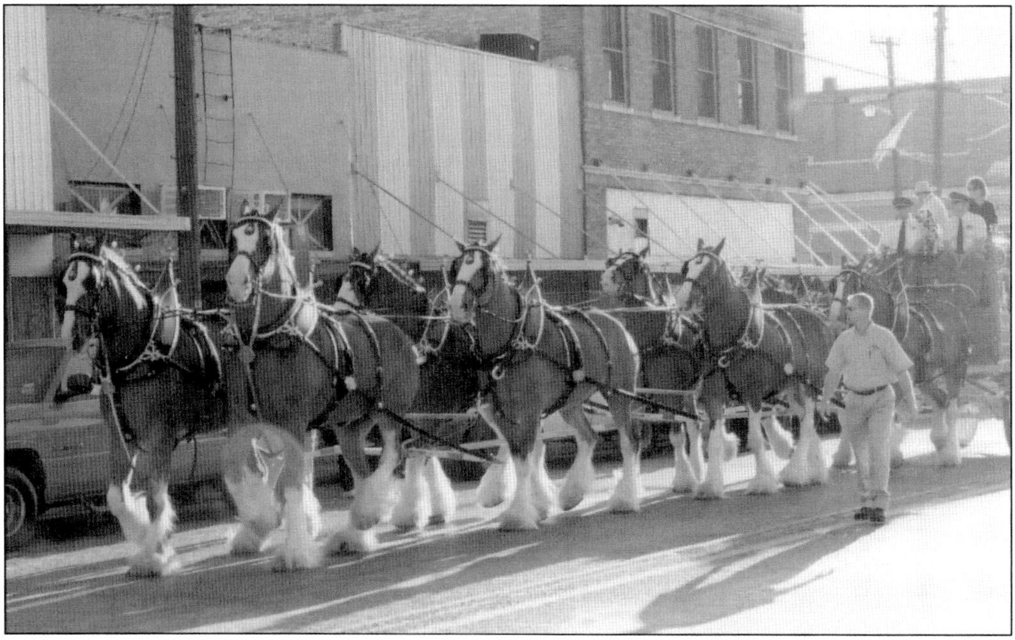

In October 2008, Yorktown Western Days celebrated its 50th anniversary. The highlight of the parade was the Budweiser Clydesdale horses and wagon. Yorktown Western Days are celebrated the third weekend in October. (Courtesy Yorktown Chamber of Commerce.)

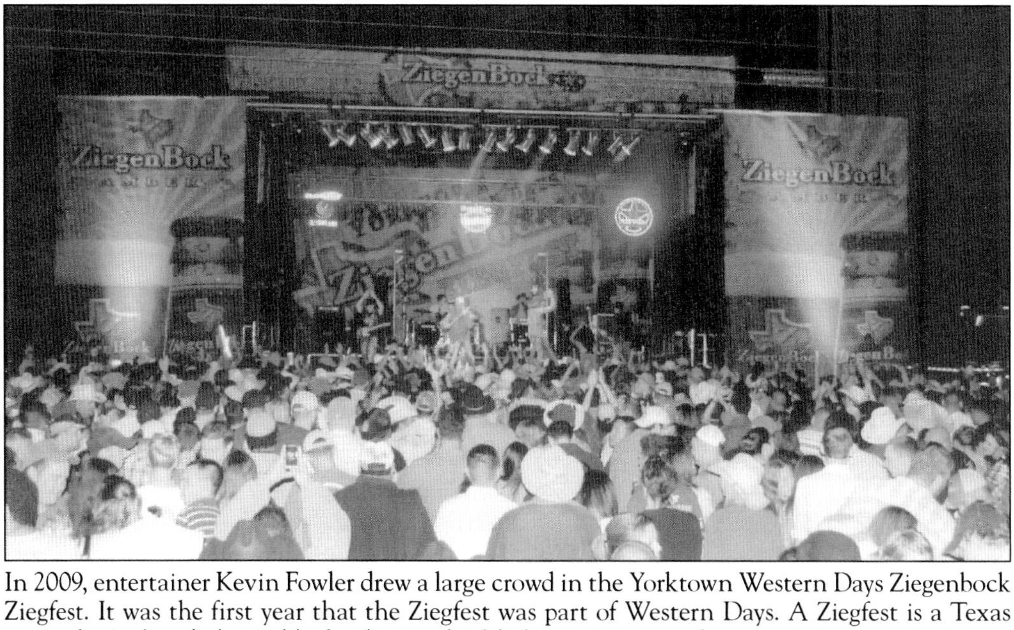

In 2009, entertainer Kevin Fowler drew a large crowd in the Yorktown Western Days Ziegenbock Ziegfest. It was the first year that the Ziegfest was part of Western Days. A Ziegfest is a Texas music festival and charitable fund-raiser highlighting Texas performers. (Courtesy Yorktown Chamber of Commerce.)

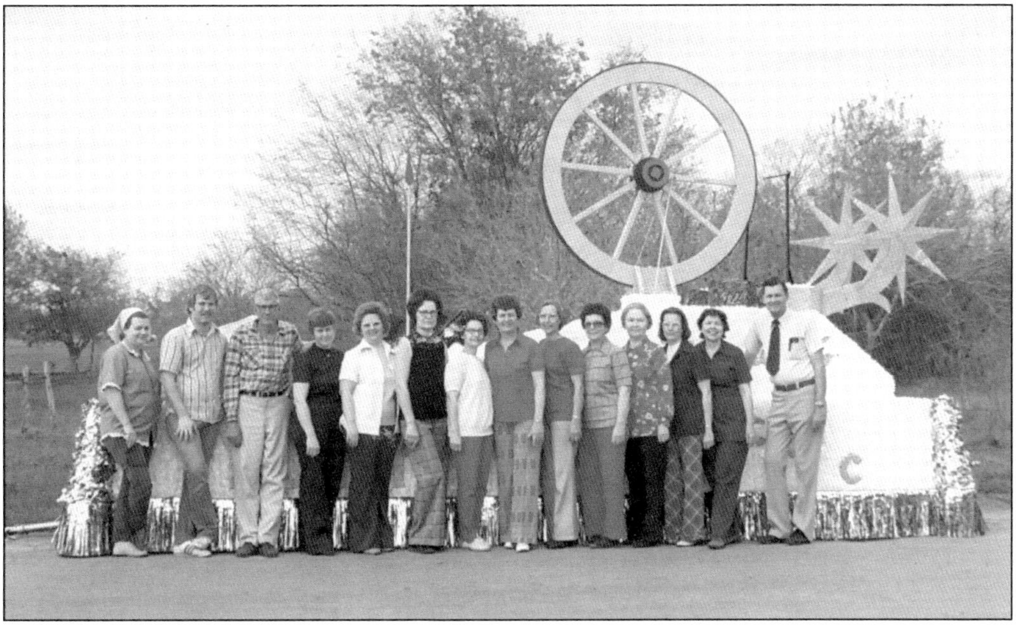

To make the Western Days Parade a success, many volunteers, both out front with the public and behind the scenes, see that everything meshes for the weekend of events. Here are the volunteers who helped decorate the 1976 Chamber of Commerce parade float. From left to right are Loretta Burge, John Koopmann, August Riedesel, Doris Koehler, Earlene Jalufka, Olivia Janssen, Lucille Klein, June Schwab, Alice Potcinske, Gladys Haun, Mae Kubala, Gail Riedesel, Jewel Weischwill, and Claud Chaney.

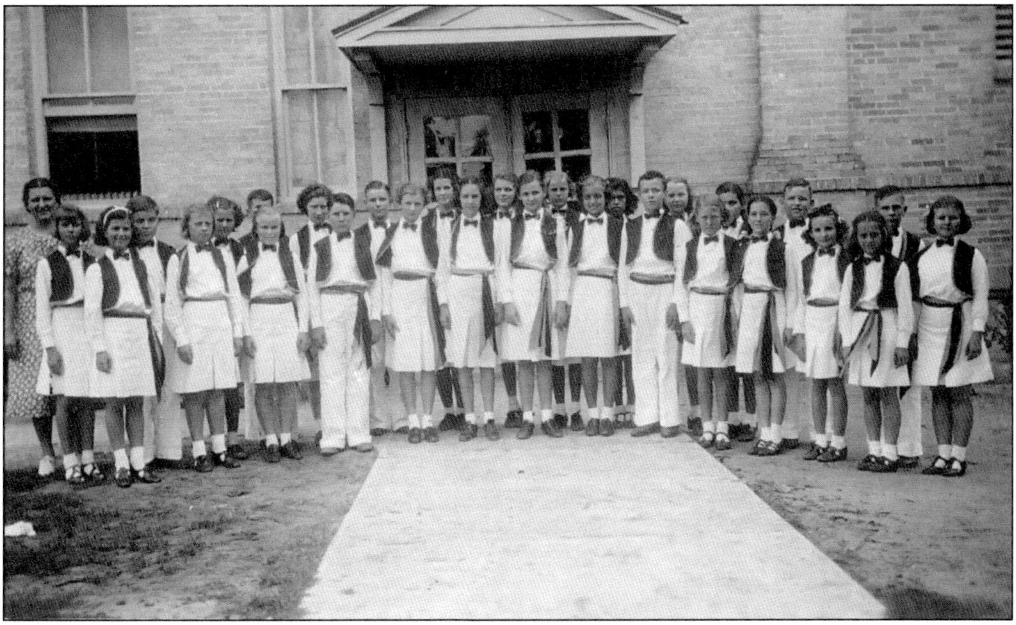

Throughout its history, music, whether vocal or instrumental, played a large part in the lives of Yorktowners. This is a school glee club under the direction of Bertha Gras in the 1950s. The students wore white uniforms with colored vests, bow ties, and sashes for their performances. (Courtesy Jay Heil.)

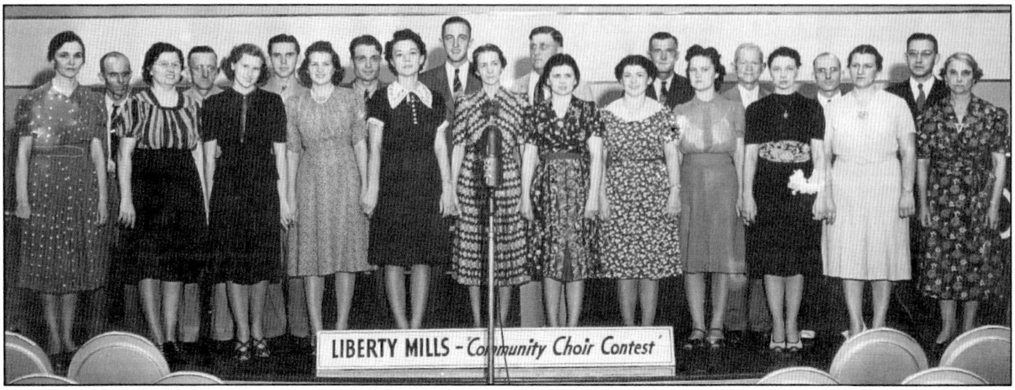

This Yorktown choir group performed at the Liberty Mills "Community Choir Contest" at the WOAI Studio in San Antonio either in 1939 or 1941. Performing are (first row) ? Metz, ? Hardwick, ? Gaida, Dora Gras, ? Miller, Olie Smith, Anita Jacob, Kathleen Jacob, ? Miller, Ada Grace Ladner, Bertha Gras, and Mrs. Vic Ladner (accompanist); (second row) C. M. Jacob, F. C. Adix, Norman Jacob Jr., John Schmidt, Leroy Potcinske, John Kerlick, ? Morisse, Herman Riedel, Robert Jacob, and Dr. Paul Kromer (director). (Courtesy Jay Heil.)

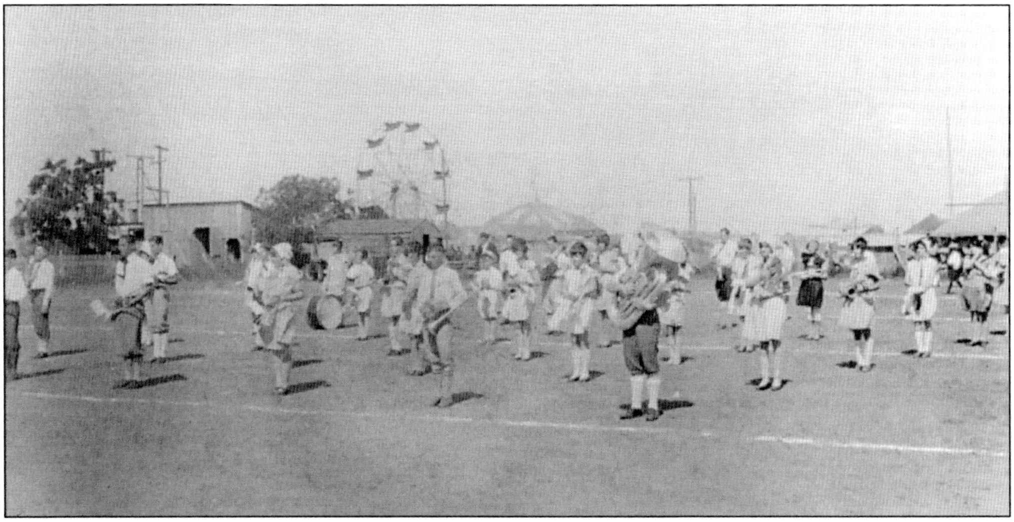

The Yorktown High School band stands at attention as they practice marching. Knickers and knee-high socks for boys and bonnets and knee-high socks for the girls seem to be the uniform on this day. In the background are tents and a Ferris wheel, indicating another celebration is underway.

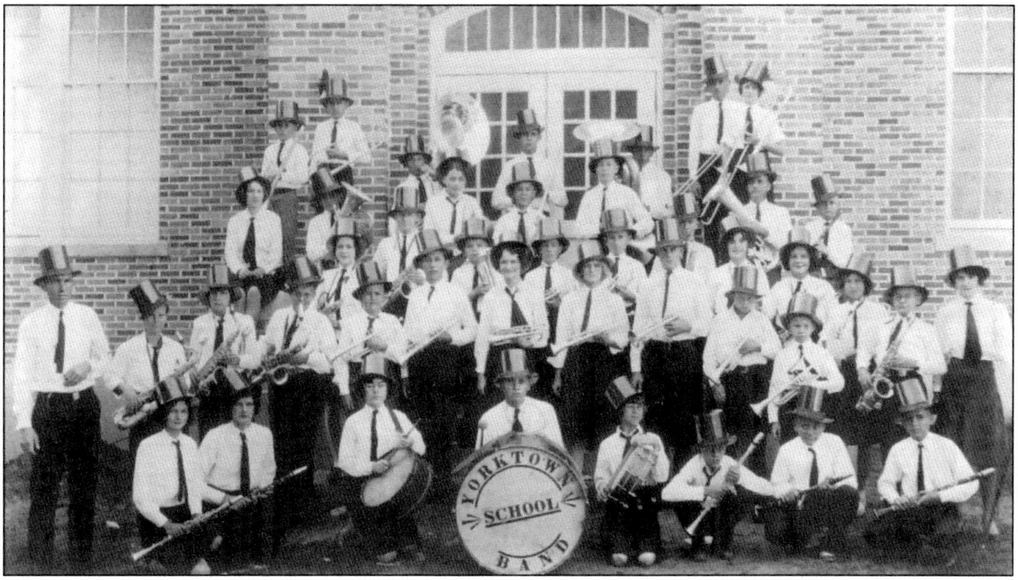

This 1931 Yorktown High School band was directed by Lou Sloma. Members are, from left to right, (first row) Gladys Mueller, Carlyn Geffert, Doris Anderson, Edmond Lemke, Lou Ellen Thuem, Fred Braunig, Ray Gips, and Ed Gaida; (second row) Carlyn Randow, Joyce Ehlers, Will Paul Menn, Carter Kraege, Lloyd Metz, Delores Strieber, Elenora Muschalek, and Alton Gips; (third row) Doris Hinsey, E. R. Sauermilch, L. C. Duderstadt, Clarence Alex, Raymond Fritsche, Rosemond Viereck, Carlyn Stuermer, Alice Horn, and Lloyd Newtown Smith; (fourth row) George Roeder, Hilda Lamprecht, Glenn Shockley, Frances Dunn, and Roland Kraege Jr.; (fifth row) Norman Jacob Jr., J. G. Kerlick, Charles Kolodzey, H. P. Eckhardt, Doris Neumayer, and Joe Kolodzey.

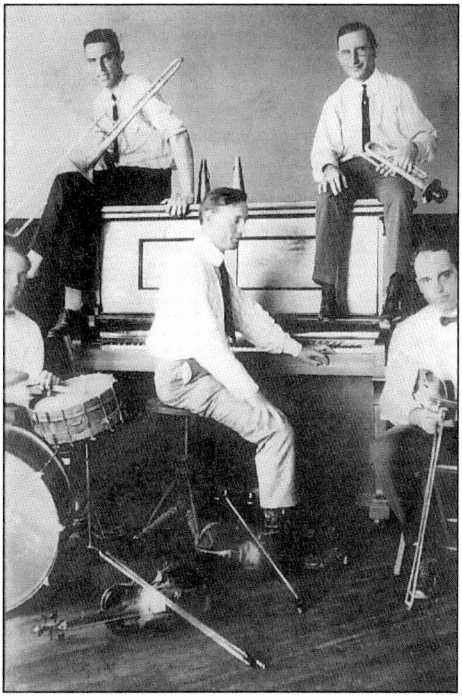

The Yorktown Dance Orchestra performed upstairs in the Nau building from 1919 to 1927. Members of the orchestra were, from left to right, Otto Pieper on drums, Lou Sloma holding his trombone, Paul Schmidt on piano, Robert Jacob who played trumpet and violin, and Wendel Leonard, the director who played banjo, violin, clarinet, and saxophone.

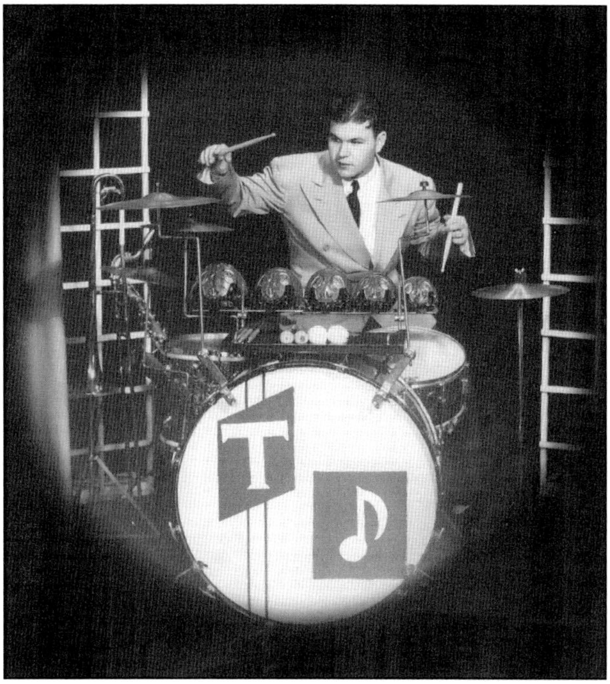

Harold Weber "Tee" Tiemann was involved with music from an early age, playing the drums. During World War II, he was in the 36th Division Band. He led the Tee Tiemann, His Drums and Orchestra for 23 years. In 1947, Tiemann opened an instrument repair business that was reputed to be "the largest and most complete home instrument repair facility in Texas." (Courtesy Arlene Schroeder.)

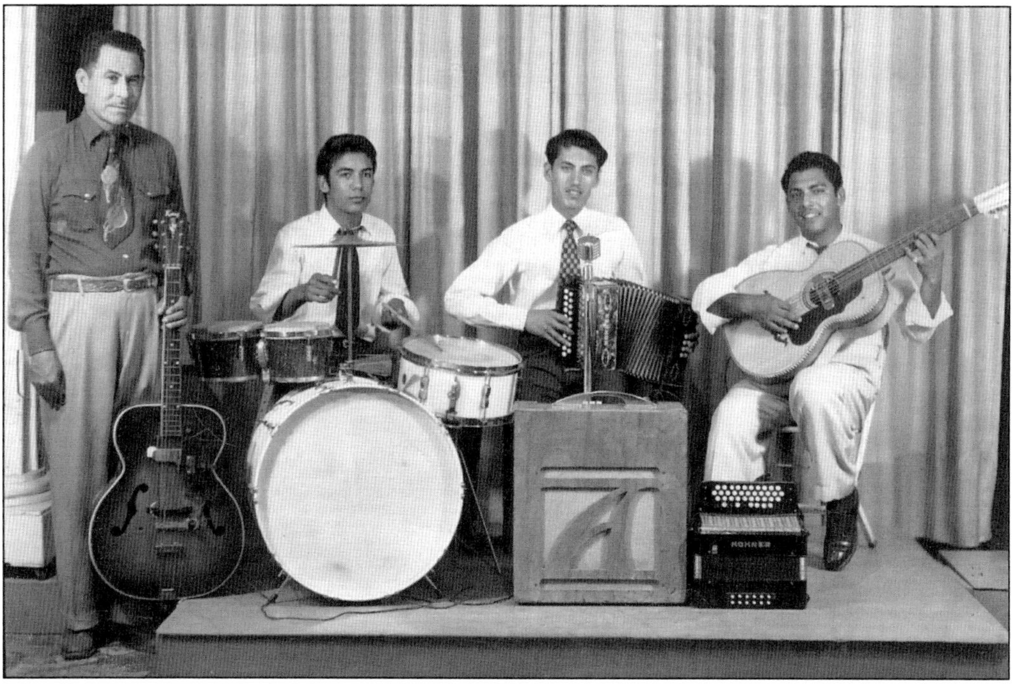

The El Conjunto Falcon was a Tejano band that began in 1955. Many of their performances were at the El Tejano Club on Highway 240, north of Yorktown, until it closed in 1980. Members of the 1955 band were, from left to right, Chon Portilla on guitar, Eloy Rosales on drums, Cleo Mungia on accordion, and Aurelio Morales on guitar. In the 1970s, the group was composed of Cleo Mungia Sr., Cleo Mungia Jr., Louis Mungia, Joe Ochoa, and Isario Mejia Jr. Cleo Mungia Sr. continued to play music until the day he died on stage, August 24, 2000. (Courtesy Karen Swain.)

Five

NORDHEIM BEGINNINGS

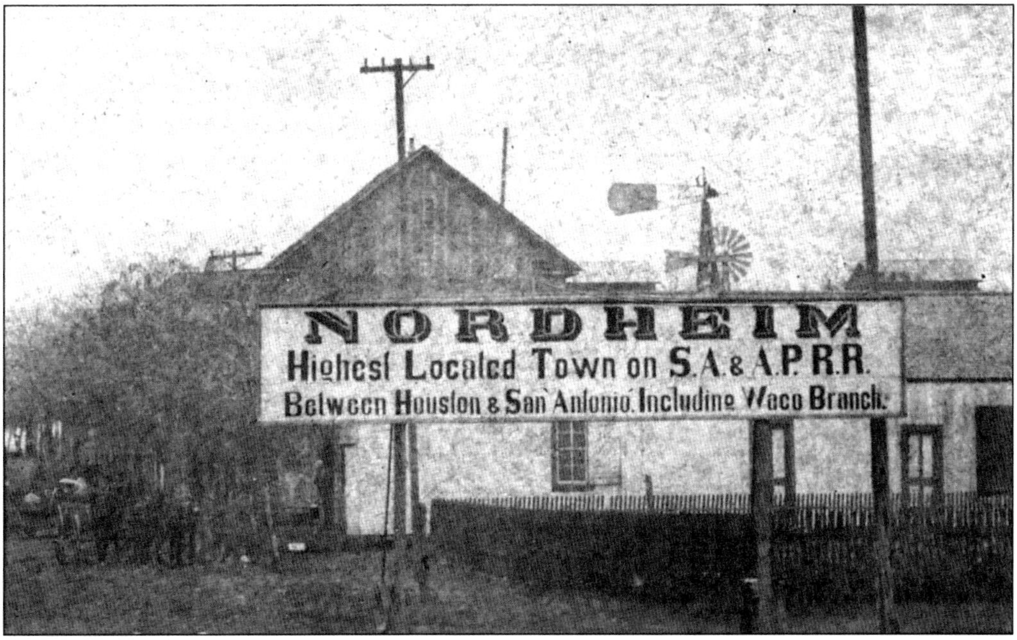

In 1886, Nordheim, originally known as Weldon Switch, was proclaimed to be the highest spot between Houston, San Antonio, and Waco by the SA&AP Railroad when they came through and established a station in Nordheim. The Nordhiem Businessmen's Club erected this sign in 1909 at the entrance to the town.

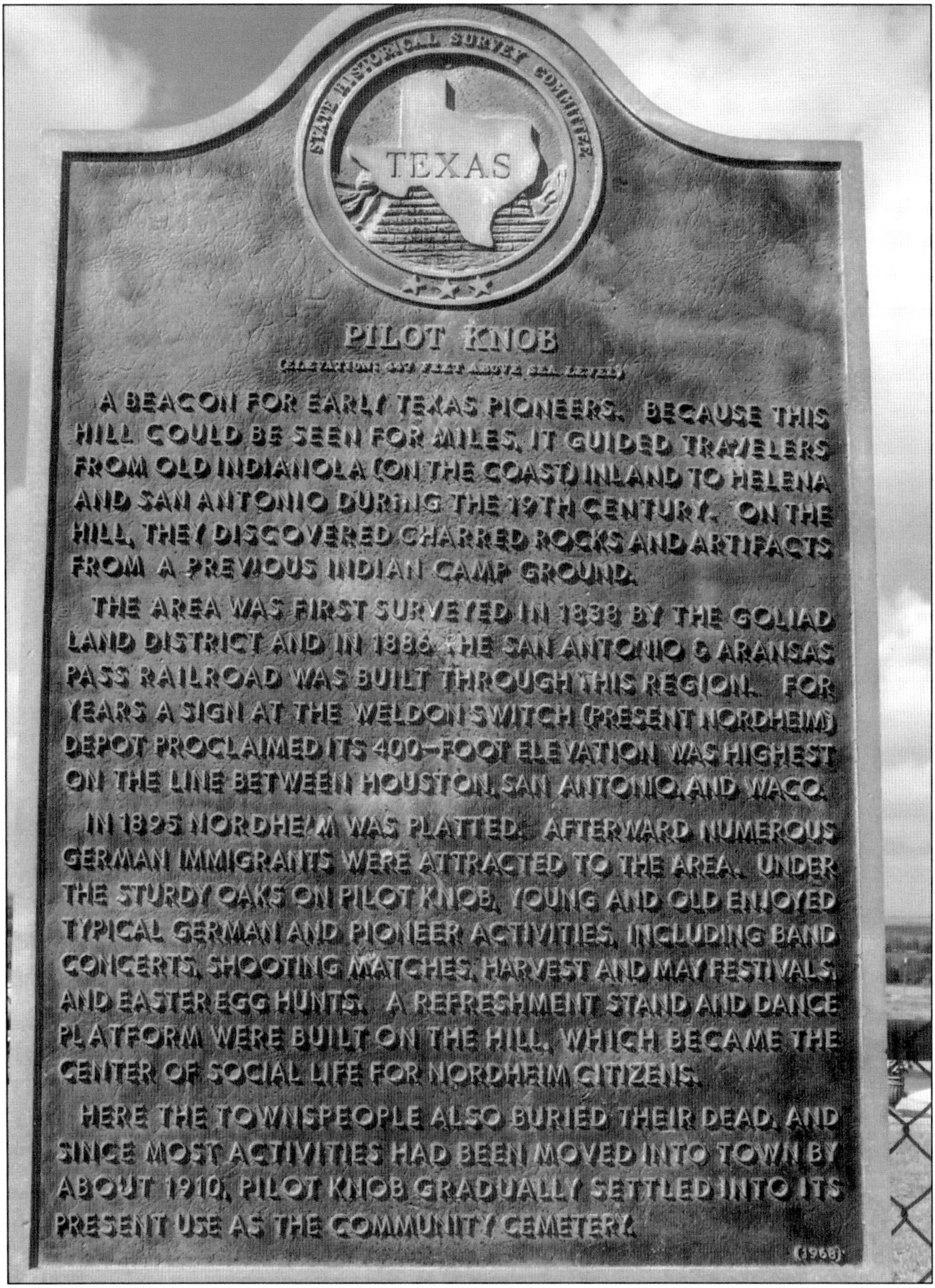

Right outside of Nordheim, a hill known as "Pilot Knob," at the elevation of 447 feet above sea level, was a beacon for early travelers of the Old Indianola Trails to Helena and San Antonio during the 1900s. Prior to this time it was an Indian campground. This Texas historical marker on Pilot Knob was dedicated in 1968. It was in the beginning and still is to this day an important part of the community. (Courtesy Cathy Voelkel.)

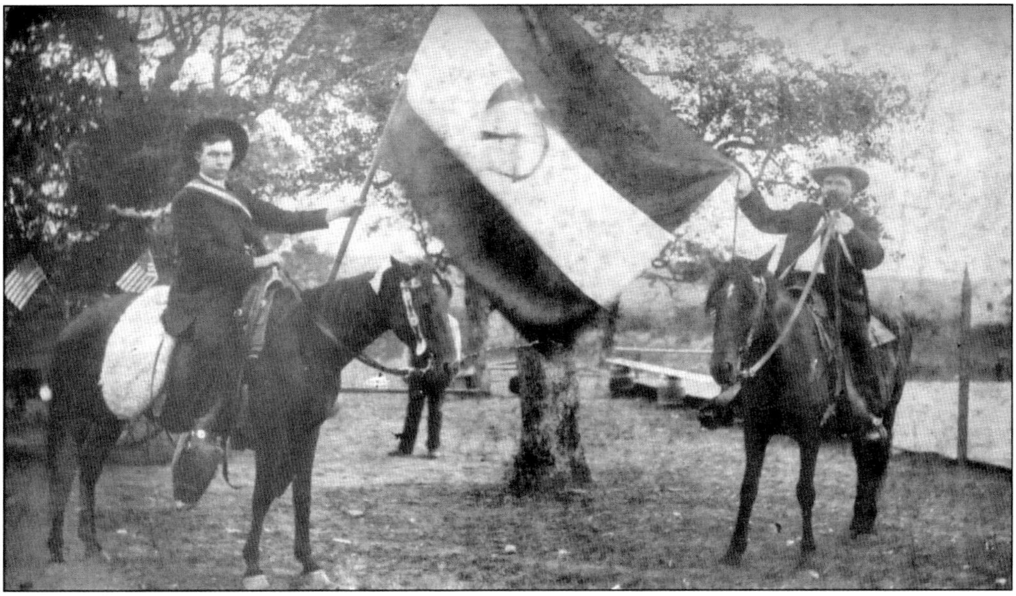

Pilot Knob was the place where the Nordheim citizens gathered. It became the center of the social life for the town. There were many celebrations held on the hill, including weddings, musical performances, shooting matches, May Feast and Harvest Festivals, dances, Easter egg hunts, and all the important events of the settlers. The flag bearer for the Nordheim Schuetzen Verein in the early 1900s on Pilot Knob was August Teiwes (right), Nordheim's mayor from 1928 to 1941. This flag and colors were lost until researched by Alfreda Huck and recreated out of wood by David Ray Whitmore and presented along with a new flag on May 21, 1986. The emblem still hangs over the Nordheim Shooting Club and Dance Hall today.

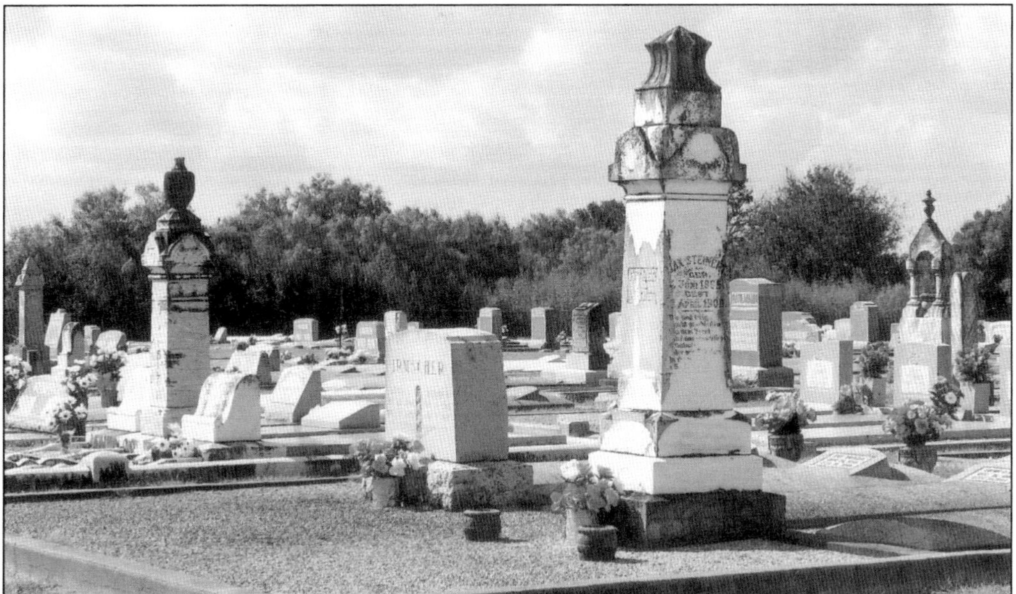

Pilot Knob was the center of the town's social events but it was also where they buried their dead. Around 1910, when the activities started moving into town, Pilot Knob became what it is today, the Community Cemetery. (Courtesy Cathy Voelkel.)

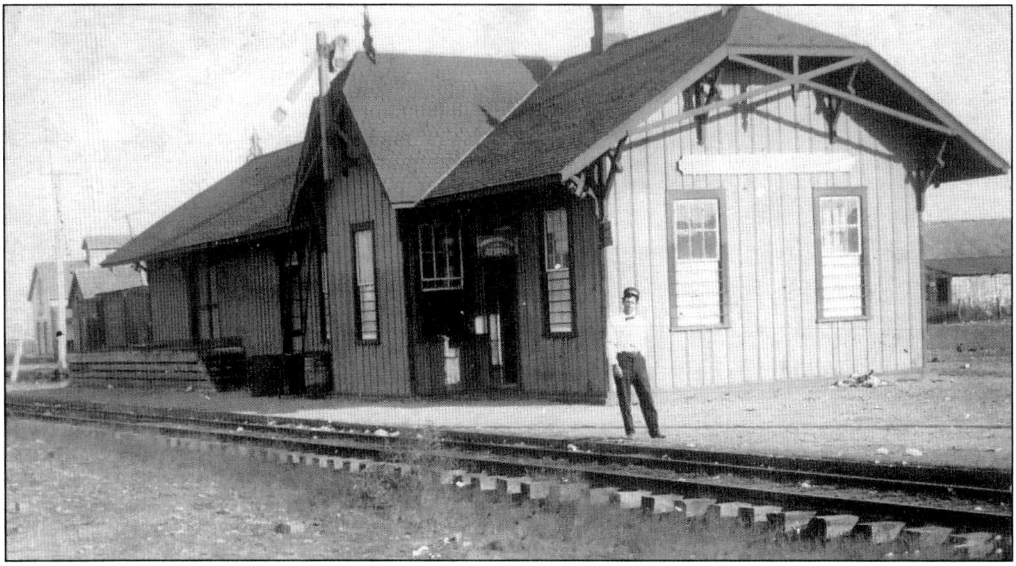

The San Antonio and Aransas Pass Railroad, later the Texas and New Orleans Railroad, was constructed in 1885. Only a small platform stood at the spot until the depot was built in 1901. Agent McKay is seen standing outside the Nordheim Depot in this picture. Aside from passenger travel, the trains took many products out of Nordheim and brought in much-needed items for the local businesses.

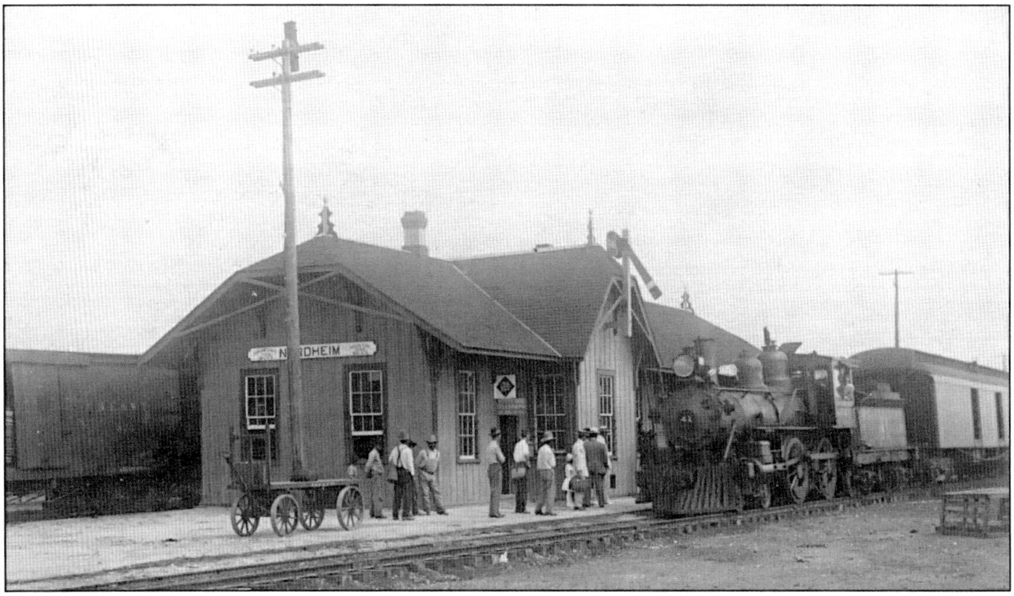

The railroad was a great asset to the community. It served as a form of transportation for the locals to go to the other communities for shopping and to travel to the coast. In this photograph, people prepare to board the passenger train in Nordheim. These trains collectively were known as the Old Salty. People would take Old Salty to Port Lavaca on weekends for a day's outing of fishing, swimming, and dancing. Others would take the daily trains to go from town to town shopping or visiting family and friends. The trains that ran from town to town were more locally known as the Little Dinky. The passenger trains were removed in 1949. (Courtesy Lindbergh and Georgie Voelkel)

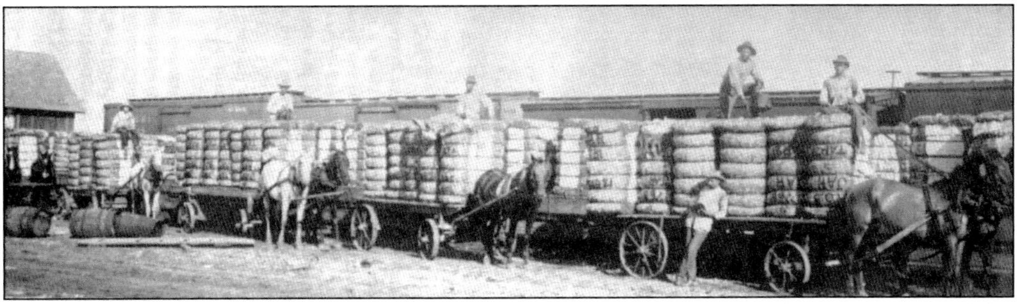

In 1914 and 1915, cotton was king and there were as many as 8,000 bales coming out of the Nordheim gins annually. Seen here are, from left to right, Ernest ?, Tom Lewis, Ernest Wolpmann, Willie Neuman, Charles Kiehl, Willie Teiwes, and Joe Wolpmann.

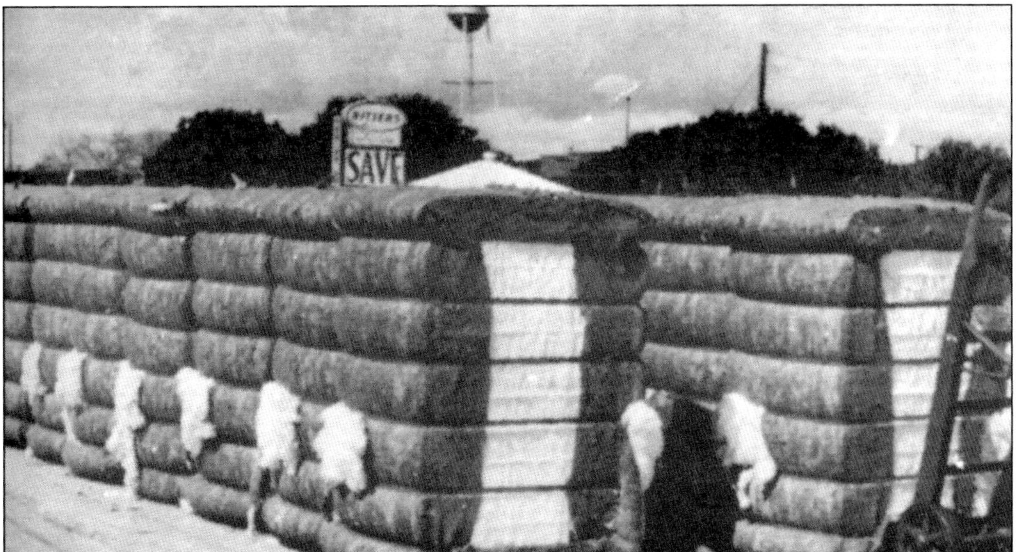

This shipment in 1970 was one of the last cotton shipments to come from the Nordheim Farmers Co-Op Gin. The gin was in business for 52 years. The cotton business was important for the Nordheim economy for many years.

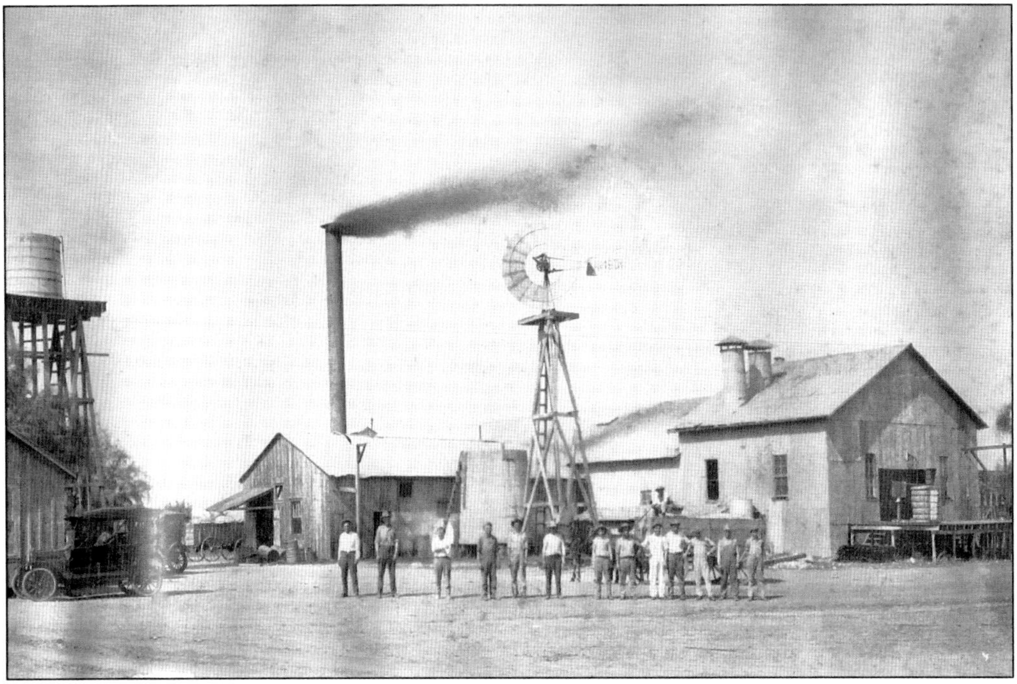

In the 1920s, there were as many as 30 gins operating in the area. Above is the Nordheim Gin Company, believed to be the forerunner of the Nordheim Farmers Co-Op Gin. Pictured in front of the gin in 1924 are John Wendt (left), Reverend Kluge (third from left), manager Fritz Onken (fourth from left), and Erwin Onken (ninth from left). The Model T car belonged to Fritz Onken. This gin was in operation for 52 years.

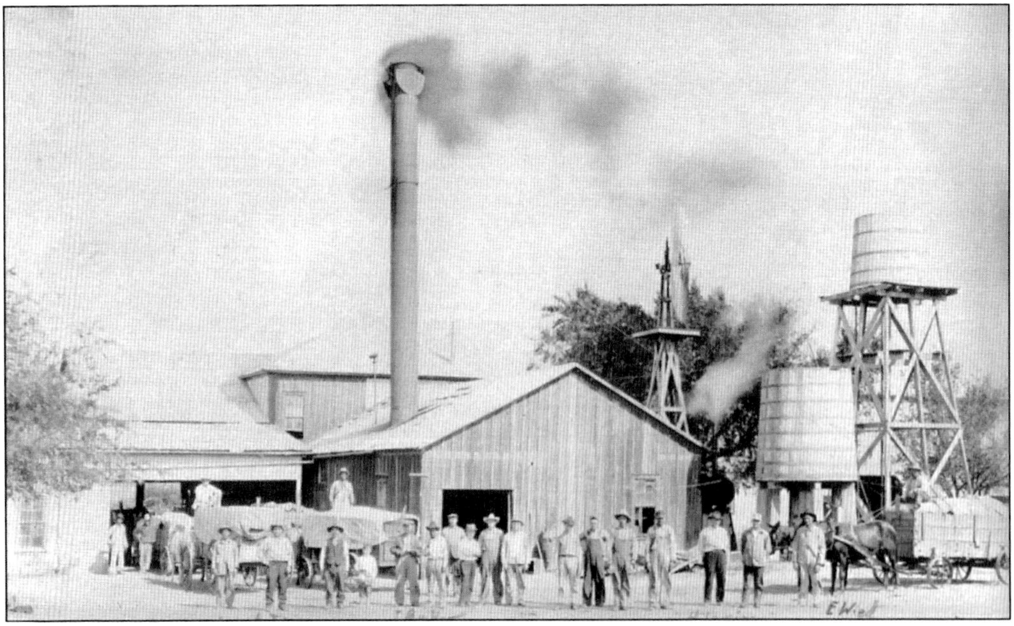

The E. H. Wied Gin, like many other gins, processed a lot of cotton when cotton was an important export from the area. In front of the gin, second from the left is A. Tam, fourth from the left is J.B. Butler, third from the right is H. Laging, and on the far right is Ed Wied.

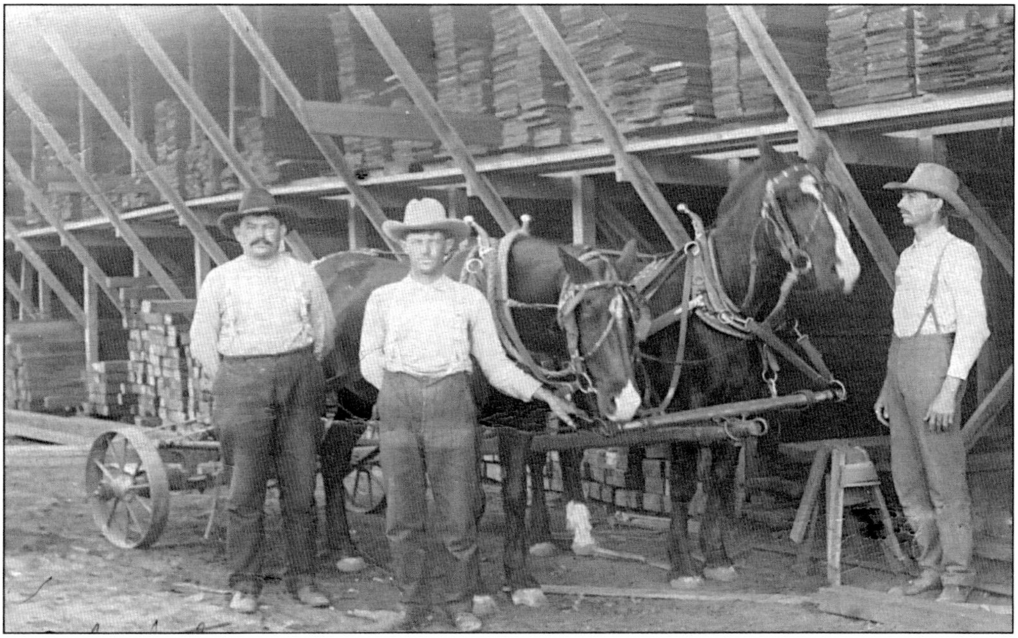

The Nordheim Lumber Company was opened by Gus Osterloh. Gus sold half interest to his father, Henry Osterloh, in 1900 and the other half to his brother Emil Osterloh in 1901. Emil bought out his father in 1902, and the business became known as E and M Osterloh Lumber Company. From left to right in this picture are Emil Osterloh, Willie Thormahlen, and Martin Osterloh standing in front of the lumber bins in the yard in the early 1900s. Emil sold the business to a Houston Company in 1914; it was managed by local men until it closed in 1957.

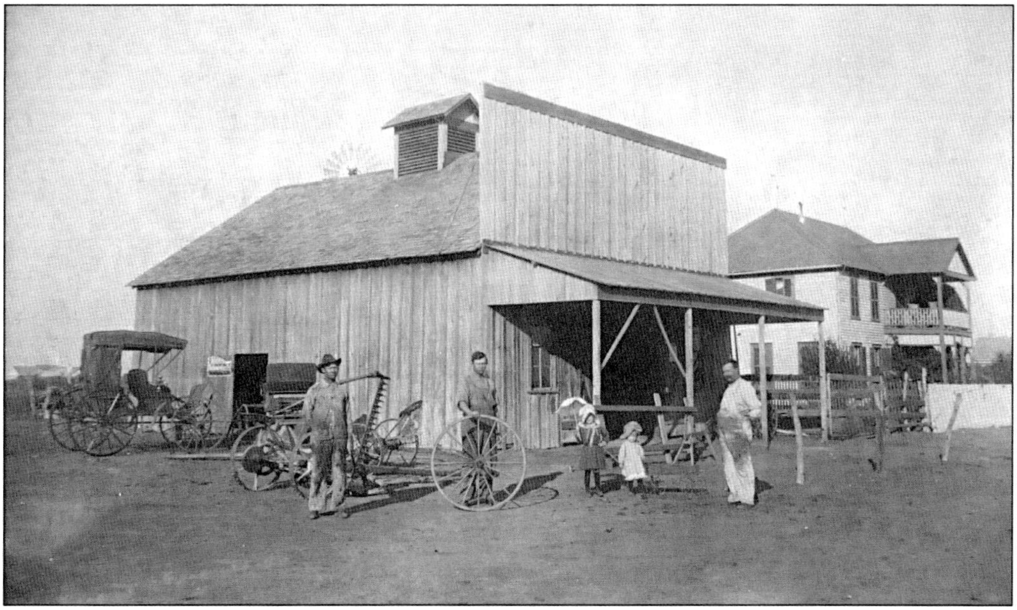

Here is the blacksmith shop owned by Paul Shulz from the late 1800s or early 1900s. The business was located on Broadway next to the August Burow home in the post office block. The men pictured here are Bennie Schulz and Paul Schulz on the right, and the children are Elenora Uhlrich and Sobena Wied.

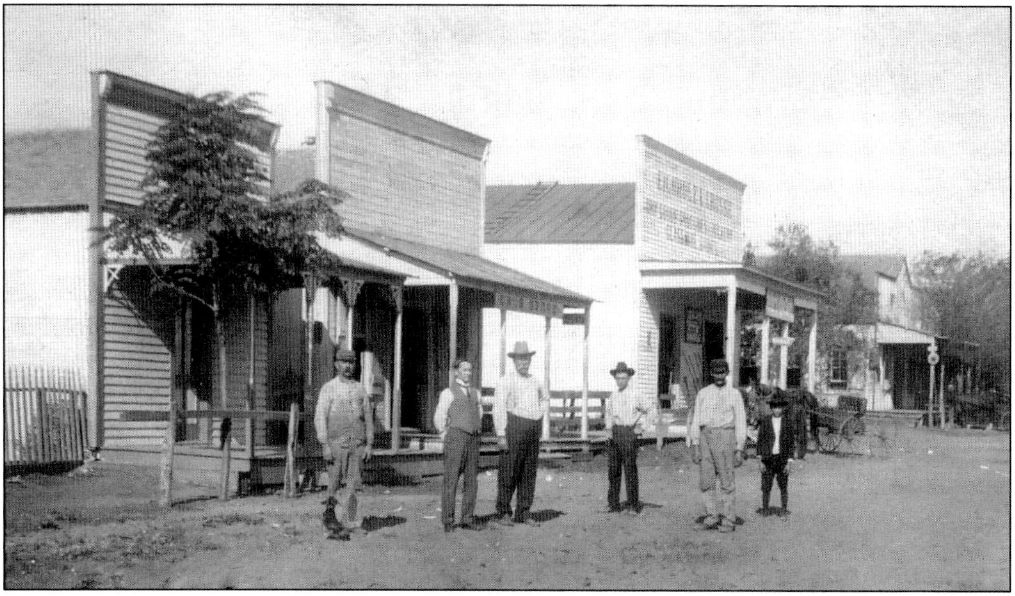

Men are standing on the dirt street in the early years of Nordheim. A trip into town was a business and social event in those days. Behind the men is Eichholz and Gross Dry Goods Store, with a horse and carriage parked in front.

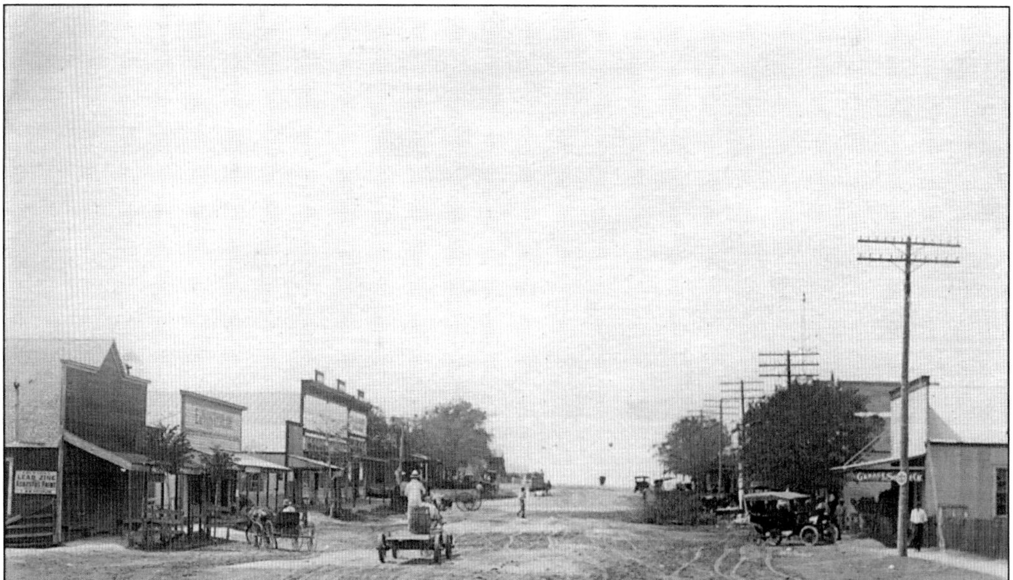

With advancements in transportation, there were both carriages and cars on Broadway, which is pictured here looking north. Times were changing, along with how people came to town and transported things from the local businesses. (Courtesy Lindbergh and Georgie Voelkel.)

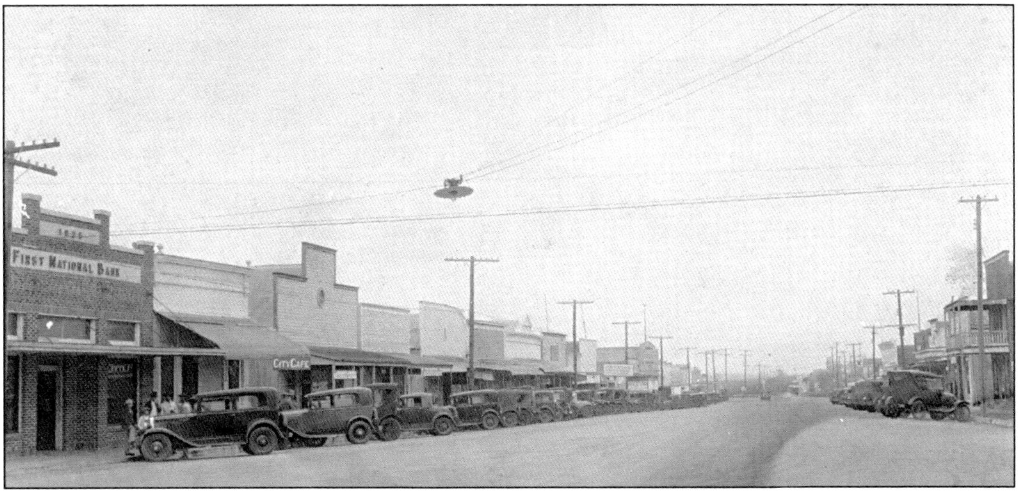

Looking south down Broadway, the streets of downtown Nordheim were lined with cars in the 1930s. In these days, the town was busy, and there were many businesses lining the streets.

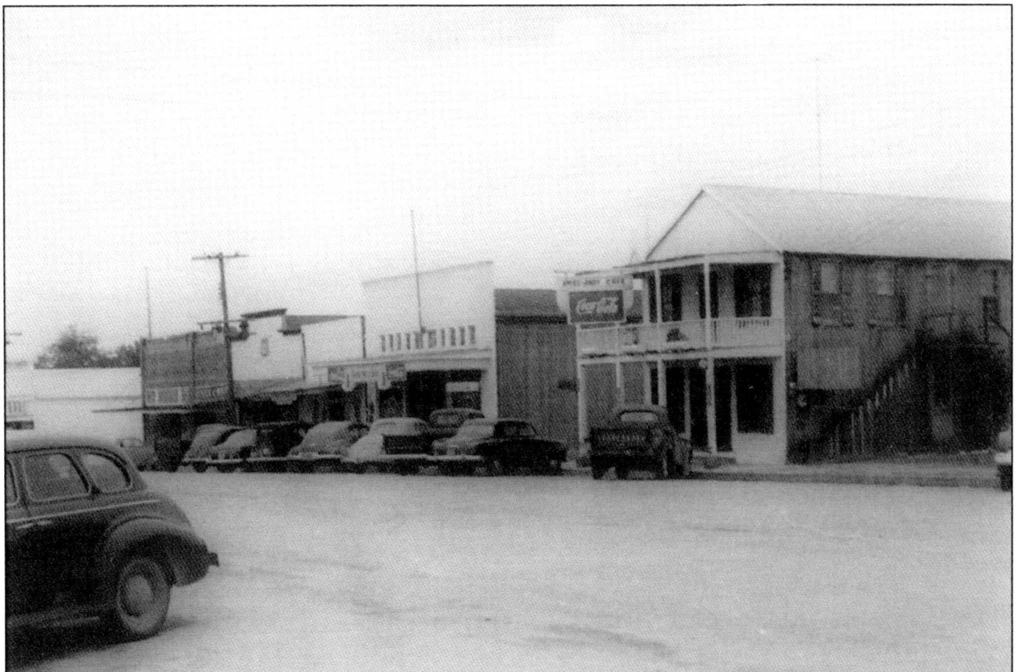

In the 1950s, cars lined the streets of Broadway in front of the Broadway Bar and Amos and Andy Café. Both these businesses were very popular in those days. Amos and Andy Café closed in 1989, but the Broadway Bar is still open and operating today.

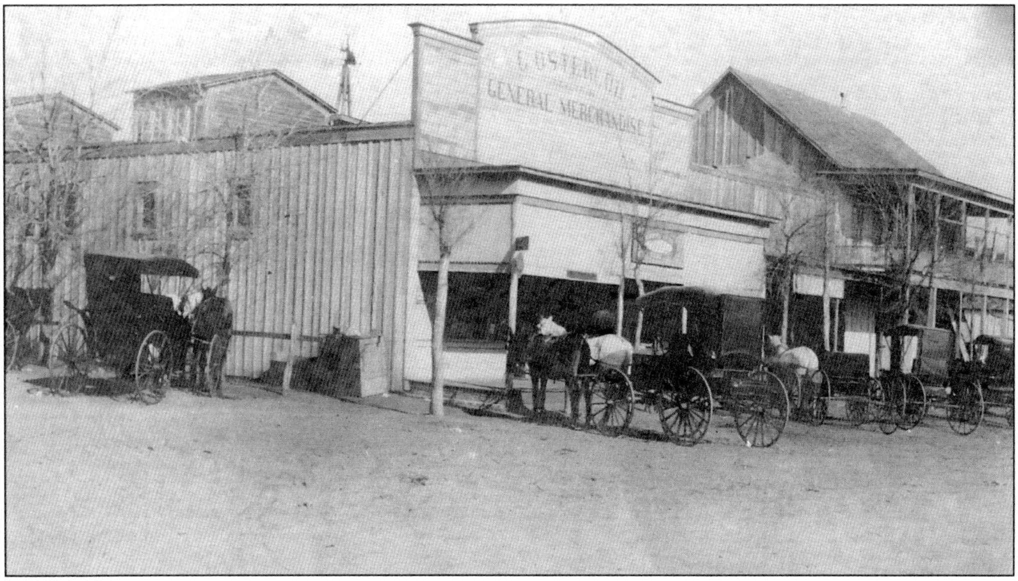

Gustav Osterloh, known as the Father of Nordheim, built his first store in 1897, which is seen in this picture. His second building, constructed in 1902, was a two-story building with his family residing on the second floor and his business operating on the first floor. It is seen to the right of the original building in this picture. In 1911, a brick building was erected and is still standing in town today. This building has been renovated without disturbing the front facade and is the office for Bob and Amanda Koricanek's businesses.

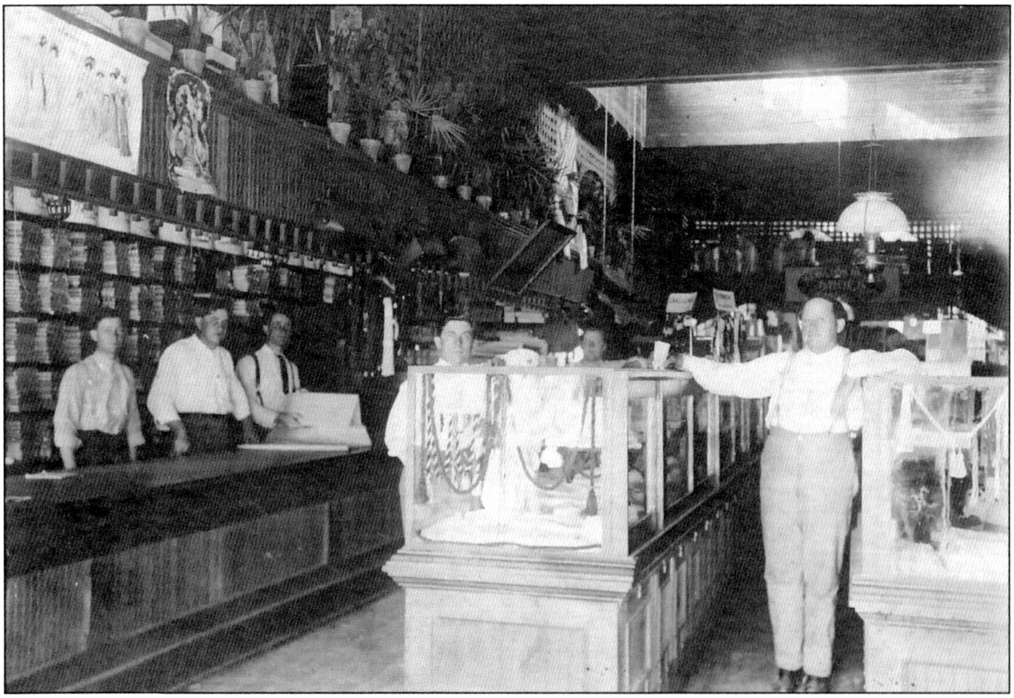

Gus Osterloh stands to the right in the first store he owned in Nordheim. Pictured here with him on the left of the showcase is Leo Neutzler, along with Willie Osterloh and Henry Schlosser. Osterloh became one of the most successful businessmen in the area.

H. A. Stuermer Dry Goods Store was in operation for many years, eventually closing in 1940. In 1942, the business was sold to Janssen, who operated it until 1968. At that time it was the last dry goods store still in business in Nordheim.

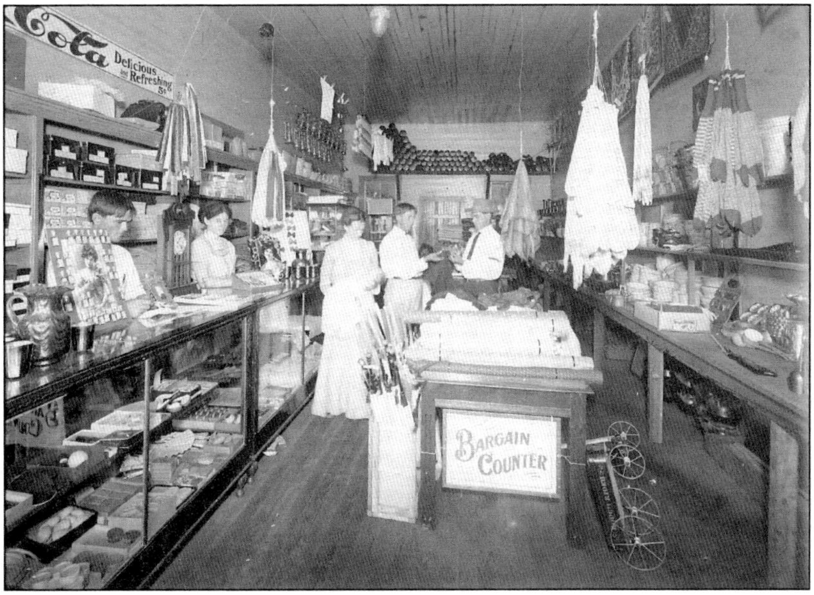

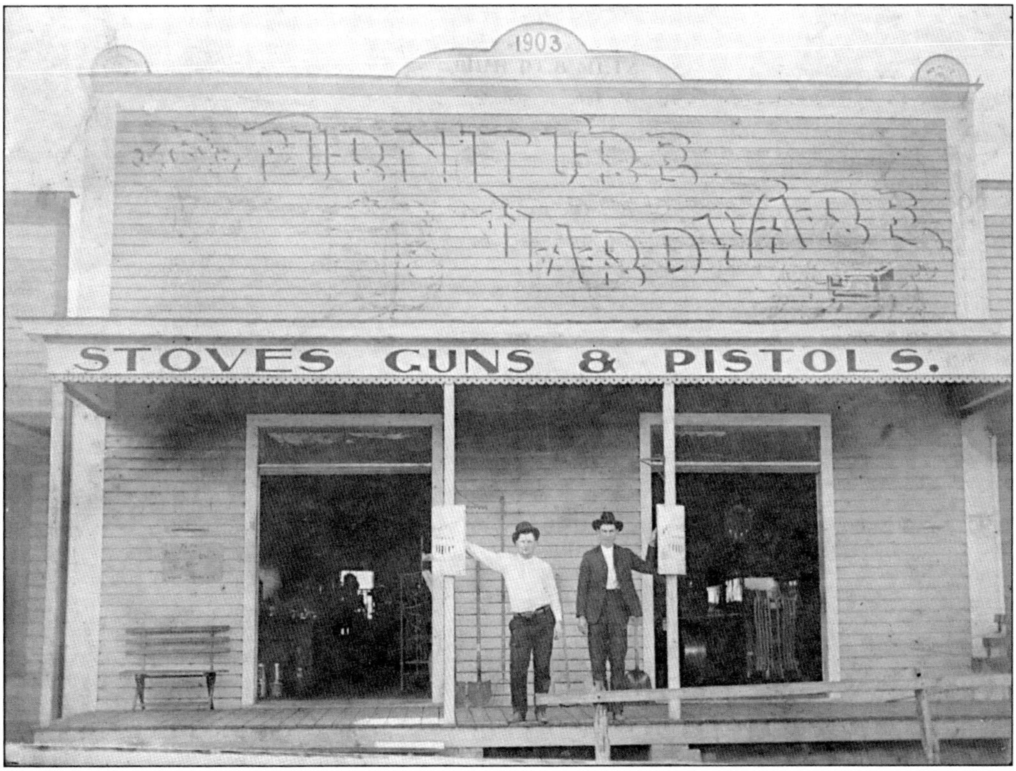

Otto Rabenaldt Hardware was built in 1903. This store sold hardware, furniture, stoves, guns, and pistols. In this photograph, Rabenaldt and W. P. Schulz stand out front. Dr. Hugo Buehring's office was in the back of the store. Dr. Buehring, the first doctor in Nordheim, was active in many aspects of the community. He organized the Modern Woodmen of the World in Nordheim, he was a member of the shooting club, and also helped with organizing the Nordheim Brass Band. This building became the Broadway Bar in 1933, which is still in business today.

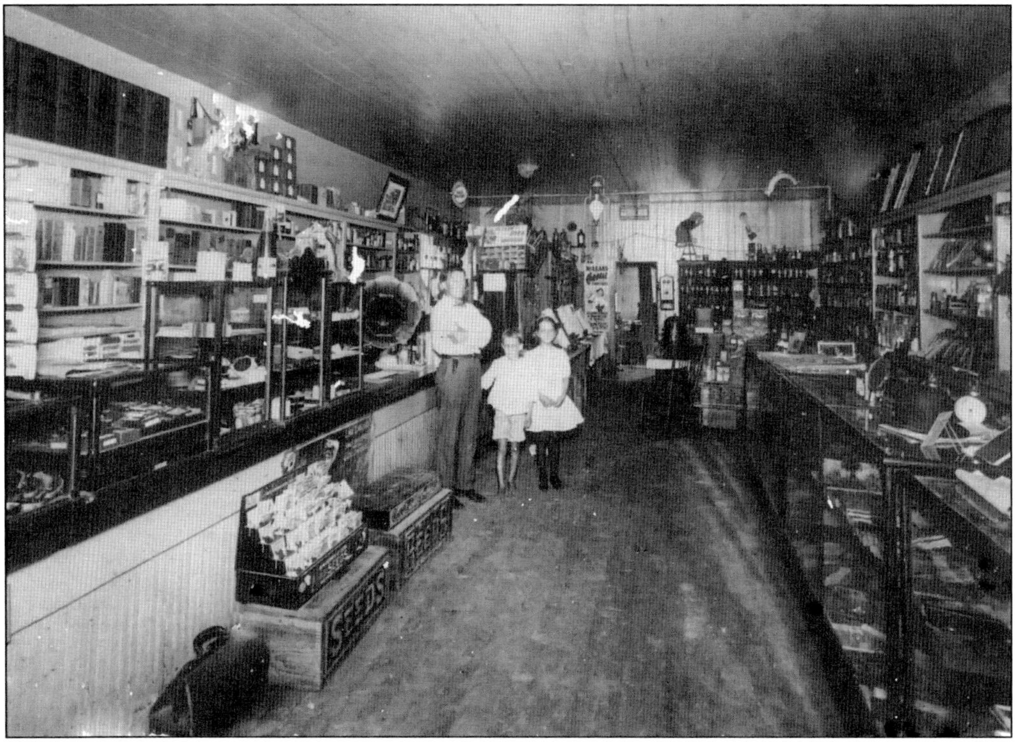

The original Nordheim Drug Company was established in 1909 by Fred Brunkenhoefer. A new building was erected in 1913. Pictured in this 1910 photograph in the first store are Fred, Roy, and Lunes Brunkenhoefer.

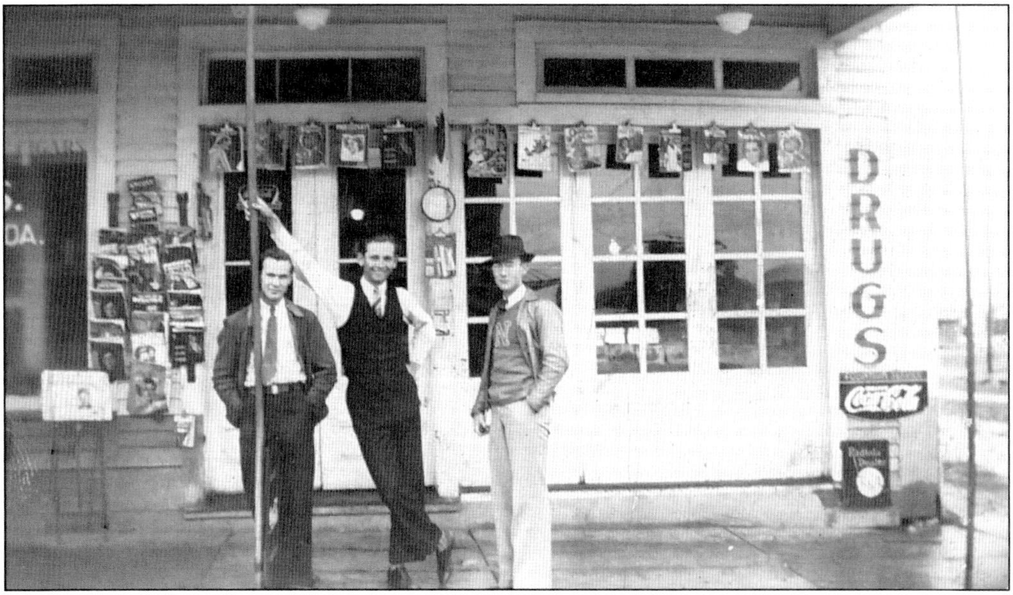

C. W. Voelkel Drugstore is pictured here with Ivie Klaevemann, Manfred Riebschlaeger, and Lester Klaevemann on the front porch of the store.

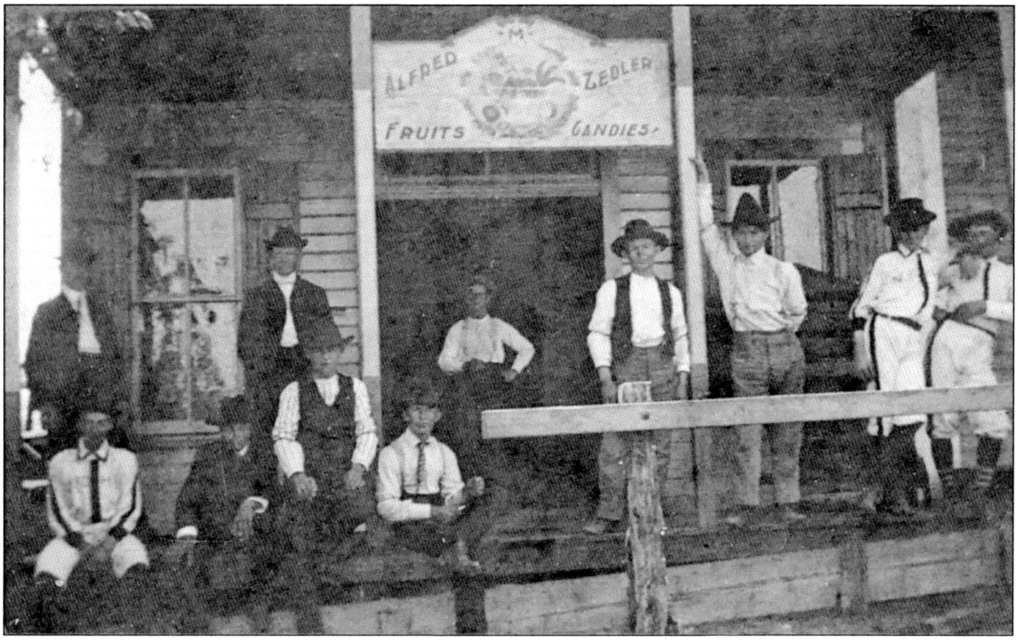

The Zedler Store, selling fruits and candies, was a popular place, as seen in this photograph.

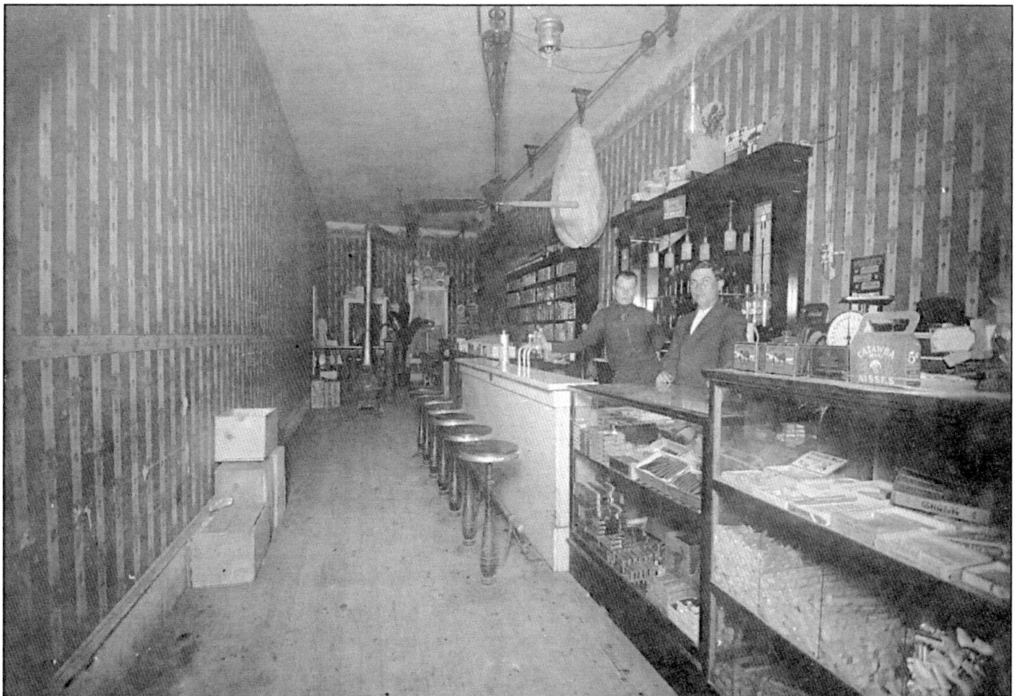
W. P. Schulz opened W.P. Schulz Confectionery after moving here in 1910. Early on Schulz went into partnership with his brother-in-law C. W. Voelkel. The business lasted until Schulz bought out the partnership in 1919. He continued the business until he opened a grocery store in 1926.

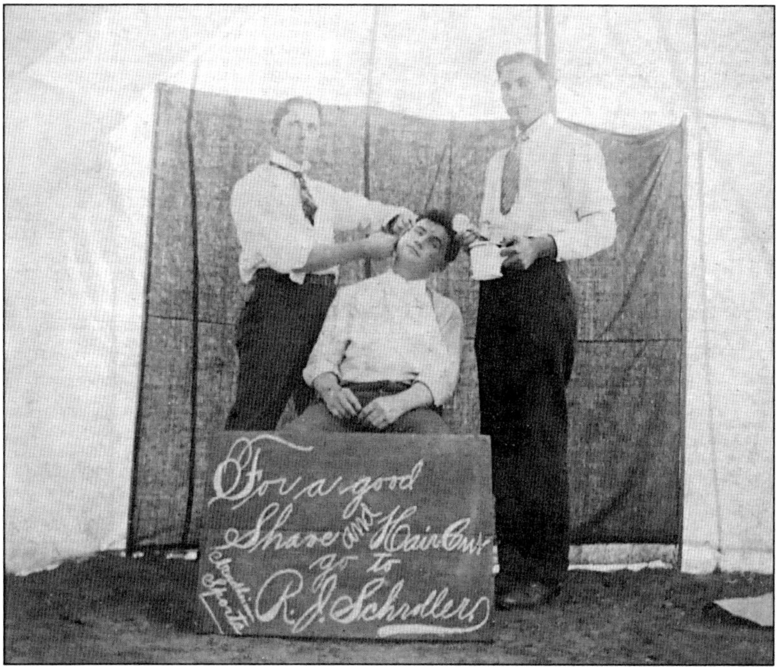

"For a good shave and haircut, go to R. J. Scholler." Scholler is pictured here giving a demonstration of his work.

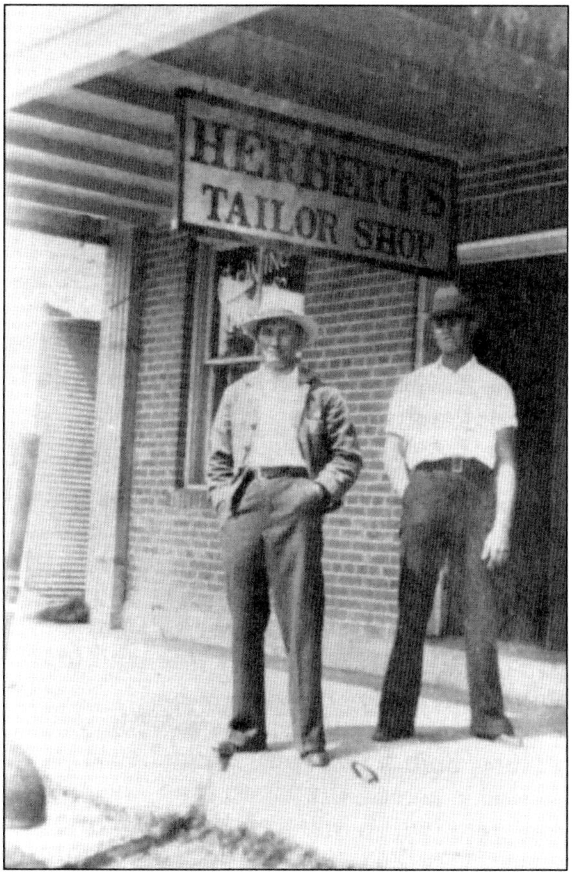

Bennie Klaevemann and Aaron Gips are seen here on the porch of Herbert Klaevemann's Tailor Shop in 1933. Clarence Reidel owned the shop until 1929, when Herbert Klaevemann purchased it. Edwin C. Klaevemann bought it from his brother in 1930 and operated the business until 1935, when Reidel bought it back. The Reidel building now houses the office of the Nordheim City Hall where the tailor shop was; the front of the building is the Nordheim Volunteer Fire Station and Oralia's Hair Station. (Courtesy Kay Klaevemann.)

C. B. Dean was the town tinsmith. He started his business in the back of the Rabenaldt Hardware Store, which is now the Broadway Bar. In 1913, the business moved across the street into what was known as C. B. Dean's Tin Shop, where he worked until his death in 1970. He devoted an amazing 52 years in the tinning and plumbing business. At right is C. B. Dean holding one of the first bathtubs built in the C. B. Dean Tin Shop. This was one of the first tubs in Nordheim, and he continued to build many tubs that graced the homes in Nordheim. Standing to Dean's left is Fritz Rogge. In the photograph below, C. B. Dean is at work in his tin shop. Dean is at the brake, and longtime employee Valentine Garcia is holding the tin snips. This photograph was taken on December 17, 1945.

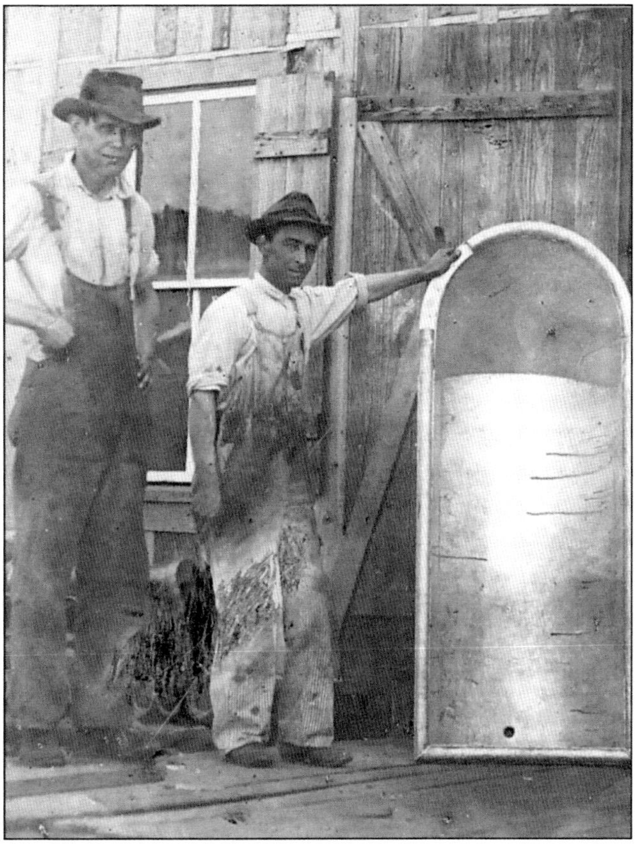

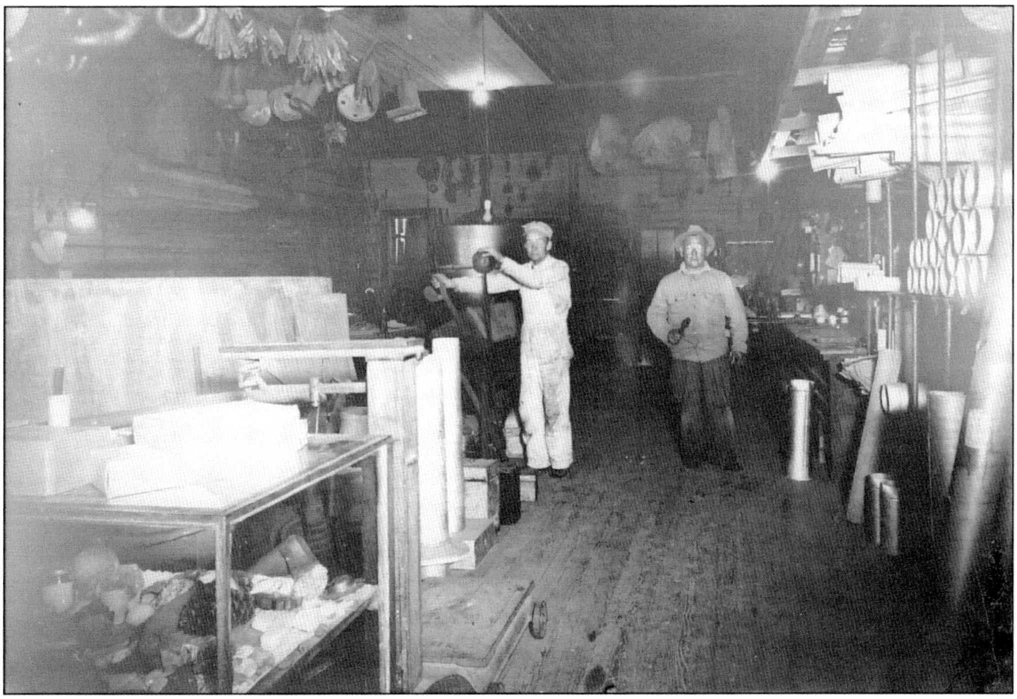

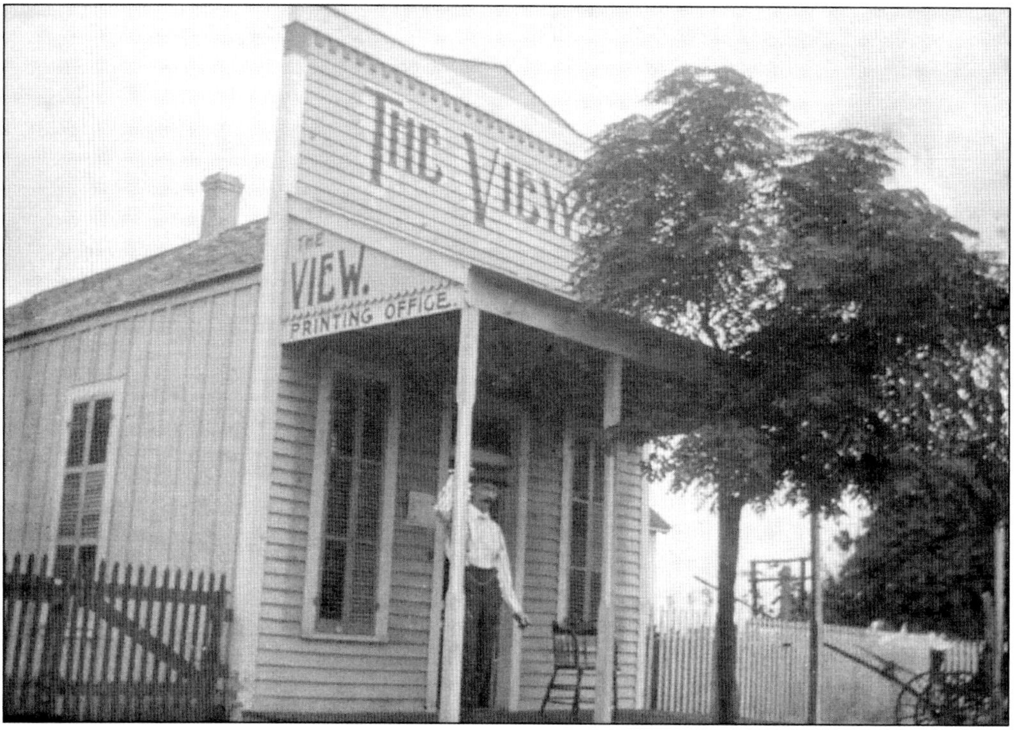

J. W. Blanton is standing on the porch of the *Nordheim View*, which he founded and began publishing in 1902 and continued doing until November 1, 1938. The picture below shows Blanton inside the office of the *Nordheim View*.

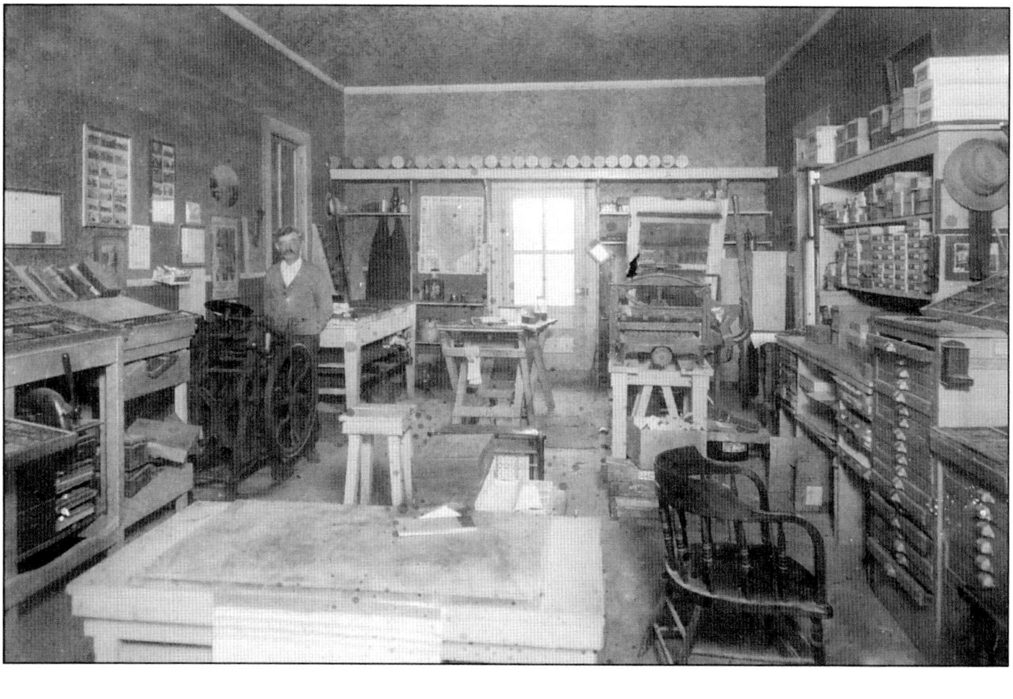

The Nordheim Fire Station and City Hall were housed in this two-story brick building. The firehouse was dedicated in 1923. The lower level was where the fire trucks were stored, and the upper level was used for the city hall. Pictured here in front of the fire station on the right is the recently purchased Model-T fire truck by Simms Company. Fire Chief J. E. Steiger is in the front row in the dark suit.

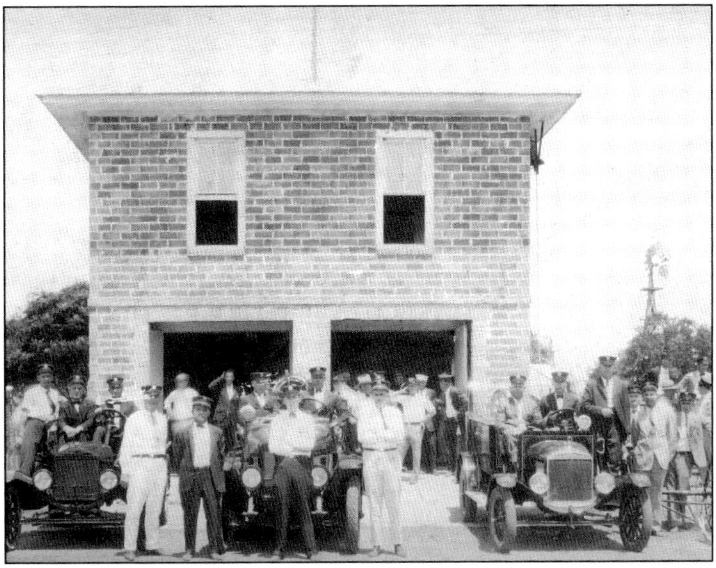

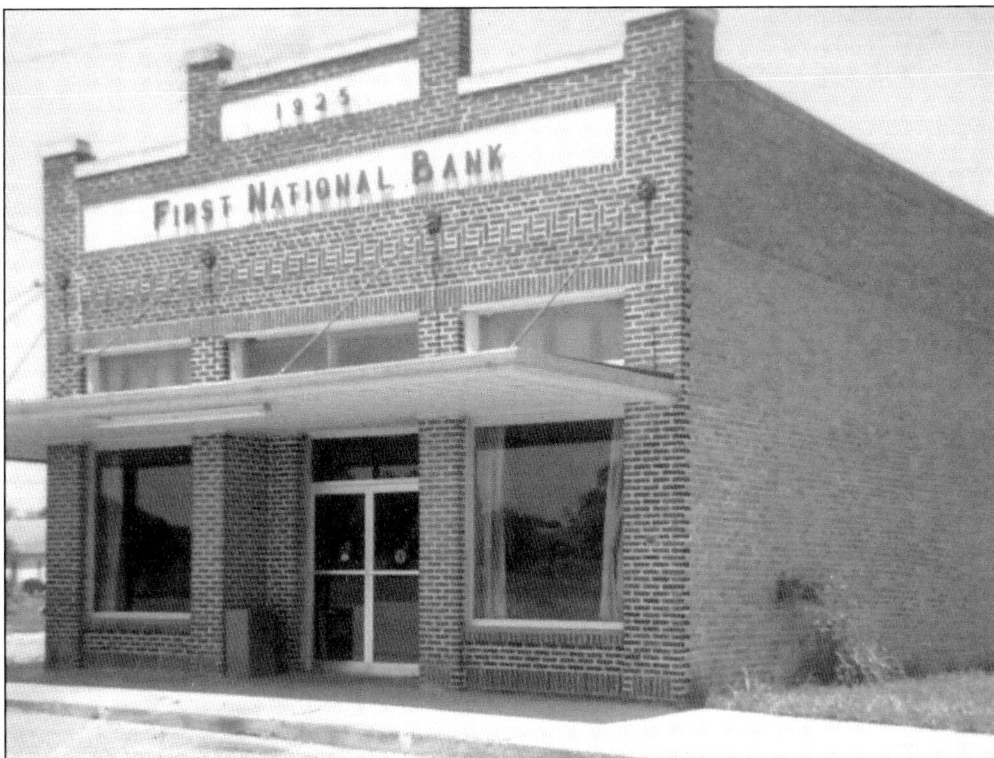

The first bank in Nordheim began as the State Bank of Nordheim in 1910. H. J. Strunck was president, Charles W. Gohmert was vice president, and F. O. A. Ladner was cashier. The State Bank became the First National Bank in 1923. F. O. A. Ladner was lead cashier from 1910 until his death in 1943. Kermit Ladner succeeded his father as cashier and served in this position for 14 years. The new brick building seen in this photograph was erected in 1925. In 1952, Lindbergh Voelkel joined the bank as cashier, and he became bank president in 1971. He retired after 37 years of service. Today Nordheim's bank is operating in a new building as Wells Fargo Bank.

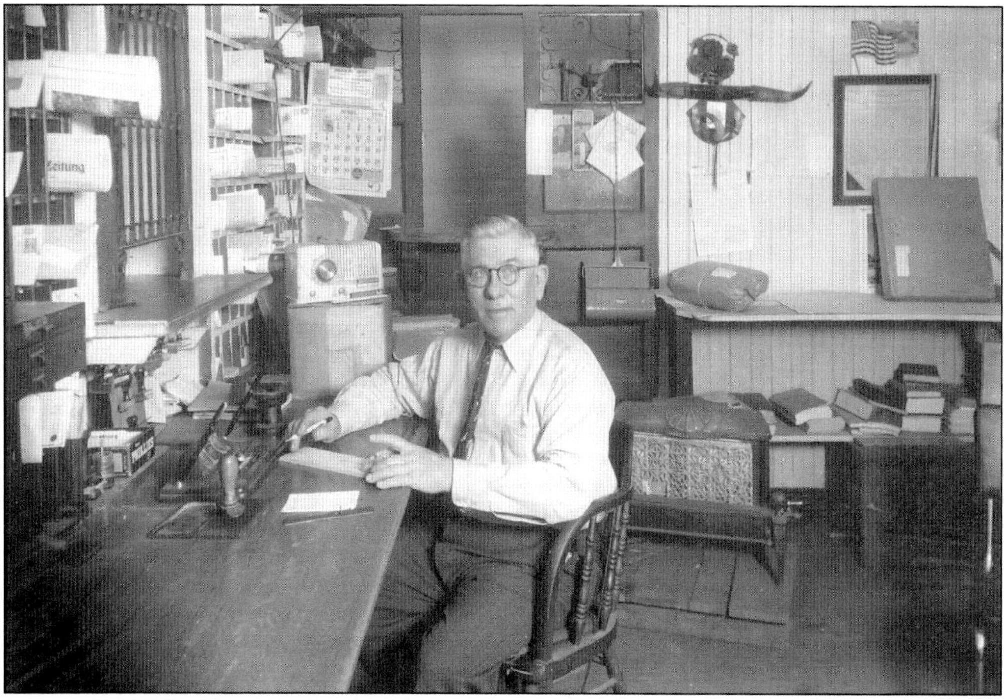

In 1941, L. C. Neutzler is pictured working as postmaster. Neutzler was postmaster from 1937 to 1948. Postal clerk Thelma Estill, who later became postmistress, assisted him.

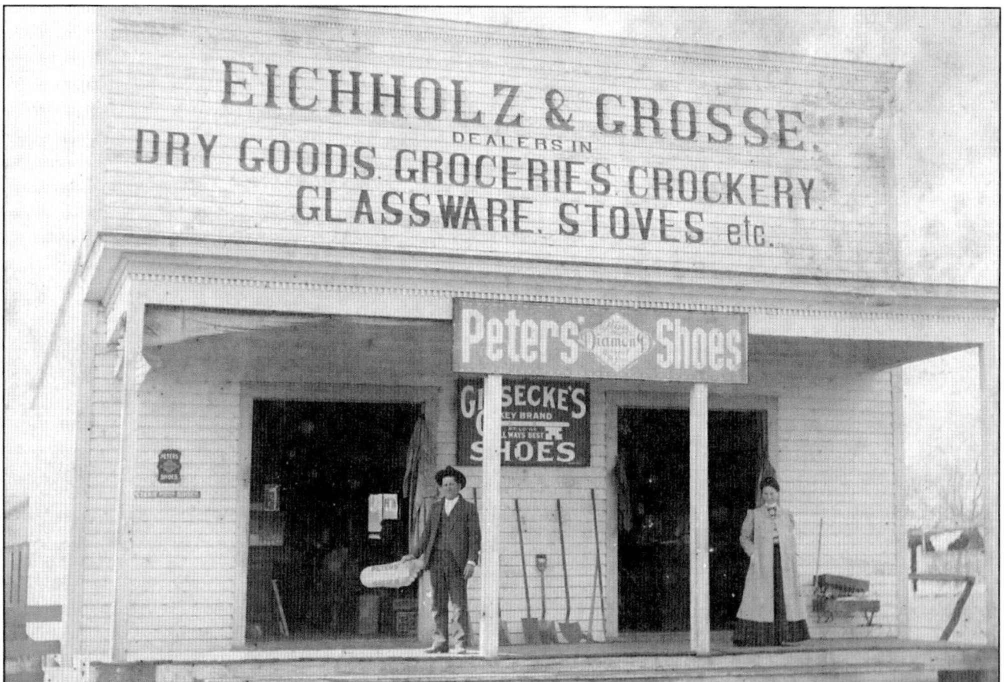

Eichholz and Grosse was one of the early dry goods stores. They handled everything from groceries, crockery, glassware, stoves, shoes, and just about anything else one could need. Pictured on the front porch of the business are Eichholz and Mrs. Grosse.

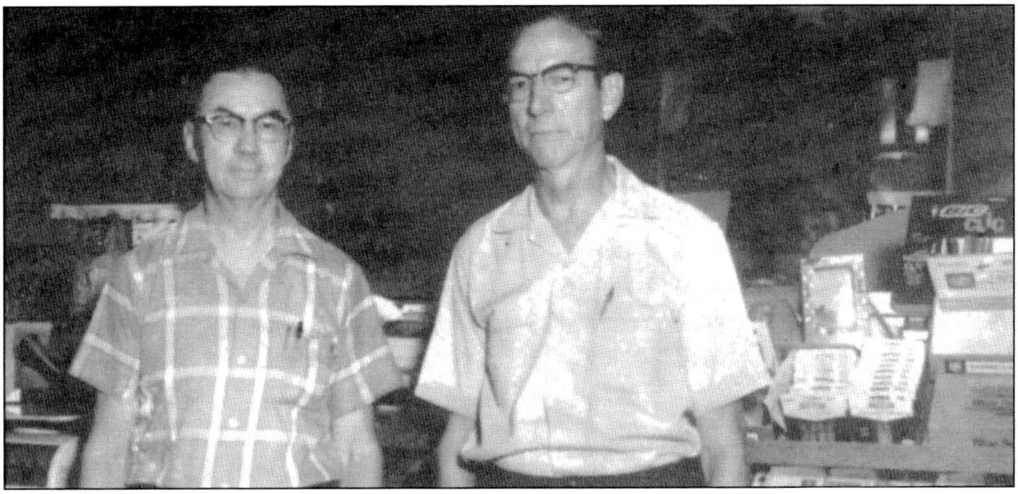

Leon and Monroe Charpentier went into business together in a confectionery store in 1926. In 1929, they expanded to a drugstore, and in 1959, the business grew to a full grocery and market. They were in business 47 years until Elo and Mary Pfeifer bought the business in 1973, and it became the Broadway Grocery. The Pfeifers still run the business in 2010 with a full line of groceries, meats, sausage, and cold cuts. On Saturdays, they offer great barbecue. The Pfeifers have been involved in various businesses in Nordheim for over 50 years.

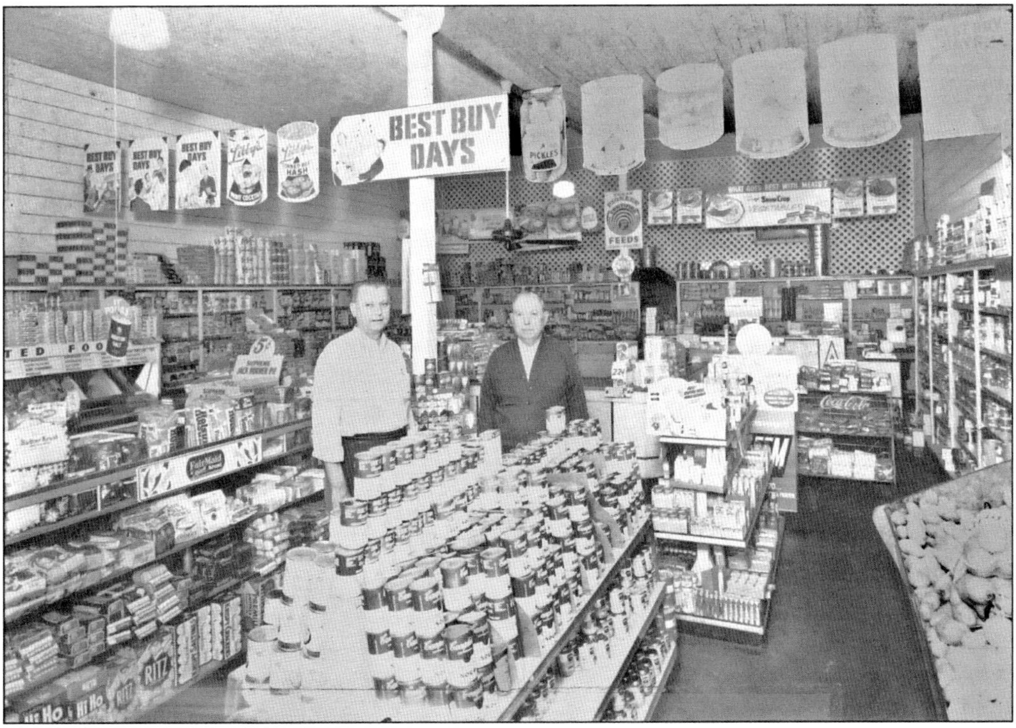

The W. P. Schulz Red and White Grocery Store was in business for 53 years. W. P. Schulz opened the store in 1926 and was joined by his son Lawrence at age 13. Lawrence took over the business after his father's death in 1961 and kept it going until 1979. Pictured here in the 1940s are W. P. Schulz on the right and his son Lawrence on the left. The building that housed Schulz's is now Sparky's Bar, currently owned and operated by Loraine Wunderlich.

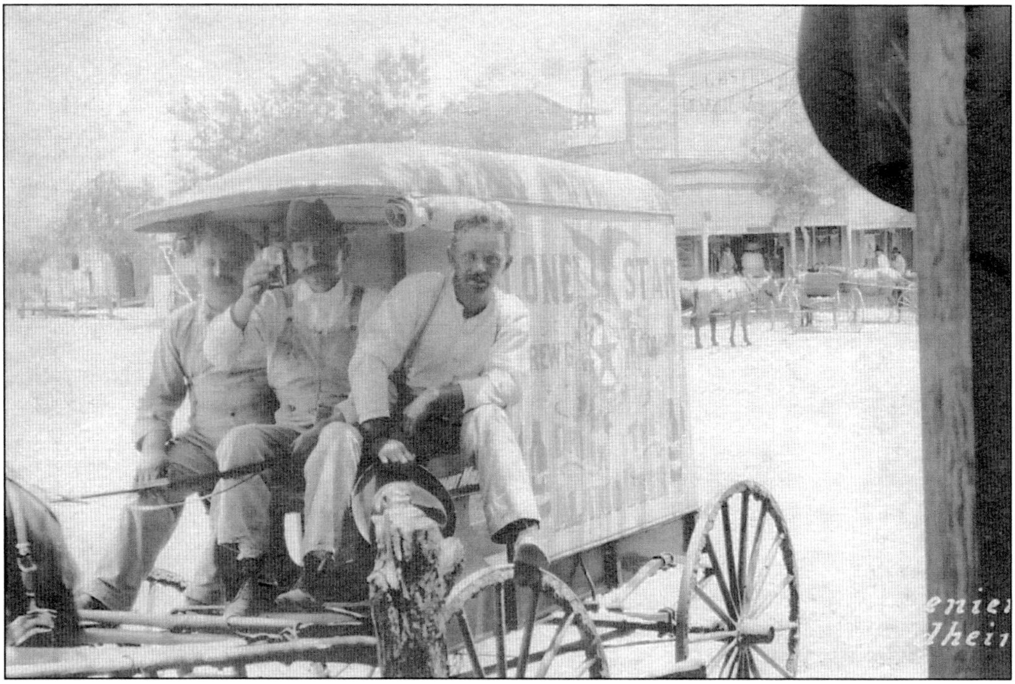

Lone Star Beer is being delivered by wagon to one of the bars in Nordheim.

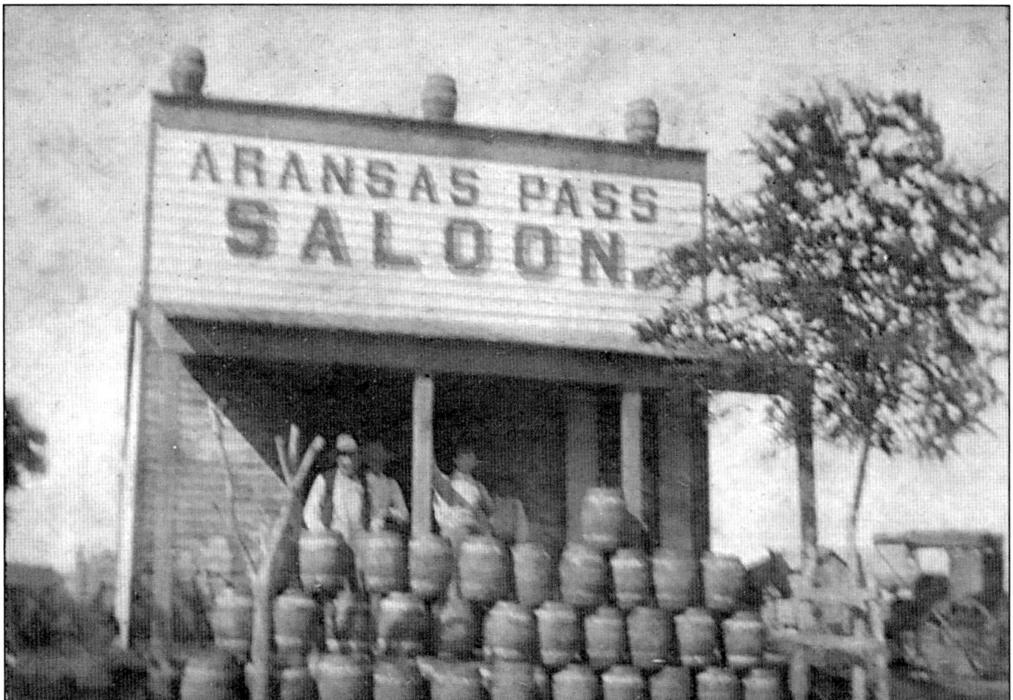

The Aransas Pass Saloon was opened in 1903 by H. Charpentier. In 1912, Emil December owned and operated the Aransas Pass Saloon, which he ran for many years. It was later remodeled into the Picture Show, Nordheim's first silent movie theater.

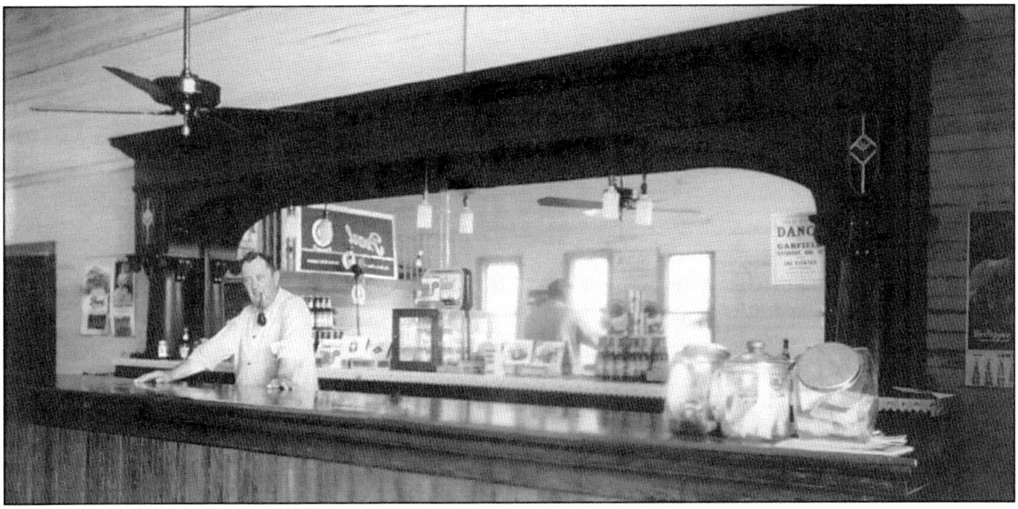

The Rabenaldt Hardware Store, built in 1903, became the Broadway Bar in 1933. In this picture, J. A. Reuser, the owner-operator in 1933, is standing behind the bar. The bar back was brought into the Nordheim area from Germany around 1903. It was first brought to the Gulf Coast by ship and the rest of the way by wagon train. It was located in two other bars before coming to rest in the Rabenaldt building. The business has changed hands several times over the years. Owned by Reueser from 1933 to 1946, Ernest Wolf and Bennie Klaevemann from 1946 to 1954, Elo Pfeifer from 1954 to 1973, Mr. and Mrs. C. C. Schroedter from 1973 until it was taken over by Johnnie Leister, and then Alvin and Elsa Leister until 1998. Since 1998, Curtis and Cathy Voelkel have owned the bar. The business has always had a family atmosphere with an old west style due to the 100-year-old bar with the brass rail. While the Schroedters owned it, part of the movie *Paris, Texas* was filmed there. The film won several awards at the Cannes Film Festival in 1984. (Courtesy Curtis and Cathy Voelkel.)

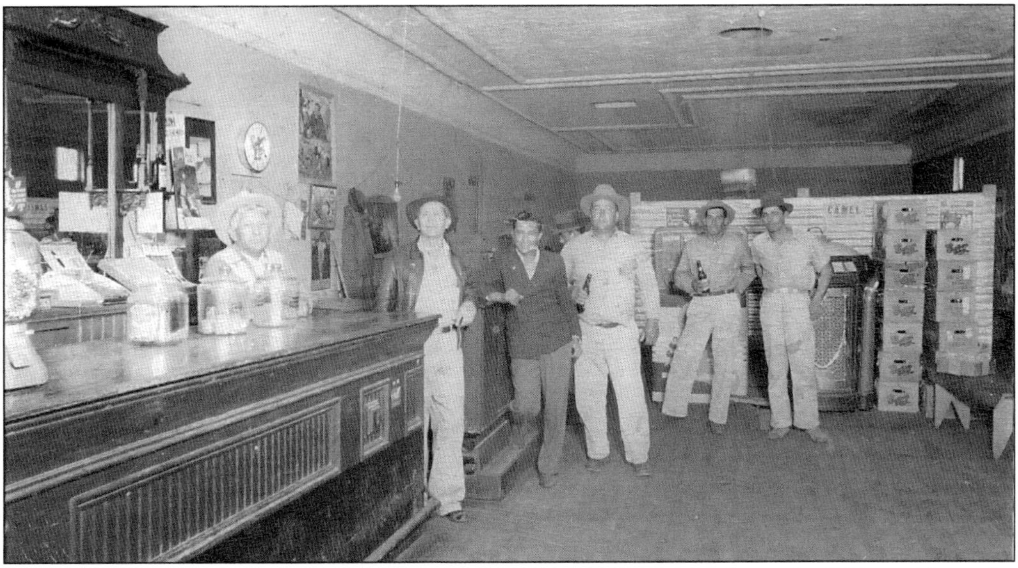

The Rancho Grande Saloon was the former Aransas Pass Saloon in the early 1900s and later the Picture Show silent movie theater. Pictured here from left to right are Francisco Munoz, Pablo Moya, Estephan Munoz, Brigido Garcia, Sebastian Saldivar, and Ernesto (Polka) Salinas. It was operated by the Munoz brothers until 1967 when it was bought by Alvin Leister to be dismantled and removed to his farm. (Courtesy Jim Salinas.)

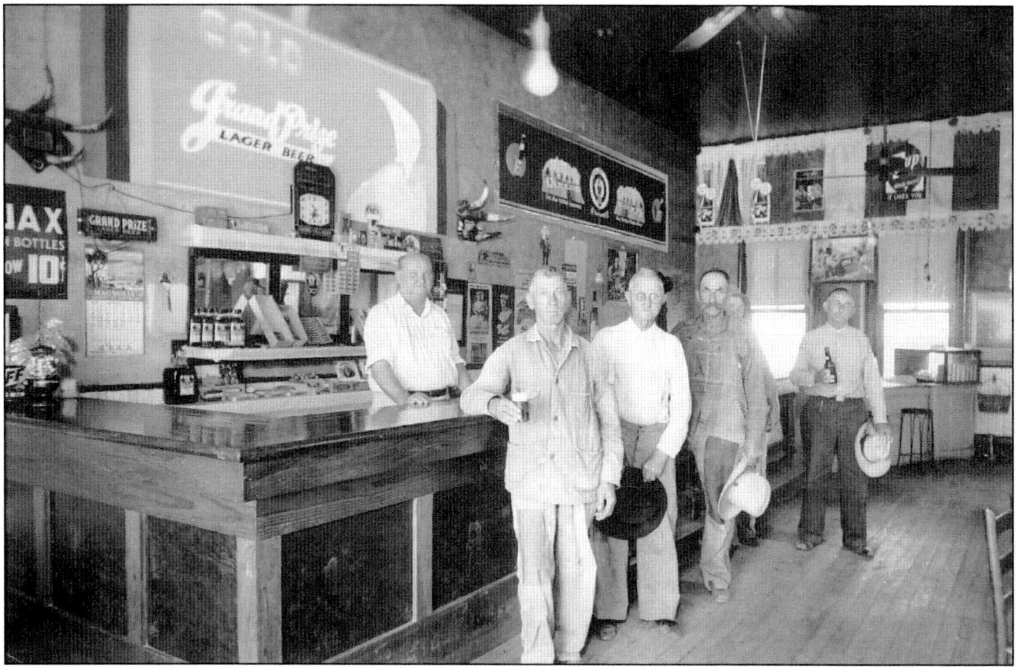

Above, Ed Beinhauer, Fred Schuenemann, Gerhart Pargmann, Otto Schroedter, Willie Tiewes, and Frank Rohan are having a drink at Ed's Place, one of the biggest sellers of Grand Prize Beer. It was a great place to stop after a long day to swap stories and have a cold one. After Ed sold the bar to Fred Schuenemann, it became Fred's Place until 1953, when he sold the bar to Alvin and Elsa Leister. Alvin's Place is pictured below in 1955 with owners Alvin and Elsa Leister. The building, known as the Arnold Dittfurth Building, was located by the First National Bank on Broadway. (Courtesy Della Evans.)

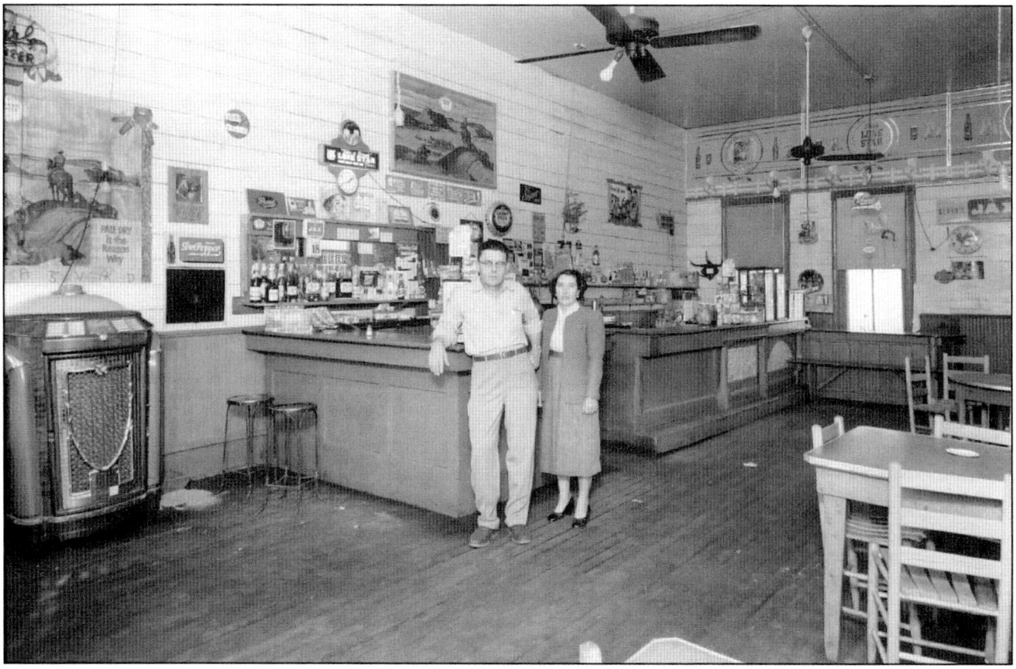

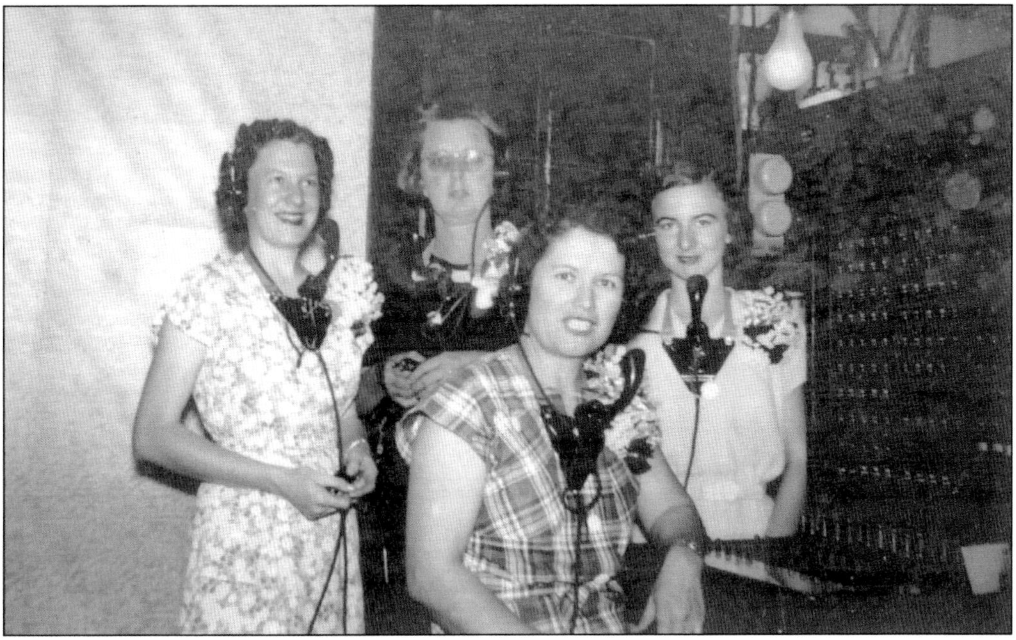

Telephone operators take a minute from their work to have their picture taken. Pictured from left to right are Nell Burow, Malinda Peters, Joyce Elaine Drapalla, and Paula Mesamoore. The first telephones were brought into Nordheim by the Eureka Telephone Company. The telephone offices were in the two-story Hill Building, which was built in 1898. This building became Amos and Andy Café in 1937.

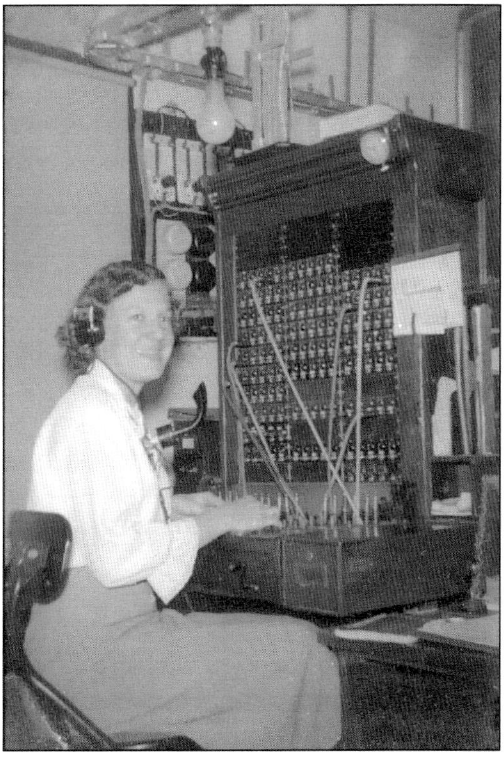

Nell Burow is seen here at the switchboard, which was quite a large piece of equipment. The operators wore headsets with mouth pieces around their neck, to leave their hands free to connect calls.

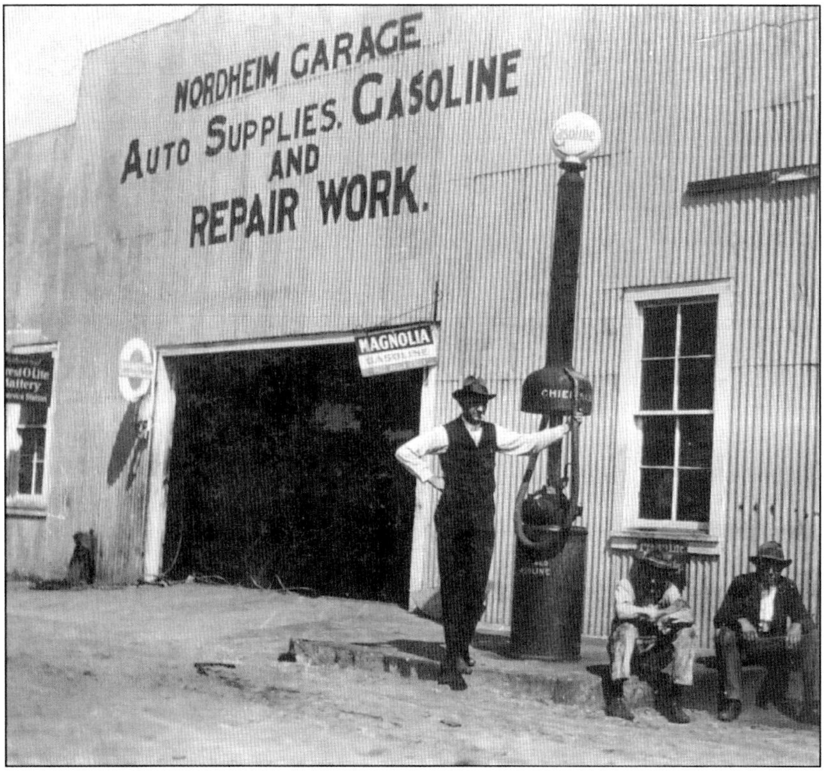

Some men are taking a break in their day while they wait outside of the Nordheim Garage, where one could get auto supplies, gasoline, and repairs done.

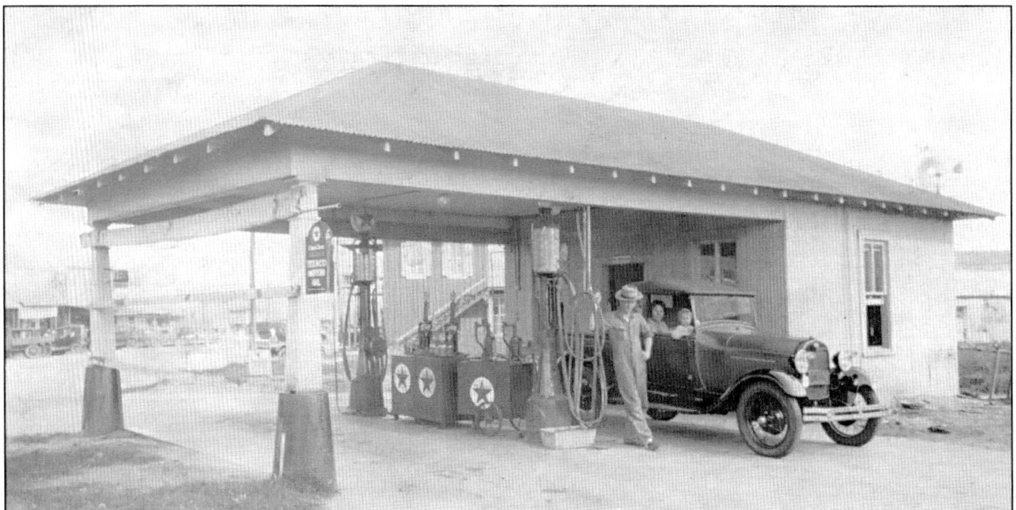

Standing outside the car in 1931 is Daniel Burow while his wife, Elma, and daughter Lora Nell sit inside the car. This gas station is on the corner of Broadway and Second Streets where the Talk School Museum is now located.

Edwin Semper and Alton Mueller pose outside the Semper Gas Station on Broadway. This building was once a gas station and is still in existence. It is owned by Lupe and Patricia Garcia and is used for equipment storage and automotive repairs for his businesses.

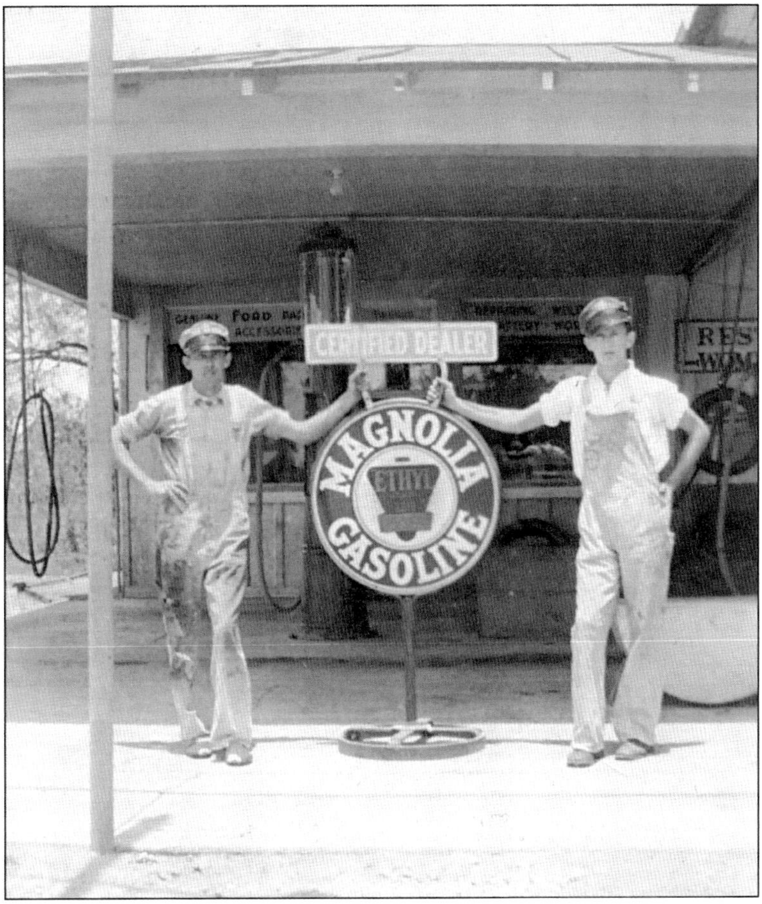

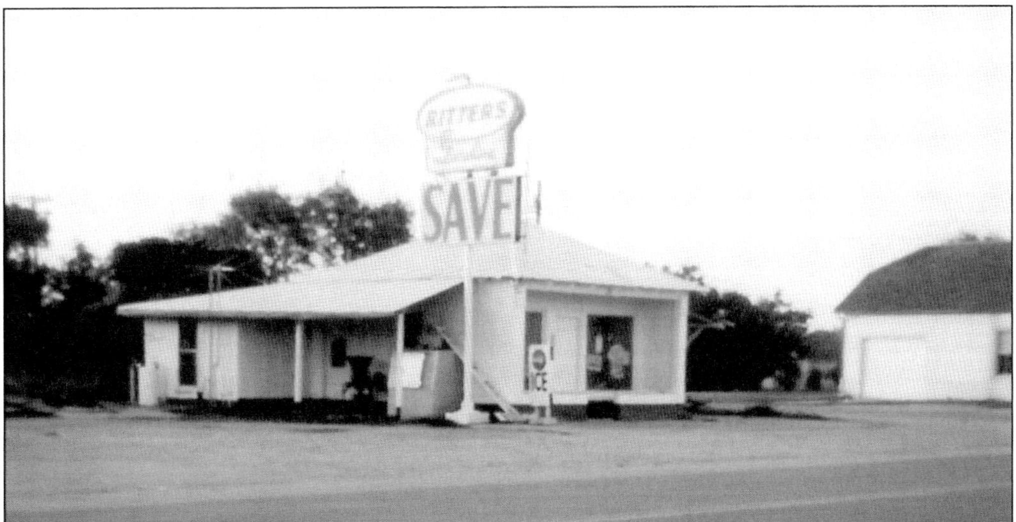

The Ritter's Station located on Highway 72 in Nordheim was owned and operated by Gilbert and Mary Pargmann from 1969 to 1981. They also had a liquor store on the premises called the Snort Shop.

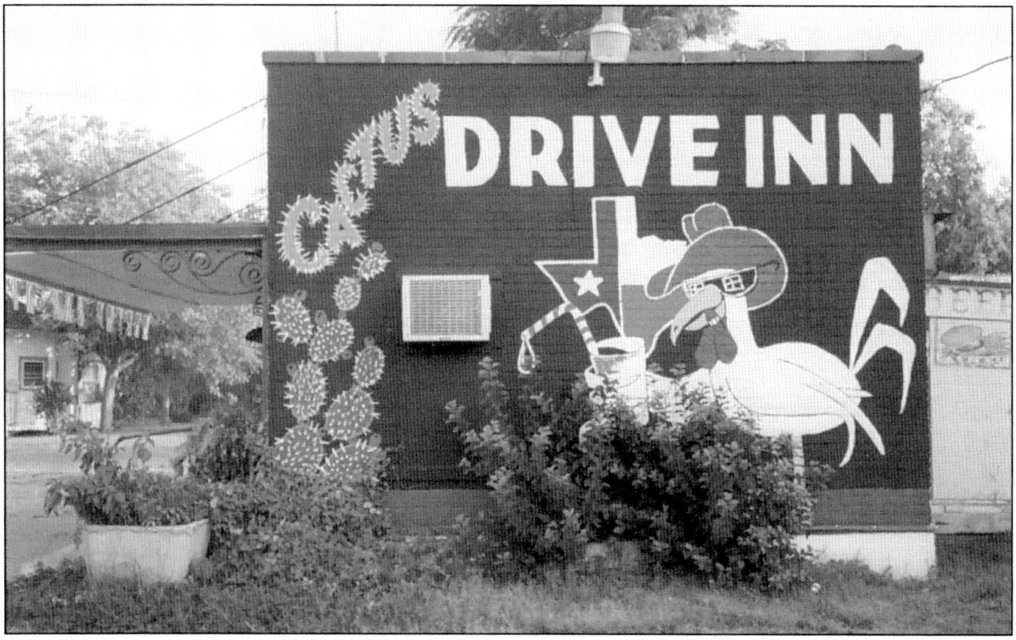

Central Power and Light Company brought electricity to Nordheim in 1924 and constructed a brick building for an icehouse and their offices in 1926. This building was vacant for many years, and during this time a cactus grew on the roof of the building. Roy McMillan moved to Nordheim and bought the building, operating it as The Cactus Drive Inn. (Courtesy Ronda Voelkel.)

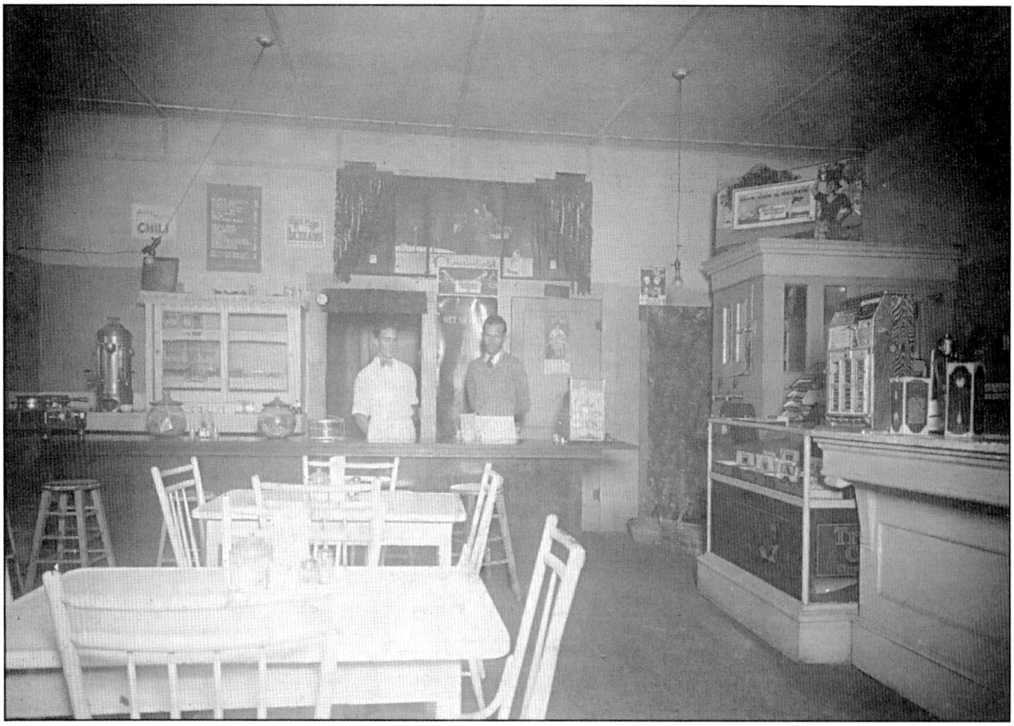

This early Nordheim café is believed to be the Emil December Café, which was famous for its chili. Werner December is pictured here on the left.

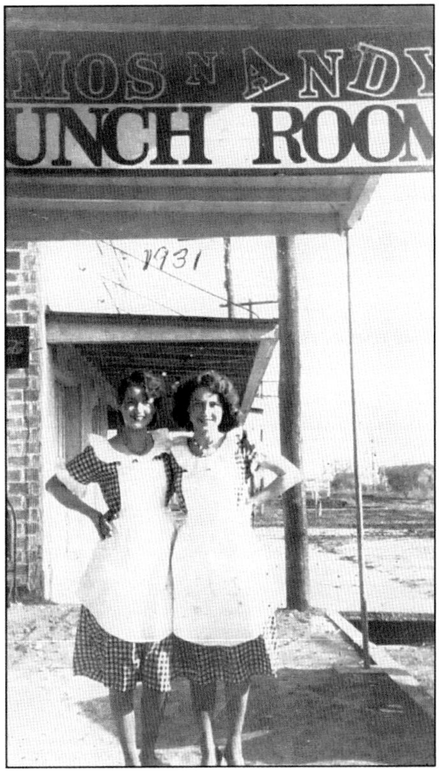

Amos and Andy Café owners Emily Wolf and Leona Krause, shown here, were just out of high school when they opened the café they had dreamed about in 1931. They named the café after the then-famous radio show "Amos and Andy." When they opened, a cup of coffee was 5¢ and a hamburger with all the trimmings was the same. A good steak would cost 35¢. (Courtesy June Buchhorn.)

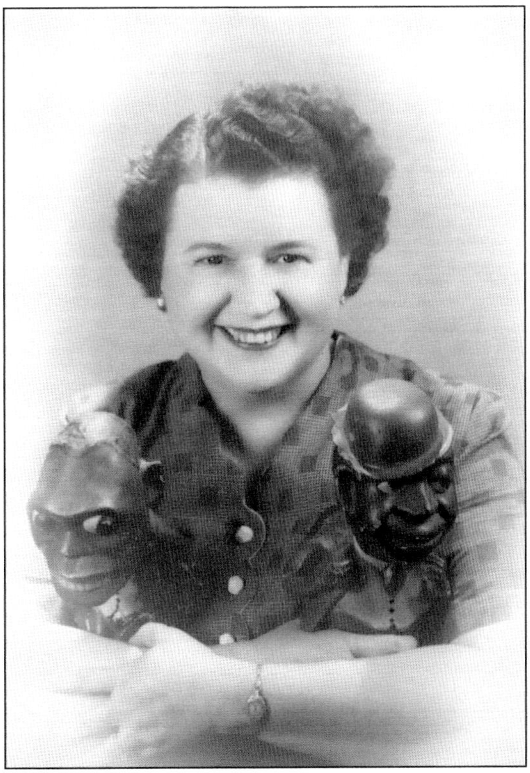

Pictured here is Emily Wolf Mullins with the famous statues of Amos and Andy. The café was a popular stop for people riding the train as well as the locals. The food was always good, and Emily was always there for customers when they came in any time of the day or night. Service was the key to this well known and loved business. Amos and Andy closed in 1989 after an amazing 58 years.

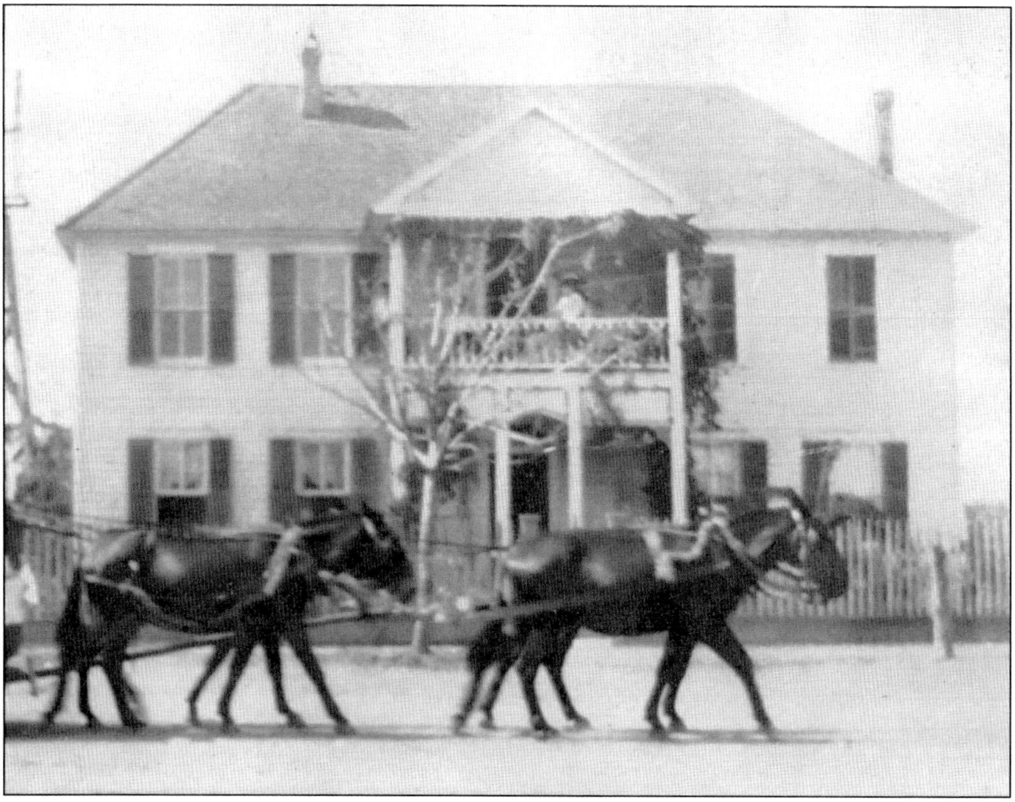

This house was built in 1903 by August Burow, one of the very successful businessmen in Nordheim. Later, it became the Nordheim Hospital and Dr. MaCaray and Dr. Prather's offices. A number of people in the community were born in this home, including Janice Ladner Brown, Paul Baumann, Shirley Voelkel Audilet, Gordon Voelkel, Ray Leister, and Iris Mueller Johnson, to name a few. The home was purchased by Curtis and Cathy Voelkel when there was talk of tearing it down. They moved it to their property on Hohn Road, where it has been renovated and turned into their home. (Courtesy Lindbergh and Georgie Voelkel.)

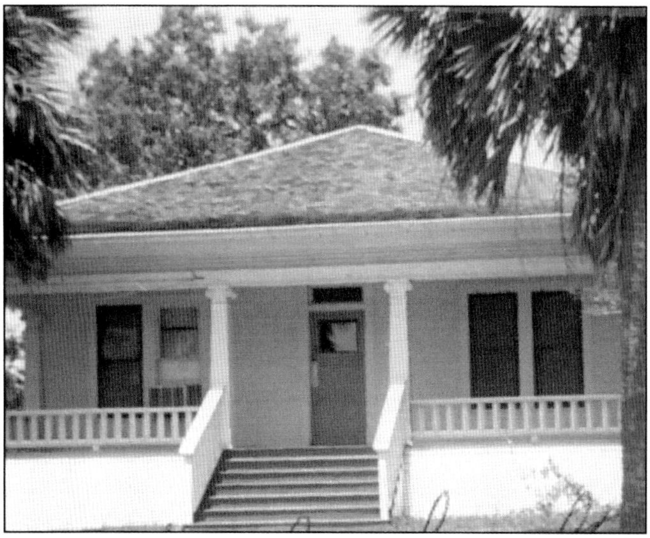

Dr. D. C. Scheffler came to Nordheim after graduating from dental college. He opened his office in 1930 and practiced for 54 years until his retirement in 1984. His practice drew people from all over south Texas. He practiced out of the home pictured here, which was built by C. D. Bolting and was also a residence for Alfreda Mueller Huck before Dr. Scheffler bought it. It is now the residence of Robert and Dorothy Ckodre, and has been relocated to their property outside of town. (Courtesy June Buchhorn.)

Six

Nordheim Organizations and Churches

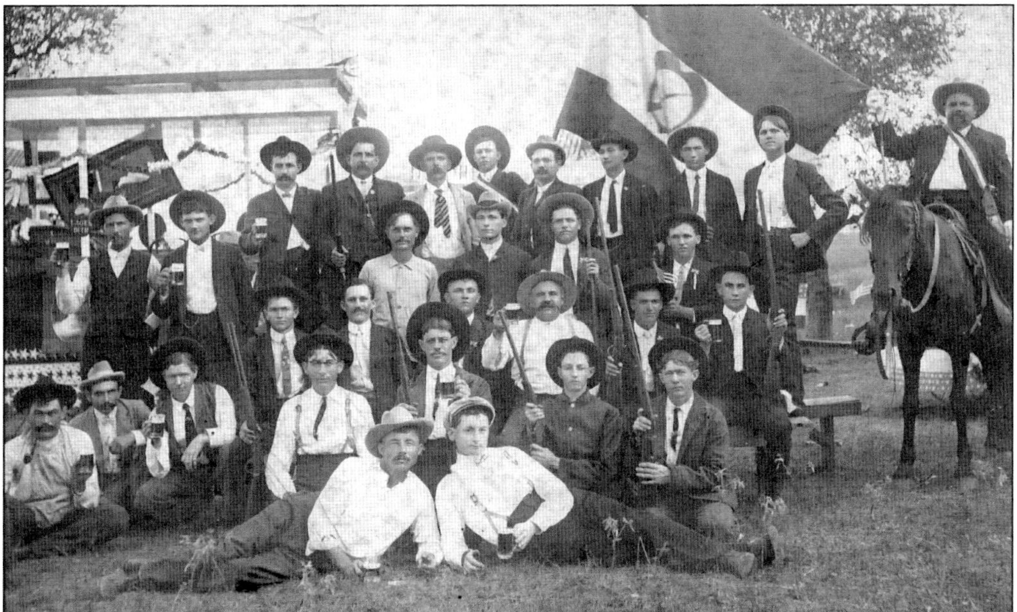

The Nordheim Schuetzen Verein (Shooting Club) was organized on September 20, 1902. Their first celebration was held on Pilot Knob and it is one of the oldest Nordheim organizations still in existence today. Pictured here are Julius Reuser, Fritz Menn, Louis Piehl, George Truede, Doctor Buchring, George Janssen, Emil Osterloh, Gerhardt Mueller, Willie Bues, Robert Sucher, Herman Charpentier, Martin Osterloh, Eugene Reinhardt, August Burow, Ernst Pfeifer, Henry Bues, Henry Morisse, Otto Reinhardt, Charlie Havaman, August Teiwes (on horse), Otto Kursel, Fritz Schulz, Fritz Ulrich, George Morisse, Emil Charpentier, Fritz Bues, Hugo Rabenaldt, and Willie Osterloh.

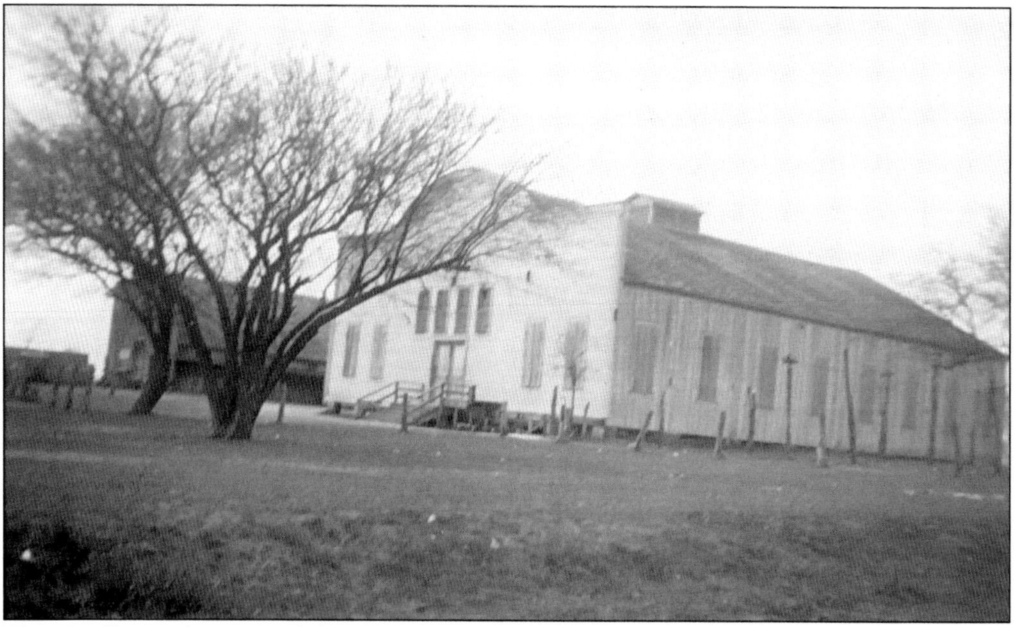

The Nordheim Shooting Club and Dance Hall, pictured here, was built in 1908 with Robert Sucher as contractor. It was the center of entertainment for people from miles around. The May Feast in those days had kings and queens and held dances with entertainment by local musicians. The May Feasts have changed some, but the dances are still held every year along with many other activities. The consolidation of the Schuetzen Verein and the Fortschritt Verein created the Nordheim Shooting Club Inc. in 1930.

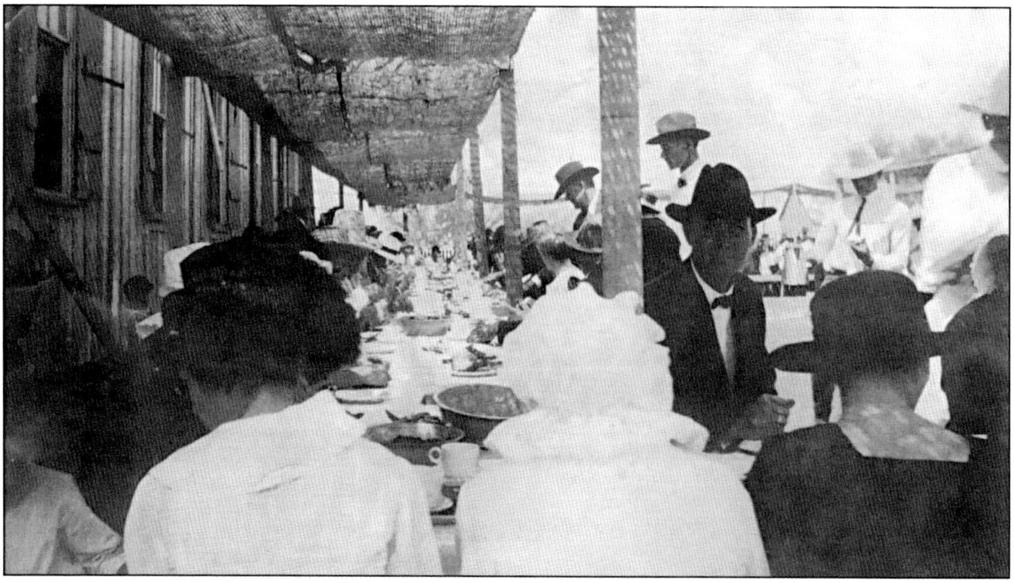

The Nordheim Shooting Club holds the May Feast every year, and one of the main attractions has always been the meal served on Sunday, as pictured here in the early 1900s. (Courtesy Lindbergh and Georgie Voelkel.)

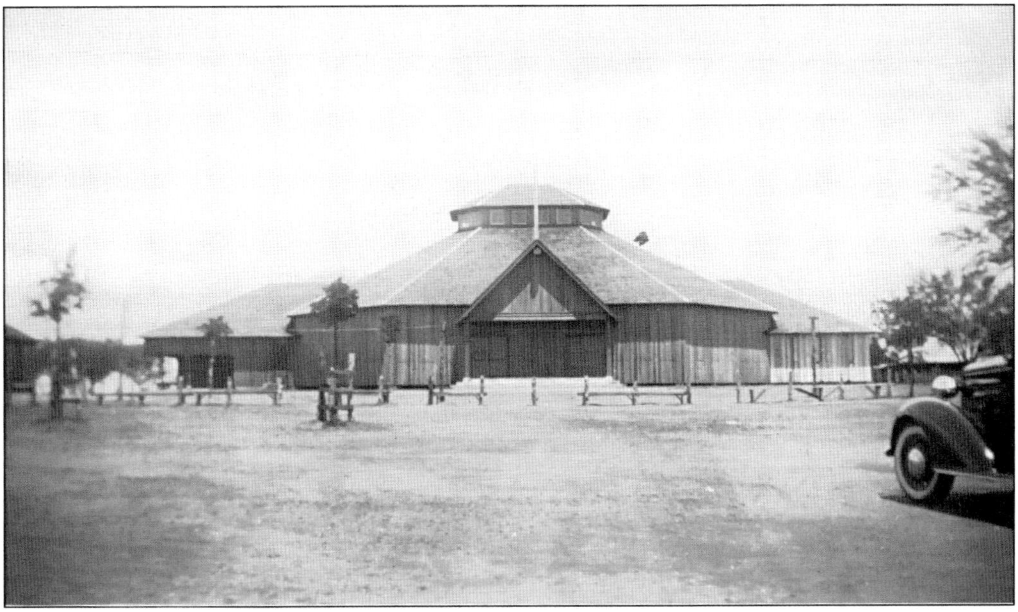

In 1937, the existing dance hall was razed and the new dance hall was built from the design of C. B. Dean. The structure was dedicated on May 21, 1939, with L. C. Neutzler as master of ceremonies.

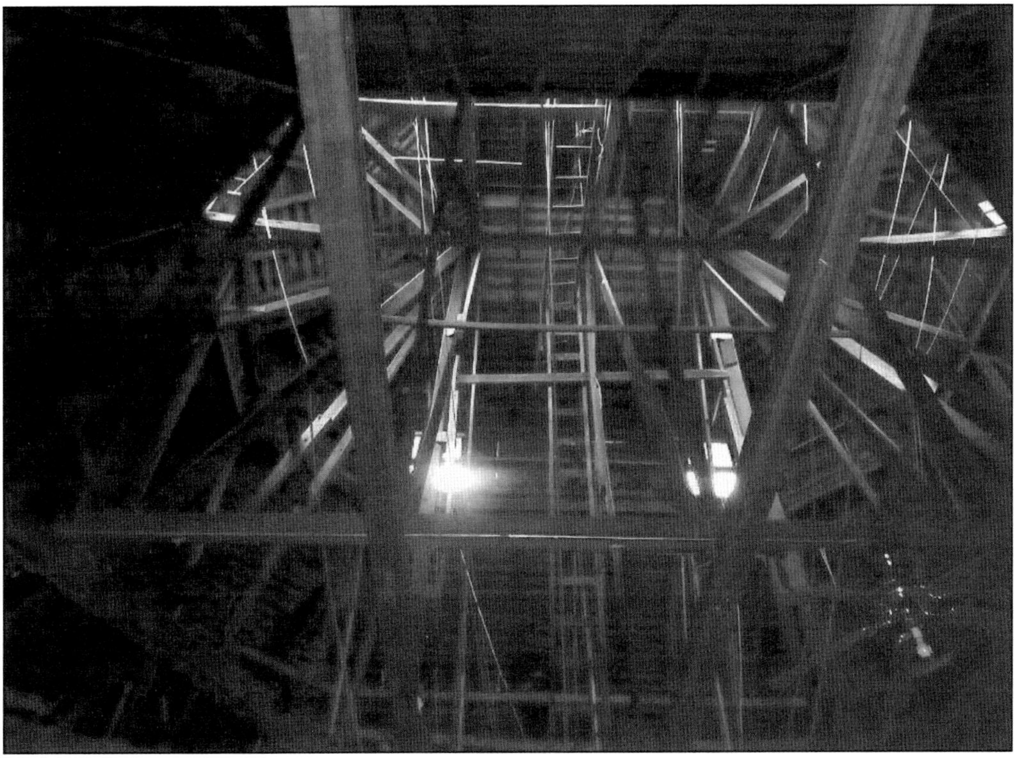

The inside of the Nordheim Shooting Club is quite impressive. One is always amazed when driving up Broadway and coming over the hill and seeing this large structure before them. It is incredible that the building was constructed without modern equipment and only simple manpower and great engineering. (Courtesy Ozzie Carrasquillo.)

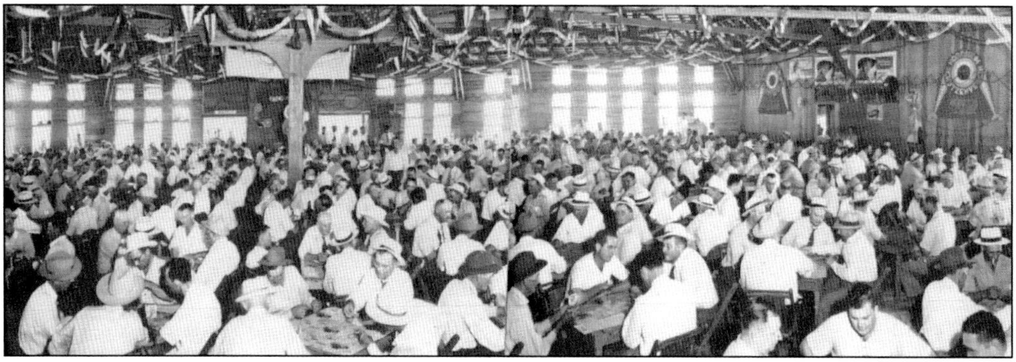

Skat tournaments (card games) were held at the large Nordheim Shooting Club and Dance Hall. As one of the most popular events at the club, they drew large crowds that either participated in or just observed the games. The tournament pictured here was the state championship and the largest ever held.

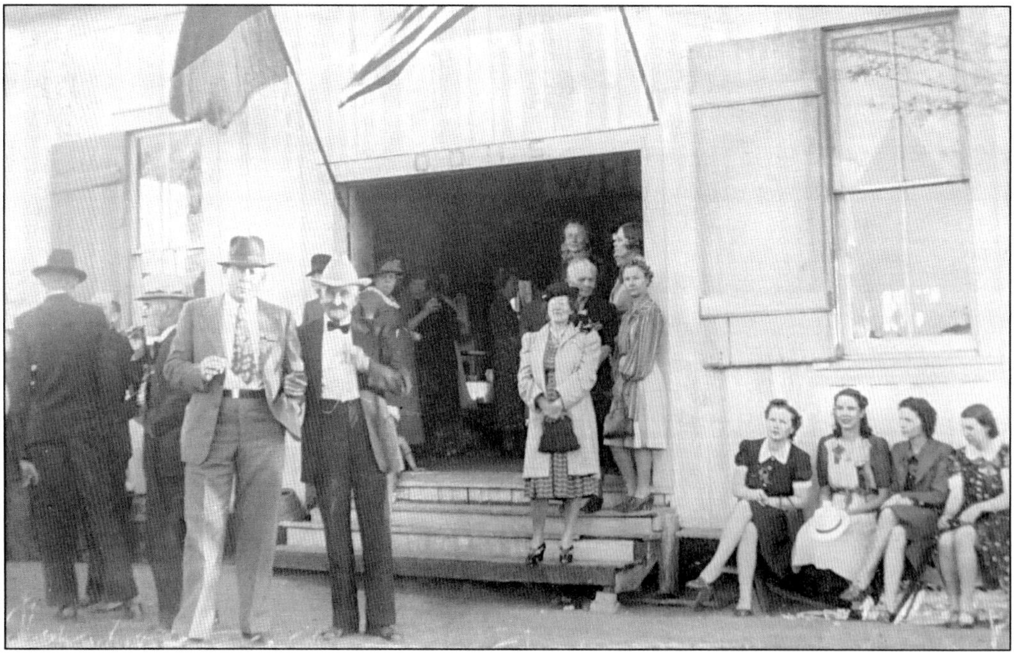

Pictured here are people gathering during an event in the early days at the Shooting Club and Dance Hall. This is how it still looks today during an event. Family and friends still gather to take part in whatever activity is going on there.

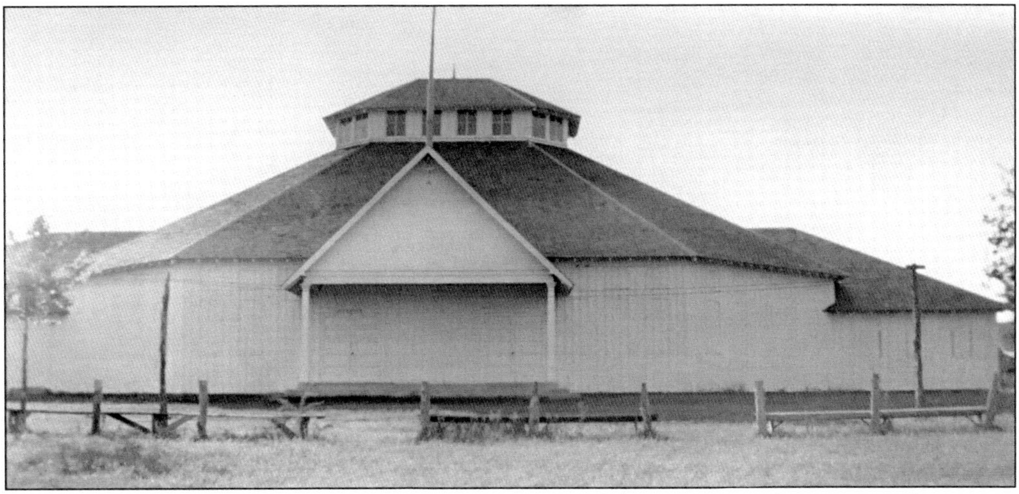

The Nordheim Shooting Club has made a number of changes over the years, and one was painting the building. As one drives up Broadway and comes over the hill, the white structure makes quite an impression sitting on the hill. The unusual structure is something that needs to be seen both inside and out to truly appreciate its craftsmanship and beauty. (Courtesy Iris Mueller Johnson.)

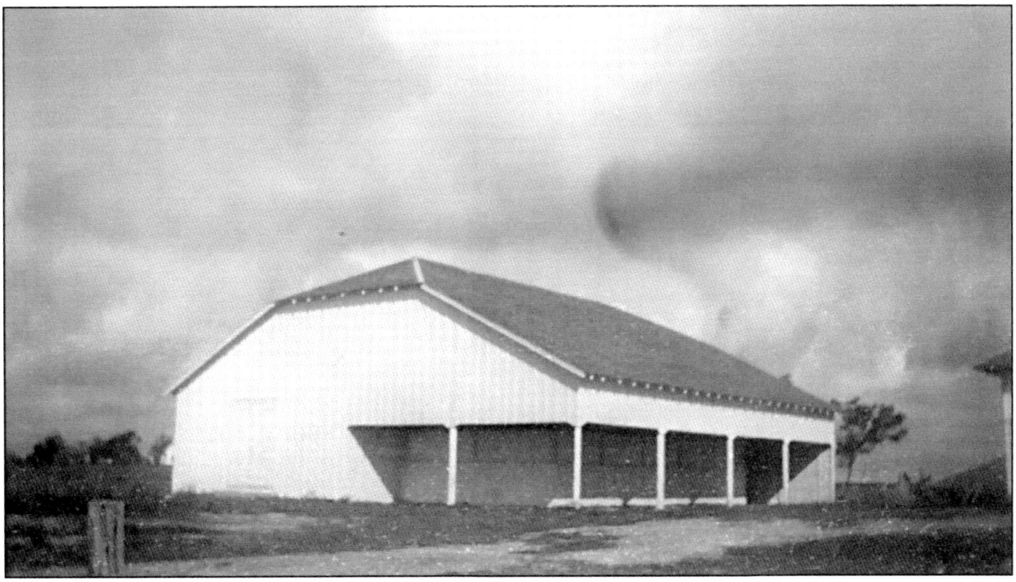

In the early years, the shooting club dining hall was used for many meals, celebrations, wedding receptions, and meetings. During the May Feast, hamburgers are served on Saturdays and a barbecue dinner on Sundays. (Courtesy Lindbergh and Georgie Voelkel.)

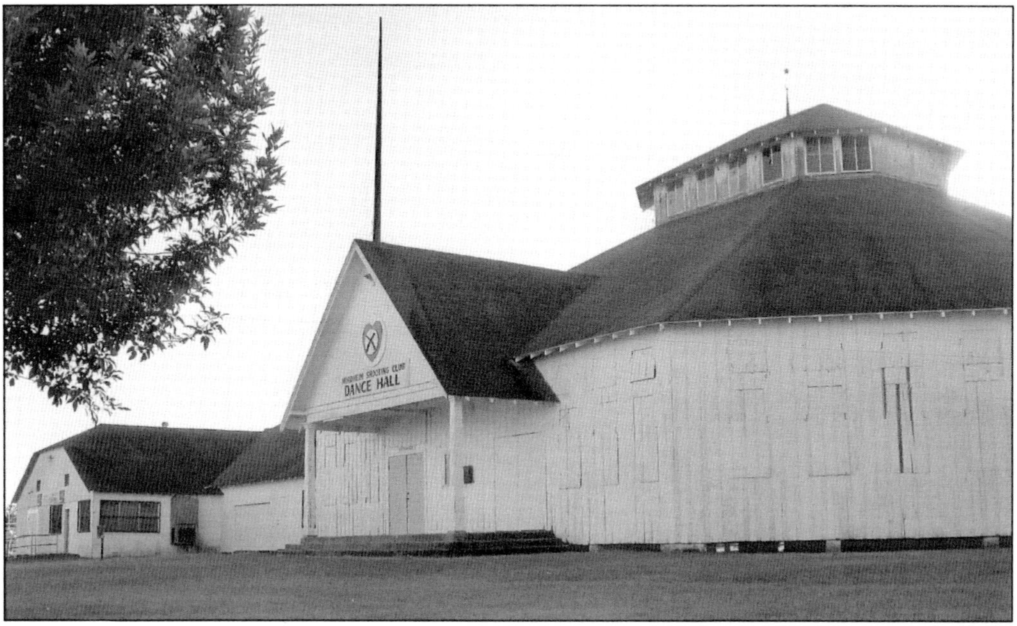

The Nordheim Shooting Club has always been a community gathering place where weddings, receptions, reunions, graduation parties, anniversaries, and the May festivals were held. It has stood the test of time and is still the same popular gathering place it was in years past. The club connected the dance hall and the dining hall with a breezeway that served as a bar, as well as a cool place to sit during big events. (Courtesy Cathy Voelkel.)

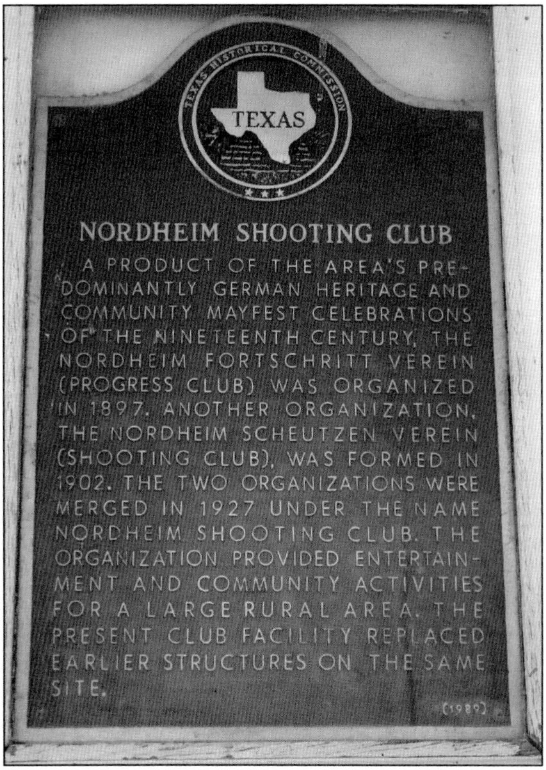

The Nordheim Shooting Club received a Texas historical marker during the 1989 May Feast. This event took place exactly 50 years after the hall was dedicated on May 21, 1939. Alfreda Huck is credited with helping the club receive this marker. Gordon Reynolds, president of the Nordheim Shooting Club, served as master of ceremonies. (Courtesy Cathy Voelkel.)

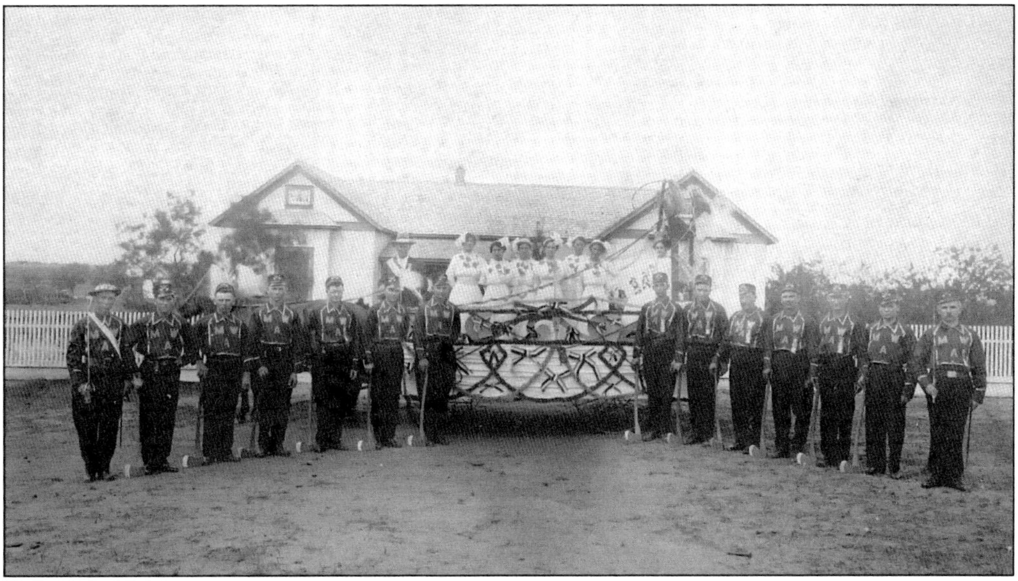

The Modern Woodsmen of the World were started in Nordheim by Dr. Buering. Pictured here on the far left with a white sash across his chest is Corvin Blake (C. B.) Dean. The woman standing alone on the far right is Frieda Anna (Reinhardt) Dean. (Courtesy Della Ruth Dean Thurman.)

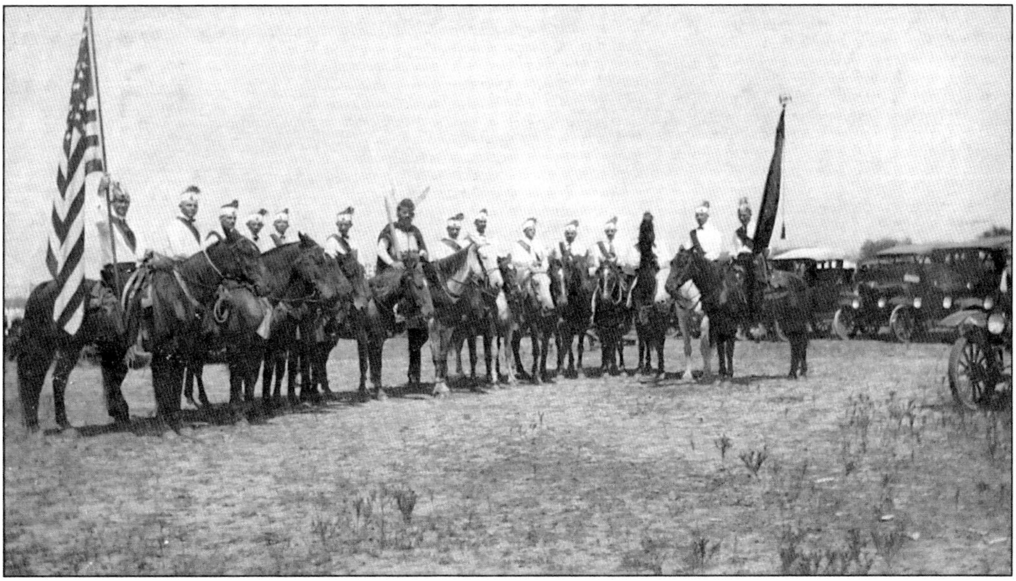

The Herman der Cheruske (Herman Sons Lodge) organization was founded in Germany. In this picture, the Herman Sons Lodge is preparing to march in Nordheim's Silver Jubilee Parade in 1922. Dressed in their Herman Sons attire, they are a professional-looking group. Centered in this picture with feathers on his headband is Joe Blaschke Sr. The red, yellow, and black bands around the horse's necks were made by Irma Onken. This group is still active in the Nordheim/Yorktown area today.

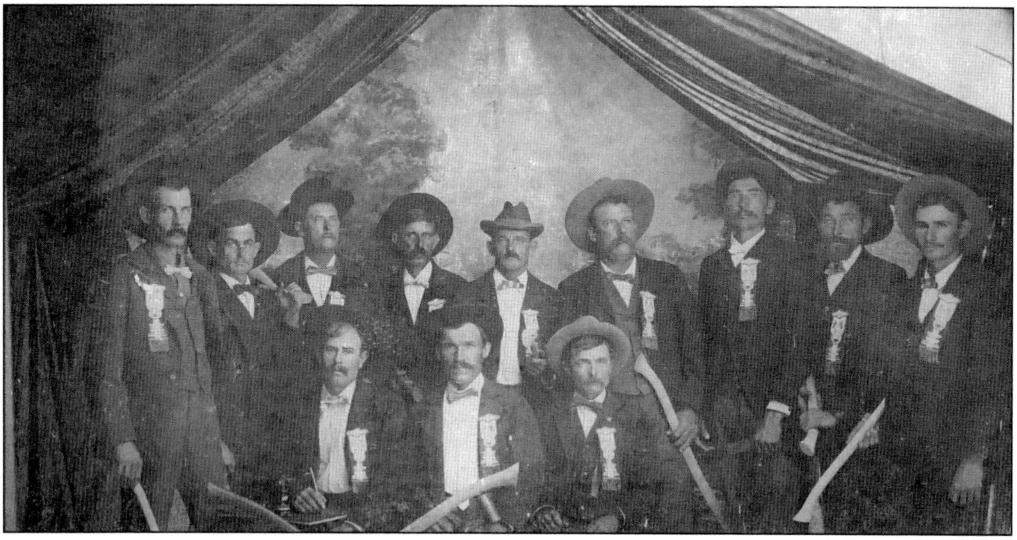

The Masonic Lodge members posed for a formal photograph. In the first row, left of center is John Butler of Cabeza.

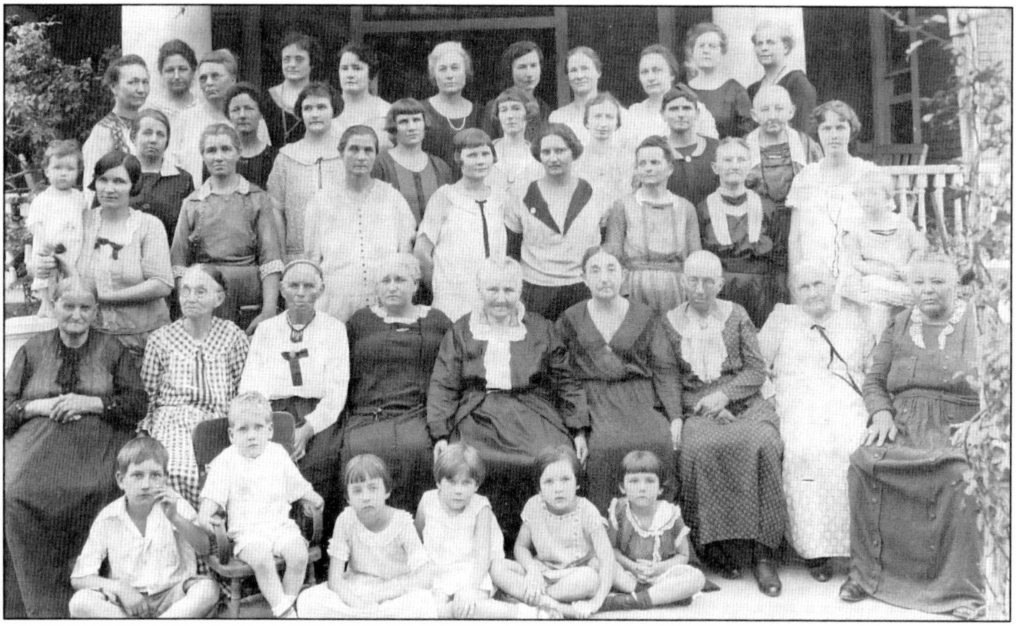

This organization was originally known as St. Paul Lutheran Church Frauen Verein (Women's Organization). Seen here in the 1920s, when they were known as the St. Paul Lutheran Church Ladies Aid, members in front of the Herman Stuermer home are (first row) Walter Kluge, Reinhardt Kluge, Elvera Charpentier, ? Kluge, ? Kluge, and Inez Lee Stuermer; (second row) Mrs. Alma Pevestorff, Mrs. H. J. Strunk, Mrs. Newmann, Mrs. Heldt, Mrs. Heinze, Mrs. D. Janssen, Mrs. Meyer, Mrs. Mueller, and Mrs. Sophia Furhken; (third row) Mrs. Kluge and daughter, Mrs. Fritz Schuenemann, Theresa Schlenstadt, Mrs. Lieschen Wied, Hilda Teiwes, Mrs. John Gaedke, Mrs. Carl Burow, Leona Gaedke, and baby Mermina Charpentier; (fourth row) Johanna Huck, Alvina Peters, Louise Stuermer, Emma Wied, Elsie Laging, Gladys Wied, Mrs. Harms, and Mrs. D. Onken; (fifth row) Theresa Westphal, Mrs. L. P. Hohn, Minna Meyer, Ida Menn, Mrs. E. Wagenschein, Anna Osterloh, Helen Charpentier, Emma Stuermer, Meta Riedesel, Mrs. Julius Reuser, and Etta Laging.

The Grandmothers Club was a group of women who were very proud to have grandchildren. Pictured in this 1951 photograph are (first row) Mrs. Neumann, Mrs. Huck, Mrs. L. Voelkel, Mrs. W. Buesing, Mrs. Mueller, and Mrs. C. Laging; (second row) Mrs. Wendel, Mrs. Wendt, Mrs. Schlennstedt, Mrs. H. Stuermer, and Mrs. Harbers.

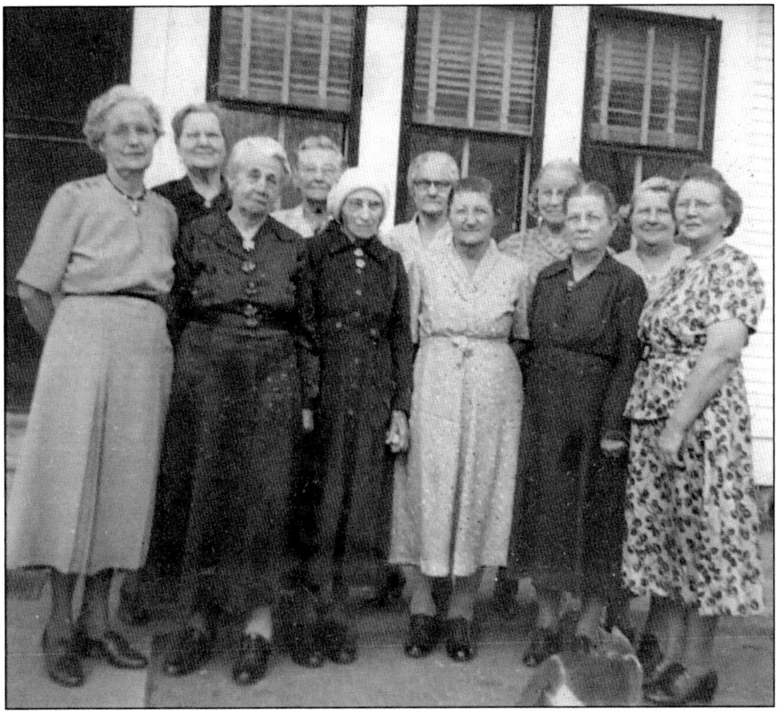

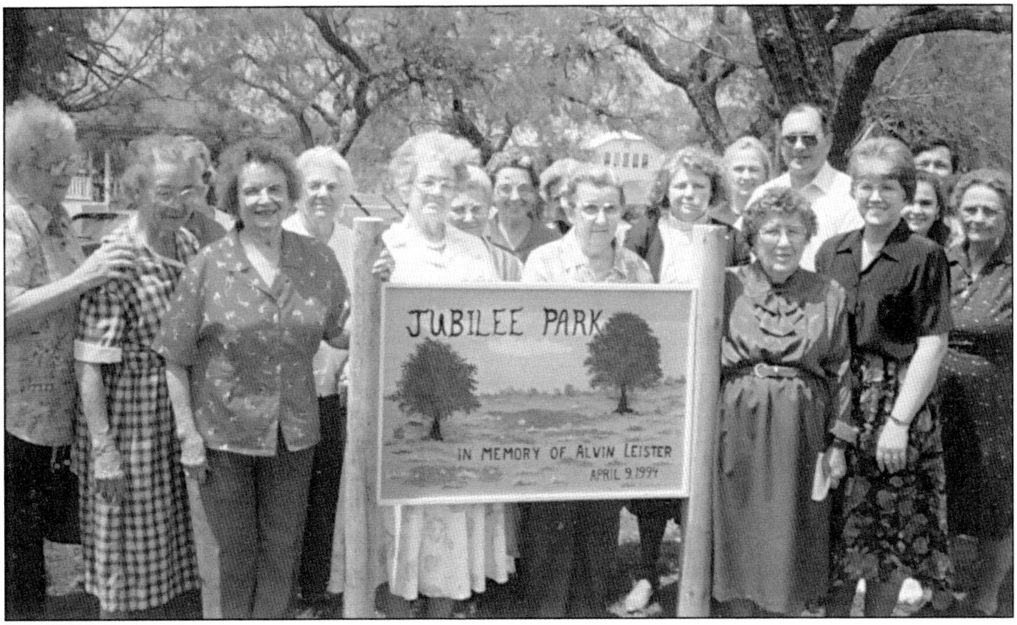

The Nordheim Garden Club was first organized in 1939. The club celebrated its 55th anniversary on April 9, 1994, with a new Jubilee Park sign. The new sign was dedicated in memory of a longtime resident and Nordheim businessman, Alvin Leister, by his widow, Elsa Leister. Pictured at the dedication in 1994 are, from left to right, Martha Baumann, Ellen Helmere, Emily Mullins, Alvina Pargmann, Hella Magee, Ailene Mueller, Doris Pfeifer, Anita Huck, Pastor Edwina Baethke, Elsie Leister, Vance Frosch Della Evans, and Lola Fuhrken. The Nordheim Garden Club is still active in 2010, 71 years later.

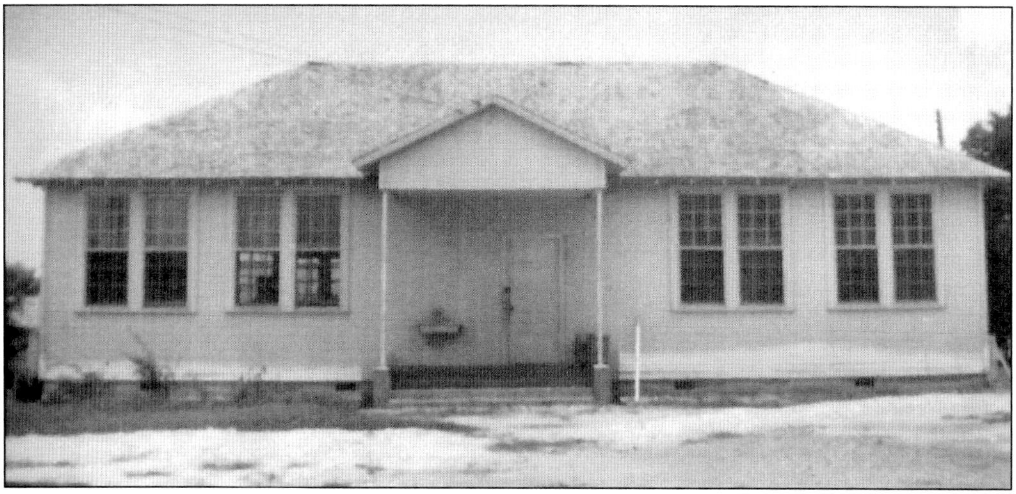

The Nordheim Historical Museum is an organization dedicated to the preservation of the history and heritage of the community. The museum is located on Second Street in Nordheim in the former Nordheim Fire Station and City Hall (page 81). The museum was formally opened on April 17, 1986. Pictured above is the Talk School, which at one time was one of the commons schools in the Nordheim area. It became the lunch room for Nordheim ISD when it was moved into town in 1946. The Nordheim ISD donated this building to the Nordheim Museum when they added a new cafeteria. The museum quickly raised the funds to move the building to lots donated by Curtis and Cathy Voelkel and the Stinson Family across from the existing Fire House Museum on Second Street. The museum has spent several years renovating the building in an effort to preserve it and prepare it for displaying precious artifacts. (Courtesy Cathy Voelkel.)

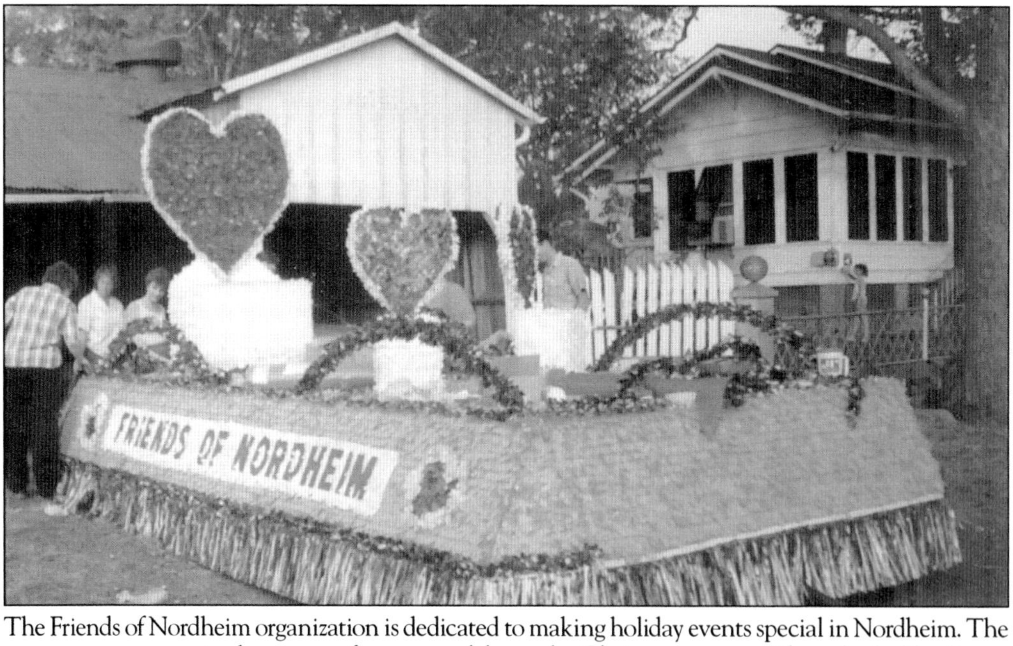

The Friends of Nordheim organization is dedicated to making holiday events special in Nordheim. The group puts up a tree in the center of town to celebrate the Christmas season. They also hold a dinner and have Santa at the fire station to make sure all the children in town get something for Christmas. In 2011, they will celebrate their 25th Easter egg hunt, which is held annually at the pavilion in Jubilee Park. They are pictured here preparing a Jubilee parade float. (Courtesy Ronda Voelkel.)

Lutheran services were held in the schoolhouse until the St. Paul Lutheran Church building was constructed in 1908. The cost of this building was $1,500. The church was 50 feet by 30 feet with a steeple.

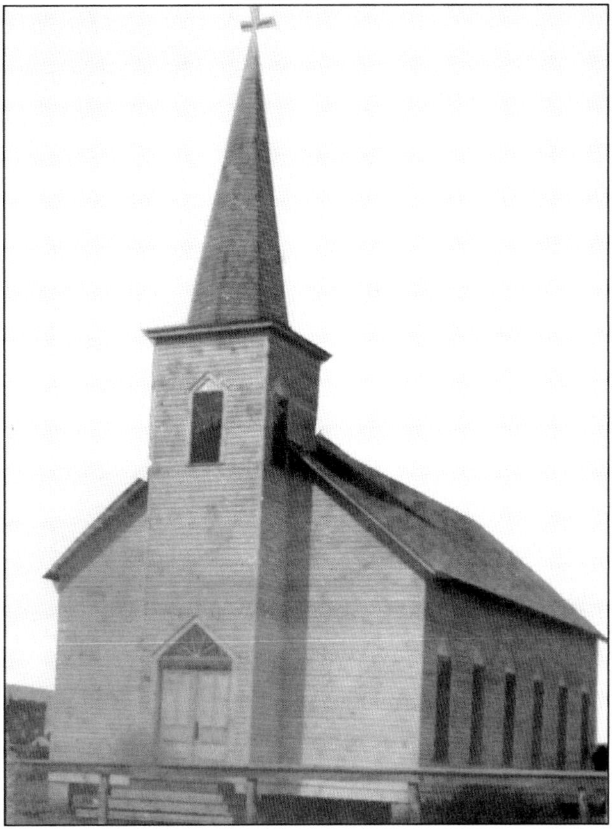

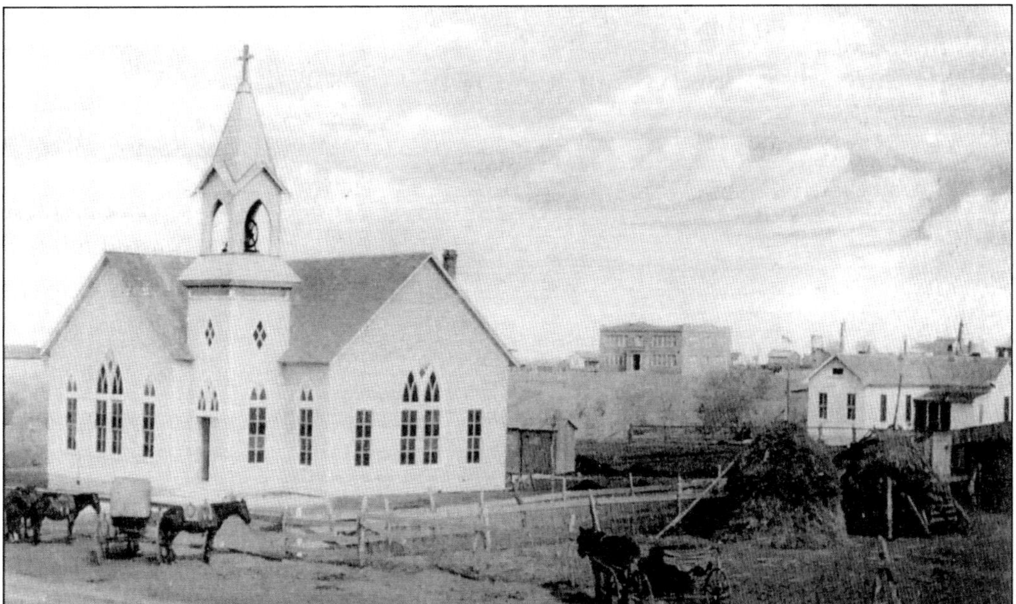

The St. Paul Lutheran Church pictured here is the remodeled church after the old building was damaged in a storm. The new shape of the building would give the church room to grow and help keep a storm from damaging it again. This building is still standing strong in 2010.

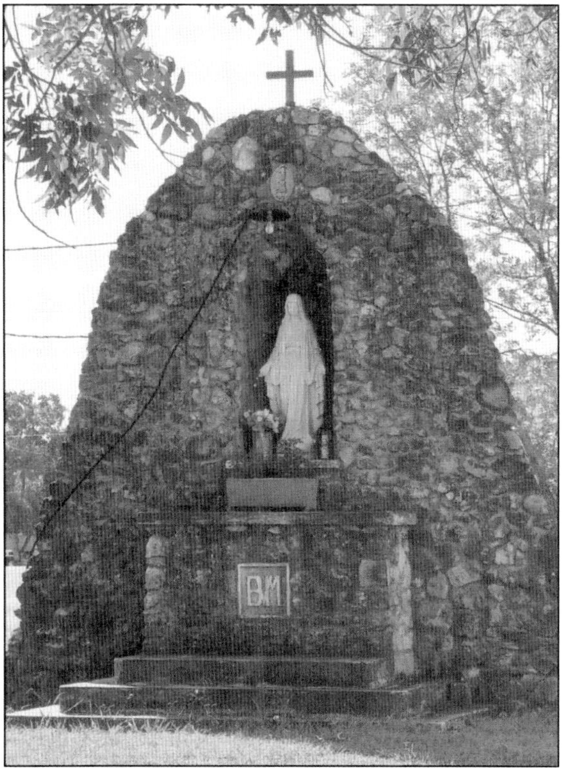

The first mass was held on March 11, 1922, in the new St. Ann's Church. In 1948, the A. W. Wagner and Wyatt Woods families constructed a grotto on the grounds of St. Ann's Church to mark the end of World War II and the return of peace. (Courtesy Cathy Voelkel.)

Socieda De Cementerio Union Mexicana was established in 1907. It was later renamed St. Ann's Cemetery. With its historic relevance to the community, the cemetery received a State Historical Recognition in 2007 in celebration of its 100th year. It is located north of Nordheim off Cabeza Road. This old cemetery has served as the burial place for the Hispanic population of Nordheim. This is the grave of one of the grandfathers of a Hispanic family who are very active members of the community. (Courtesy Cathy Voelkel.)

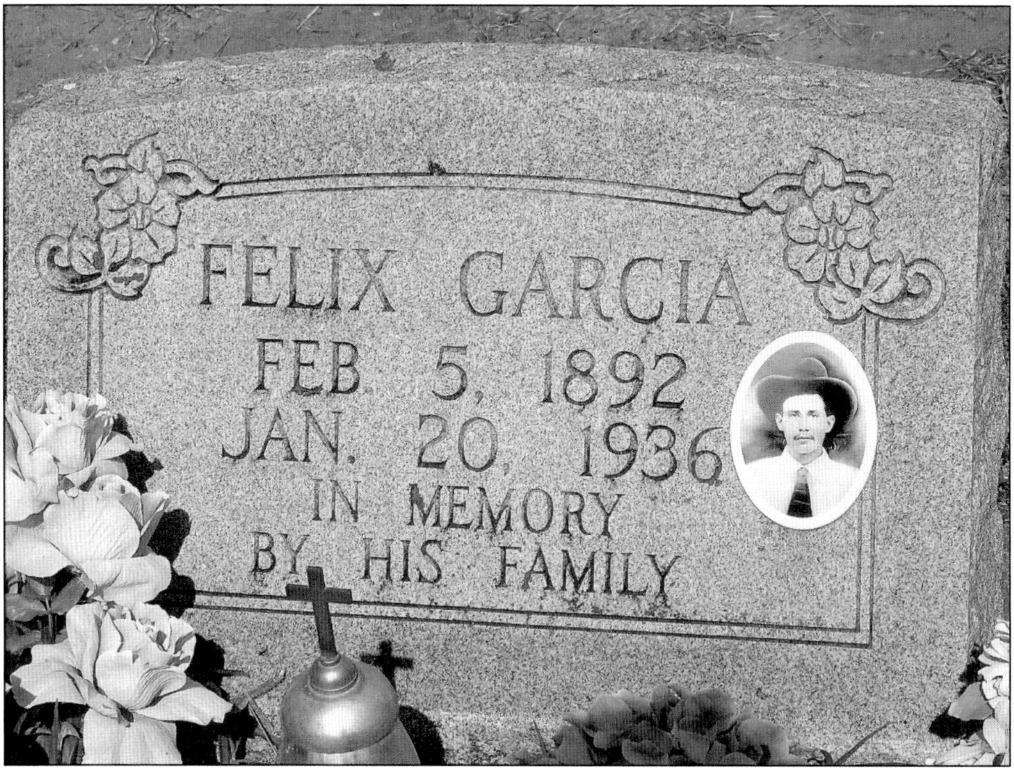

Seven

Nordheim Jubilees, Music, Sports, and Schools

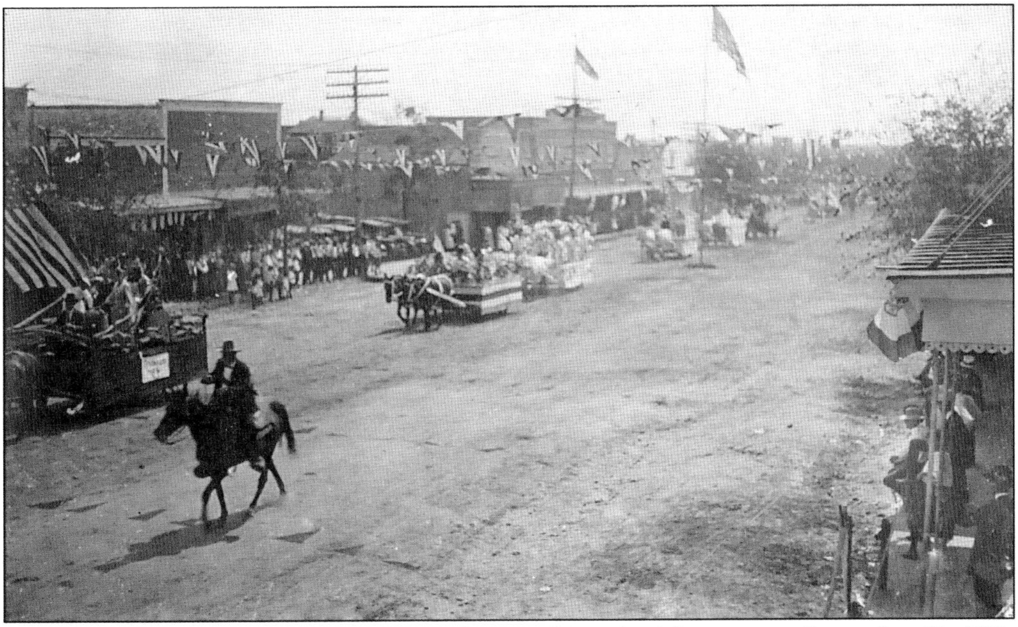

Nordheim celebrated its birthday with Jubilee parades and celebrations on September 28, 1922. Julius Reuser led the 25th Anniversary Silver Jubilee parade on horseback. The banners and large crowds line the dirt main street of Nordheim. The parade began at the Farmers Union Gin and went up Broadway and down several streets before turning back onto Broadway to end at the Feast Grounds. Four bands played at the celebrations, including the Nordheim Brass Band, Runge Texas Orchestra, Lienhard-Sloma Orchestra, and the Zedler Brothers Band.

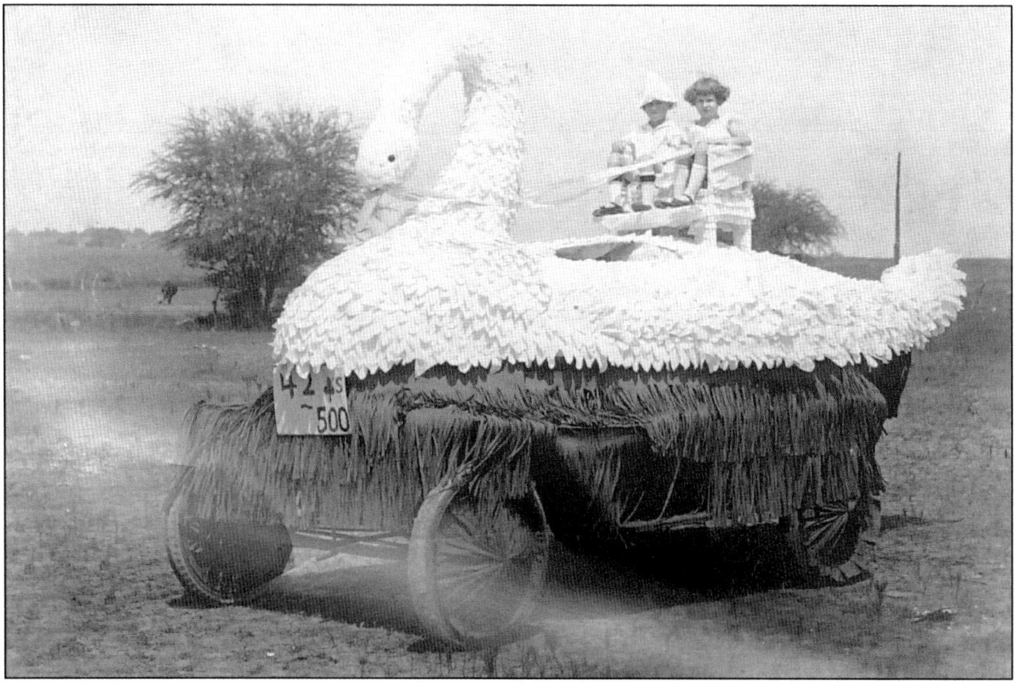

The second-place float was the "White Swan" of the 500 and 42 Club in the Silver Jubilee Parade. Alberta Brunkenhoefer and Anson Rabenaldt were the children riding the swan. The swan was built on top of an old motor vehicle. The second place winner received $8 in prize money. (Courtesy Lindbergh and Georgie Voelkel.)

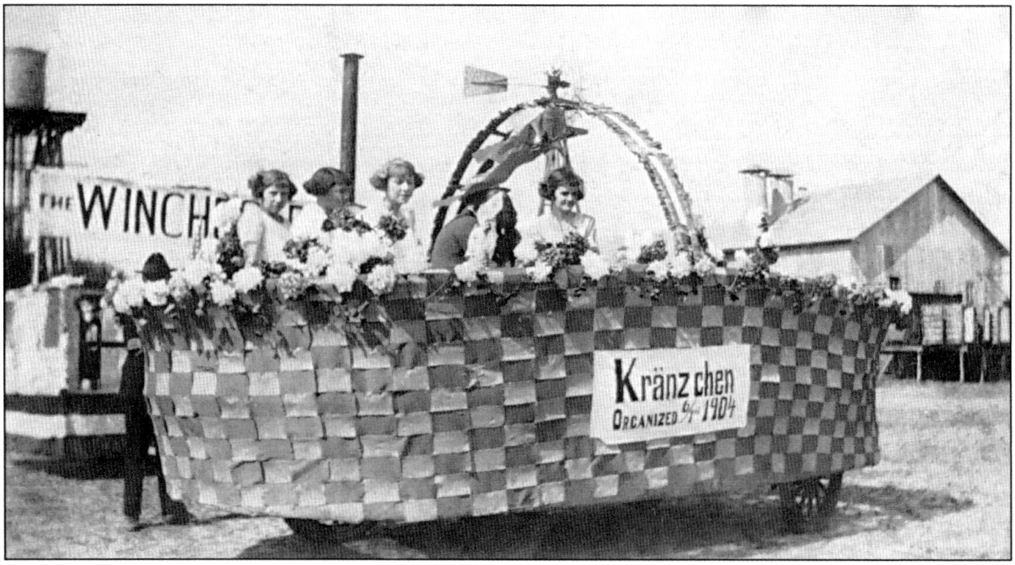

The fourth place winner in the Silver Jublilee Parade was the "Flower Basket," which was entered by the Halkelkmennzchen. The winning prize for this float was $3. Riding on the float are Lucille Menn, Anita Riedesel, Caroline Peters, Georgia Treude, and Edna Wied. Herbert Wied was the driver. This float was a beautiful woven basket filled with beautiful girls. The Kränzchen, which is on the side of the float, was a group of ladies getting together to visit, sew, and have lunch. (Courtesy Lindbergh and Georgie Voelkel.)

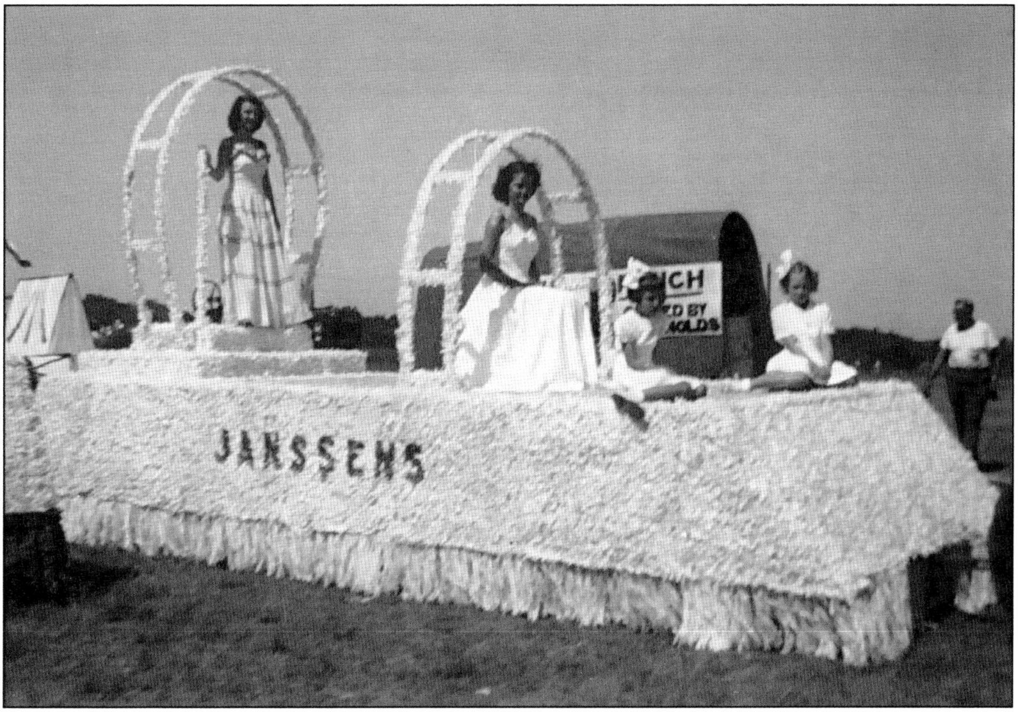

The Golden Jubilee, held on September 25, 1947, celebrated Nordheim's 50th birthday. There were more than 50 floats for the opening day. This event with its parade drew large crowds. The picture above shows an impressive float entered by Janssen's Dry Goods with beautiful young ladies riding on the top with lots of fluff and arches. The float below represented the peanut business, which is a big part of the community. Raymond Huck and his son Dick Huck ride in the float that they made out of peanut hay.

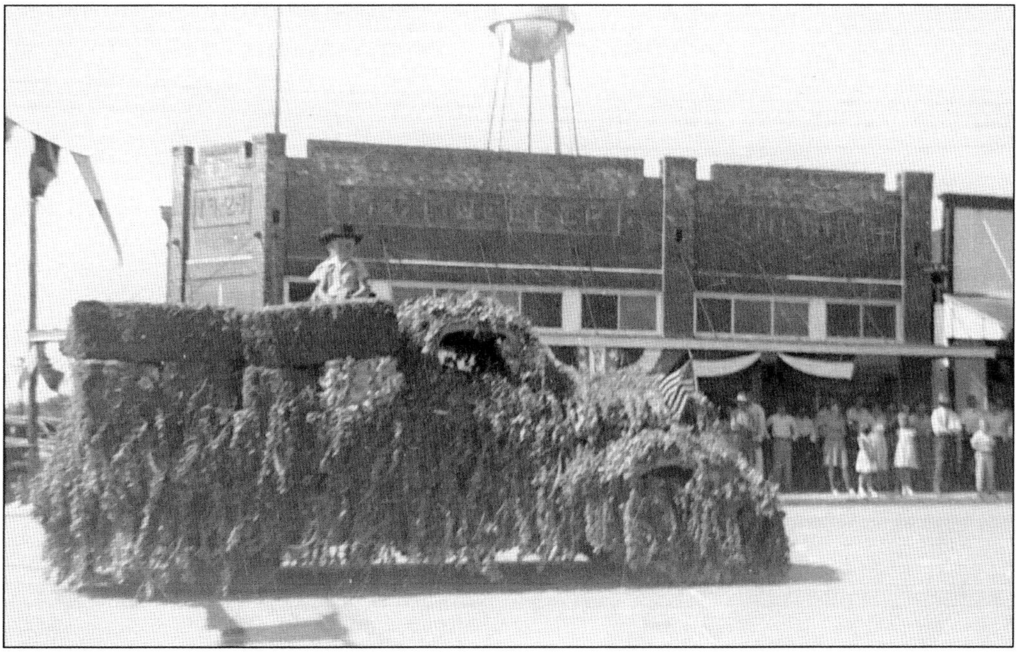

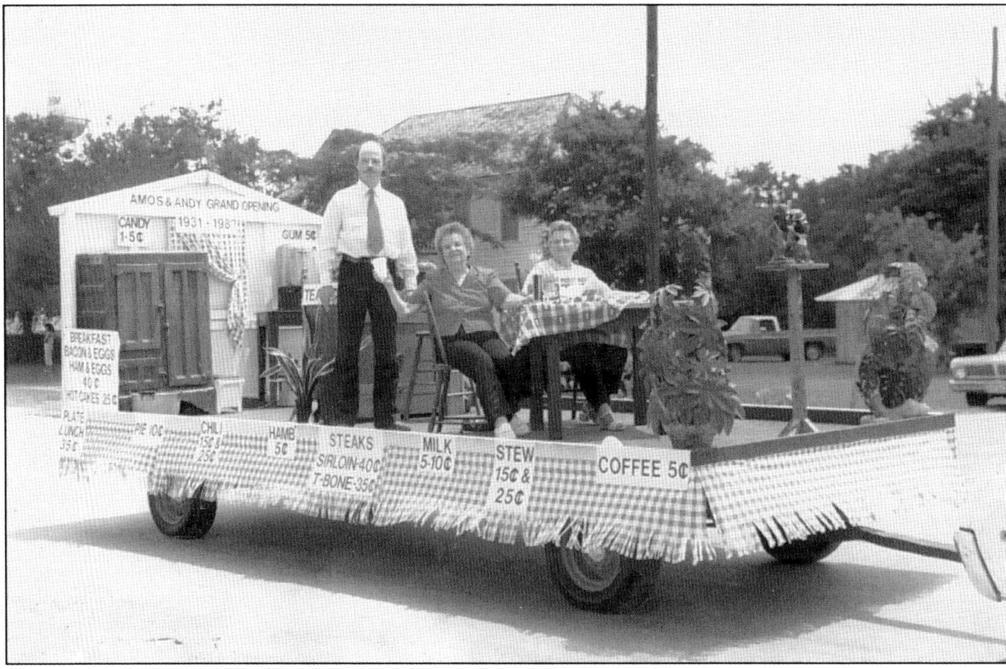

To celebrate Nordheim's 75th birthday, Nordheim held a Diamond Jubilee, which was held on September 16, 1972. Besides the parade, there was a lot of great food and concerts all weekend, along with a dance, ball games, and fun for all. Pictured in the float above is the Amos and Andy Café with Emily Mullins, Johnny Kozok, and Eileen Mueller riding on a mock-up of the café. Below is the Broadway Bar float with a replica of the bar back and customers and a bartender. The customers on this float are Carolyn Pfeifer Elizondo and Melanie Pfeifer Mica, and the bartender is Ronnie Pfeifer, all the children of Mr. and Mrs. Elo Pfeifer.

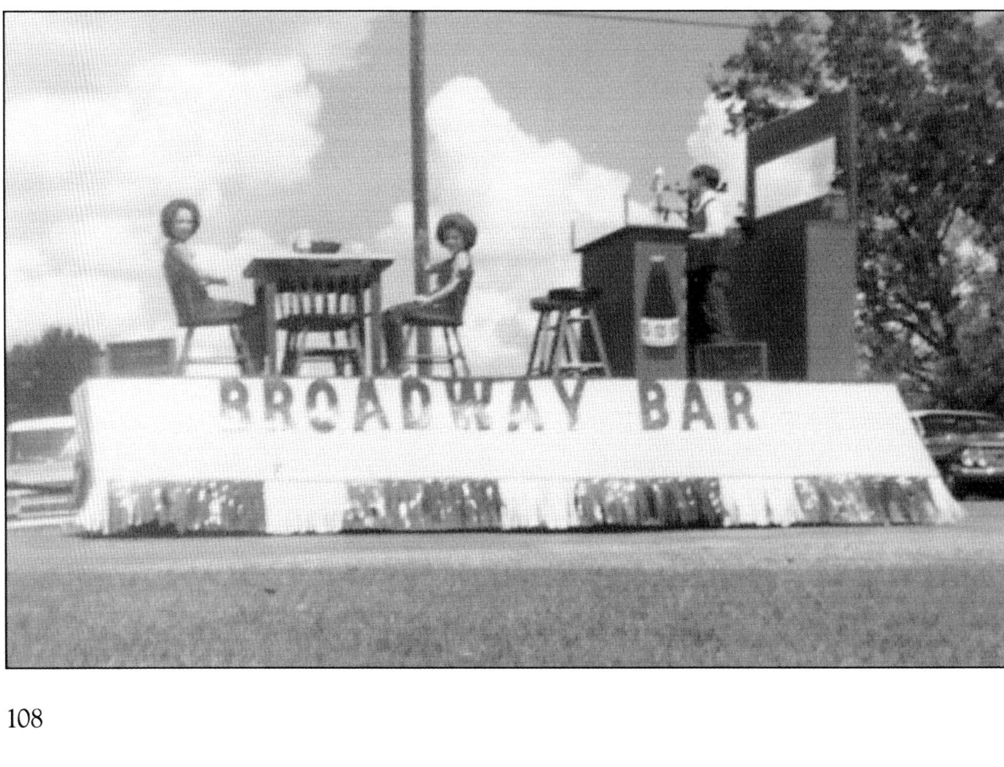

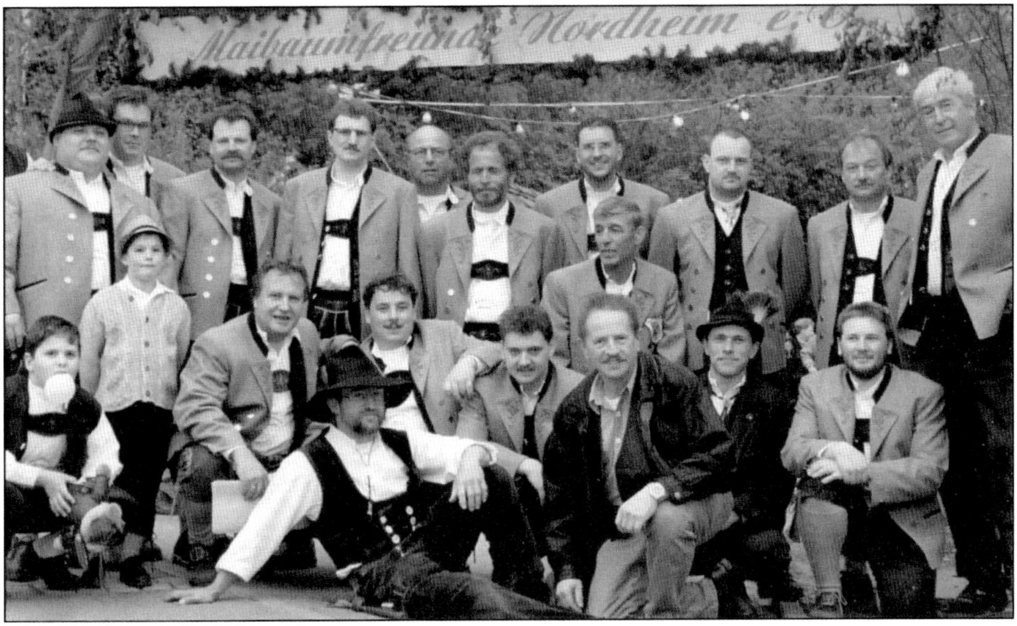

Nordheim celebrated 100 years on August 9 and 10, 1997. This birthday celebration was an important one for the community. The sister city of Nordheim, Germany, shared in the celebration by sending a group to represent them and help celebrate. The photograph above was sent to Mayor Gilbert Pargmann from our sister city. The entire group was unable to attend. The 11 delegates who came were Uwe Morlok, Herbert Weinstok, Marcel Weinstok, Stefan Weiss, Marcel Aichele, Sven Aichele, Ralf Kaiser, Stefan Schwarz, Bernd Weistok, Lothar Kircherer, and Petra Aichele. They marched in the parade and performed for the community. The costumes and entertainment were a great reminder of Nordheim's German heritage. The photograph below shows Marcel Weinstok of Nordheim, Germany, playing the accordion in front of the Broadway Grocery on parade day.

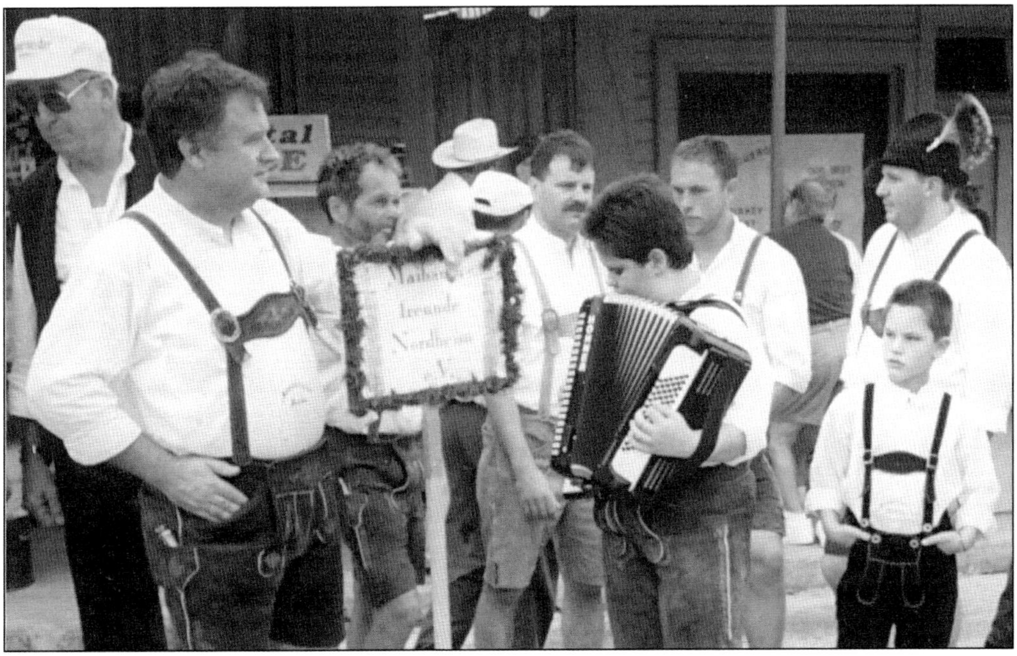

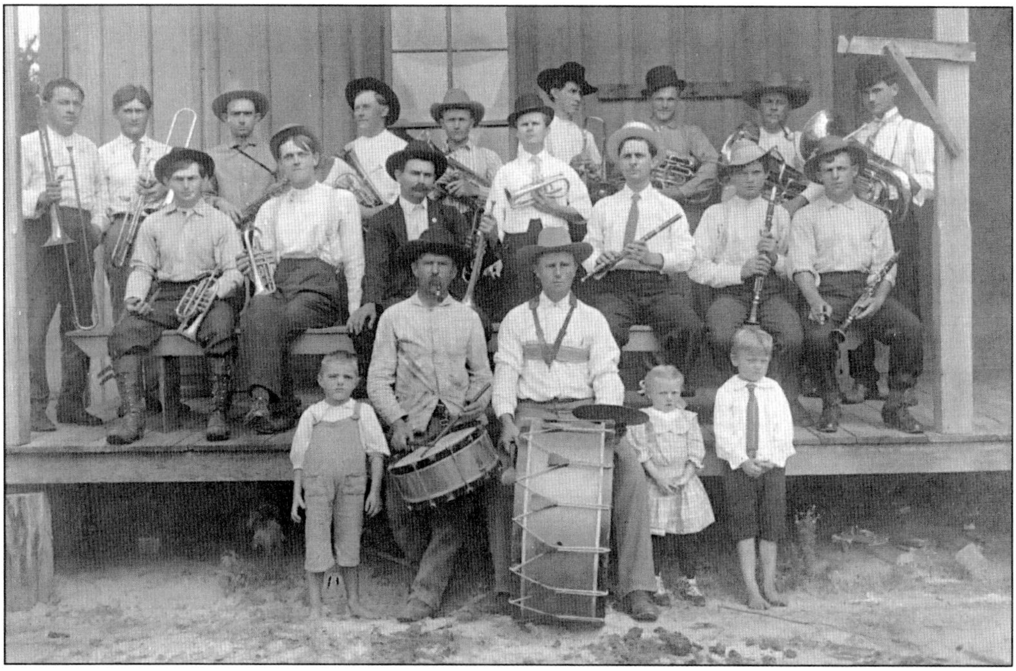

Shown here is what is thought to be the first band in Nordheim. These 18 men, brought together by their love of music and desire to entertain and celebrate, were the beginning of what would be one of the largest parts of the community. The common love of music is a large part of the heritage passed on to this day.

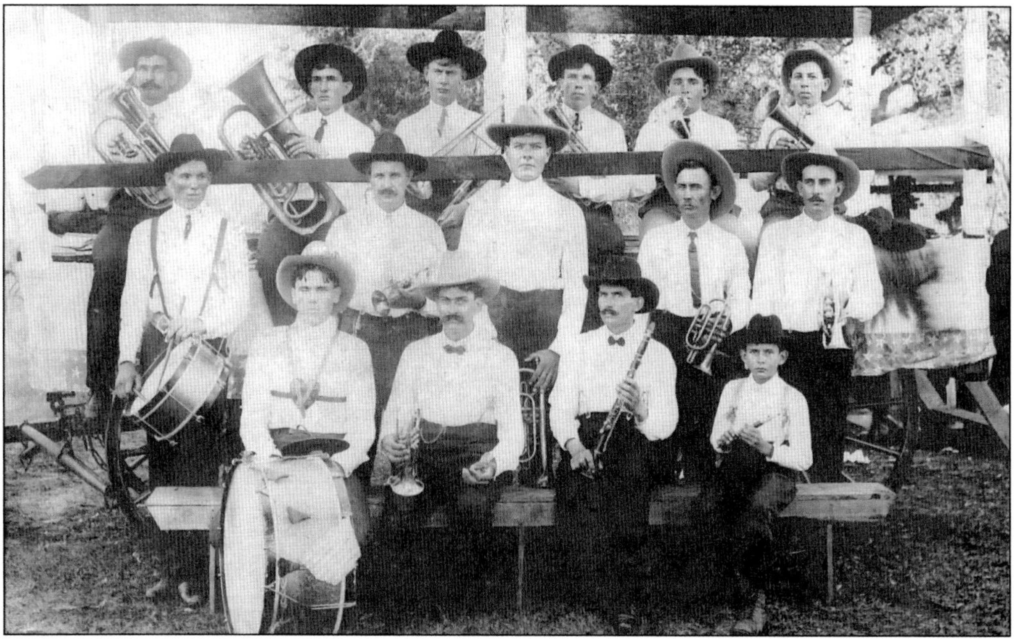

This picture of the Brieger Band was taken in 1908 at a feast on Pilot Knob. They posed on a platform built on a wagon. From left to right are (first row) all unidentified; (second row) Richard Natho, John Buelter, Albert Block, ? Ulrich, and Alfred Brieger; (third row) Henry Brieger, Robert Brieger, Walter Meischen, Otto Natho, Emil Hackfield, and Robert Natho.

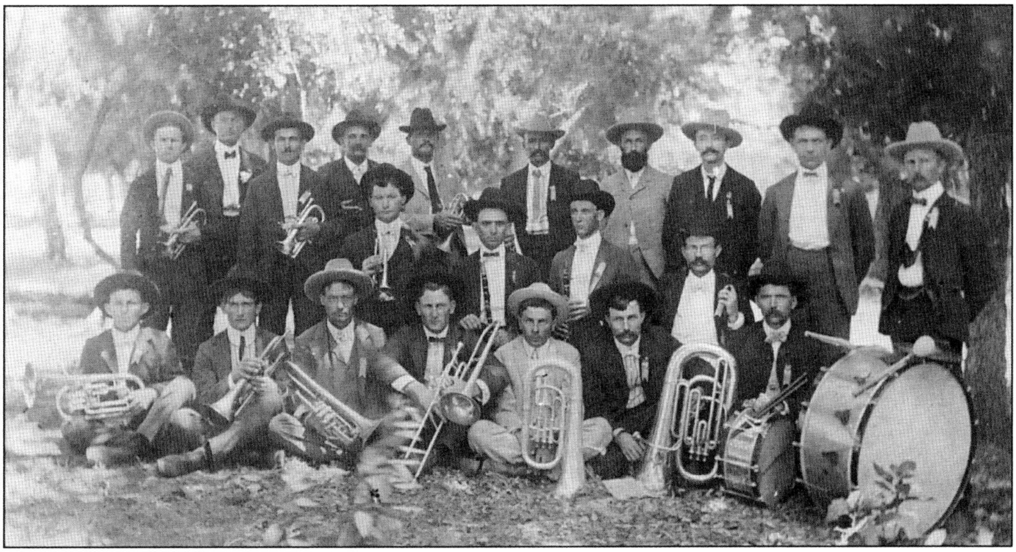

The Nordheim Brass Band is shown in 1904 at the Ottine, Texas, May Feast. Pictured are Willie Brieger, Alfred Zedler, August Burow, George Bode, Louis Phiel, Dr. Theo. Buehring, Emil December, Louis Wied, Emil Wied, Curt Reinhardt, Herman Charpentier, Gus Gross, Albert Dahlmann, Paul Ulrich, Louis Henze, and Willie Klaevemann. The Nordheim Brass Band was popular and played all over South Texas.

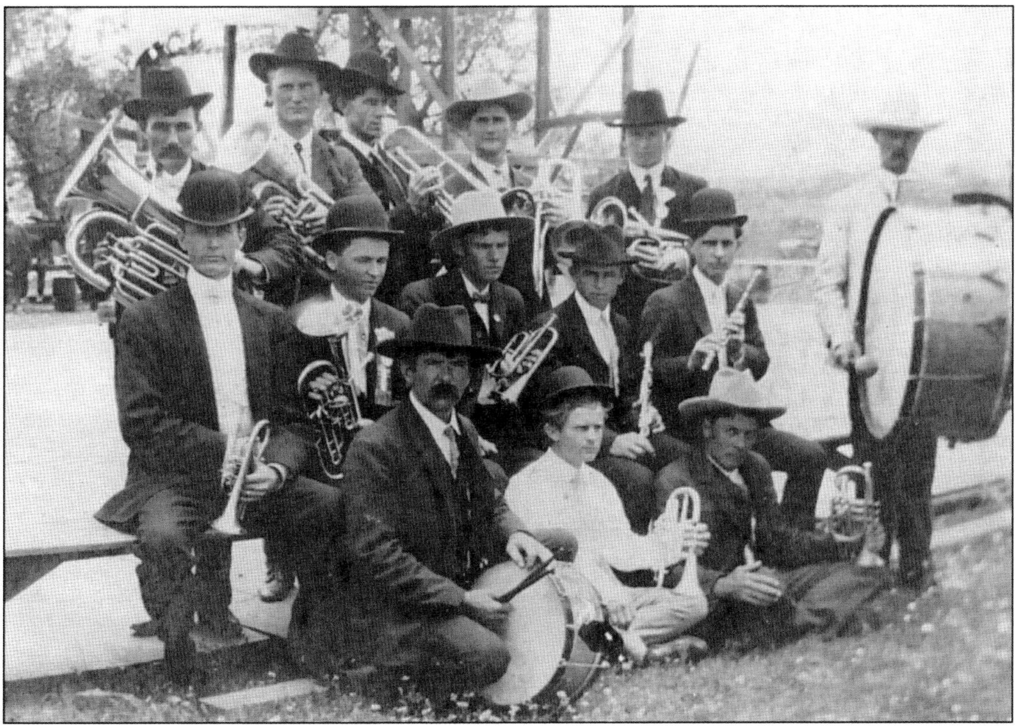

The Nordheim Brass Band in 1907 are, from left to right, (first row) Paul Uhrich, Alfred Zedler, and Emil December; (second row) Prof. Janzen, Hugo Rabenaldt, Willie Klaevemann, George Steinbach, Ben Zedler, and George Bode; (third row) Louis Piehl, Louis Wied, Louis Henze, Emil Wied, and Willie Buesing.

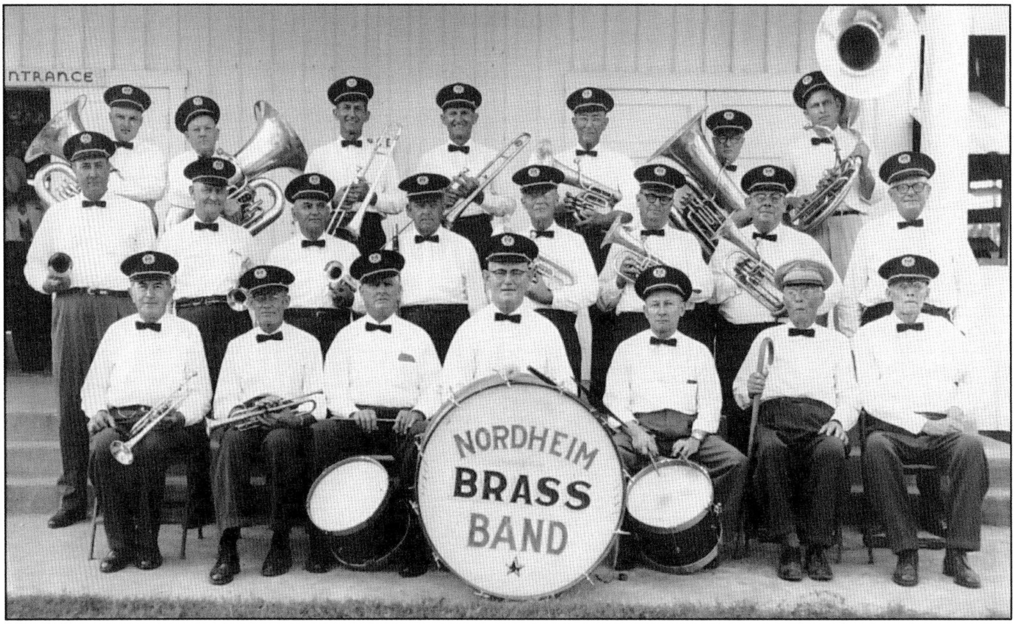

The Nordheim Brass Band is pictured here in 1963. Members are, from left to right, (first row) Joe Richter, Edwin Klaevemann, Osmar Audilet, Herman Garbe, Bennie Klaevemann, Charles Meischen and Willie Klaevemann; (second row) Ben Meischen, Alfred Schroedter, Alfred Butschek, Caesar Metting, F. A. Stirl, Emil Metting, Frank Katzmarck, and Bruno Morisse; (third row) Leroy Mueller, Roy Brunkenhoefer Sr., Louis Stoever, Eddie Stoever, E. A. Stirl, Alfred Marquis, and H. H. Stirl.

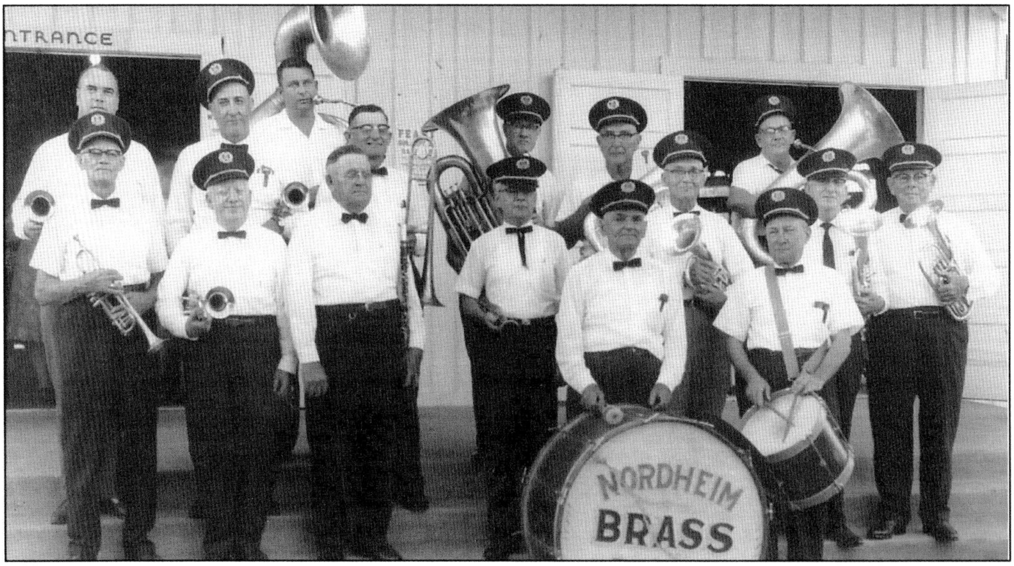

The Nordheim Brass Band posed for this picture in 1968 to celebrate their 60th year. Pictured are (first row) Alfred Butschek and Bennie Klaevemann; (second row) Edwin Klaevemann, Wilson Jacob, Caesar Metting, unidentified, Fred Stirl, unidentified, and Frank Katzmarck; (third row) Stephen Schroedter, Ben Meischen, Harold H. Stirl, Eddie Stoever, Alfred Marquis, Fred A. Stirl, and Roy Brunkenhoefer Sr. The Nordheim Brass Band went on to celebrate their 75th anniversary. They were the third-place winner in the State Band Contest in San Antonio in 1913.

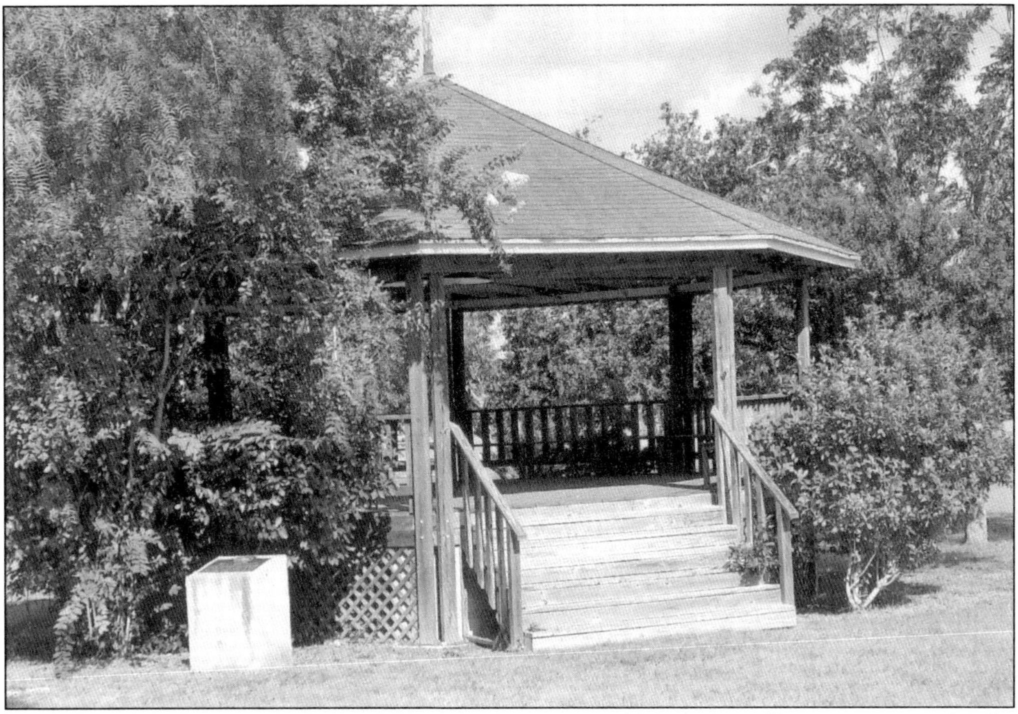

The Jubilee Park Pavilion was erected in 1923 to be used by the Nordheim Brass Band. The pavilion was made from wood used on the floats from the 25th Anniversary Silver Jubilee. The Nordheim Brass Band, first organized in 1896, has given many typical German concerts here, and through the years the pavilion has been the center of civic entertainment with annual Easter egg hunts and wedding ceremonies. (Courtesy Cathy Voelkel.)

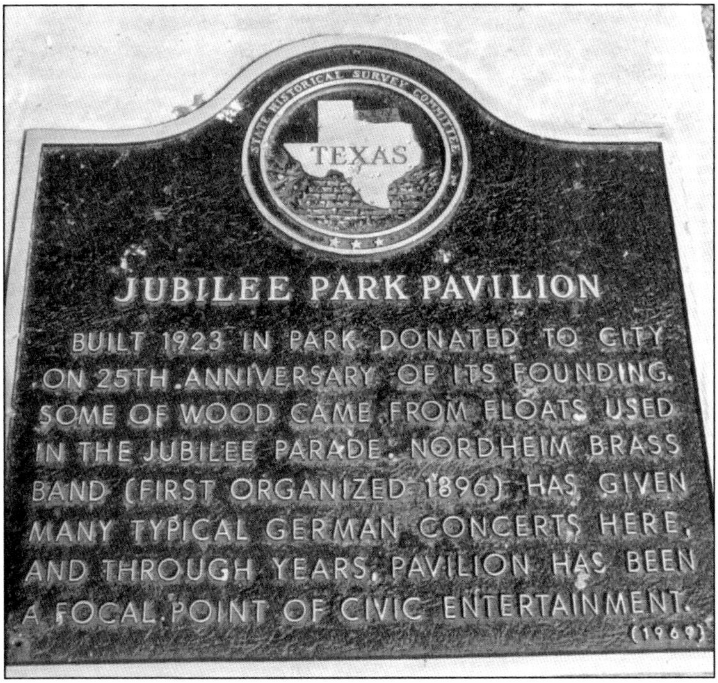

The Jubilee Park Pavilion Texas historic marker was dedicated at the park in 1969 on the 25th anniversary of its founding. The park pavilion has been the site of many events over the years. A few years ago, the City of Nordheim did restoration work on the pavilion in order to help keep this historical part of our community around for many more years. At this time the steps were moved back to their original place in an effort to maintain its history as closely as possible. (Courtesy Cathy Voelkel.)

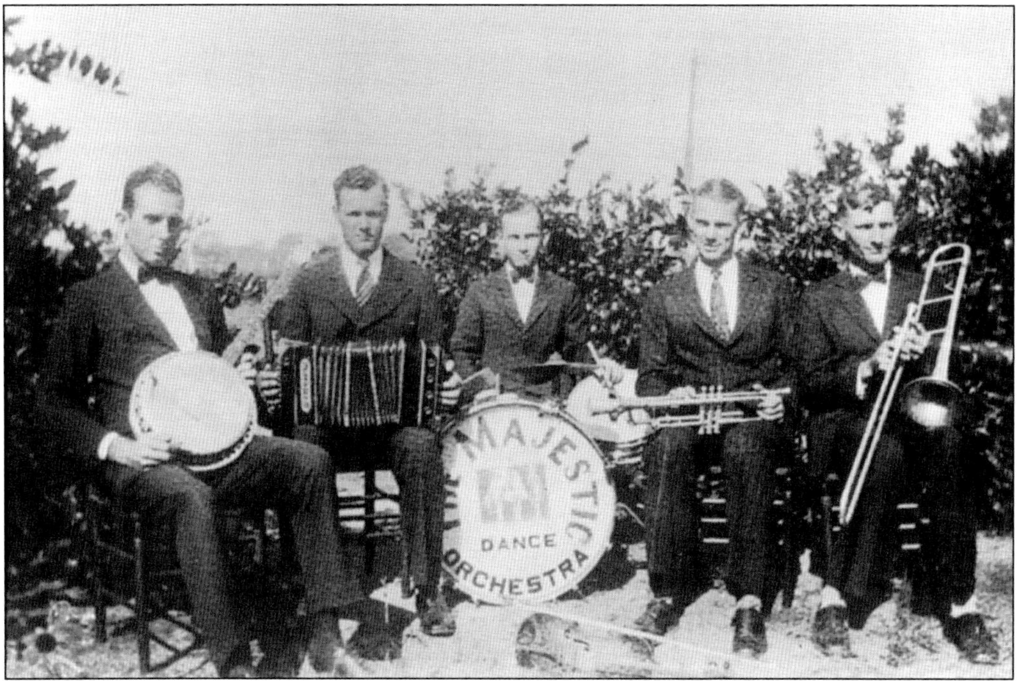

The Majestic Dance Orchestra played in the 1920s, 1930s, and early 1940s for dances all over South and South Central Texas. The members of the band in 1929 were, from left to right, Paul Dittfurth, Herbert Klaevemann, Bennie Klaevemann, and Edwin C. Klaevemann. On occasion Mrs. Edwin (Caroline Peters) Klaevemann would accompany the band on the piano.

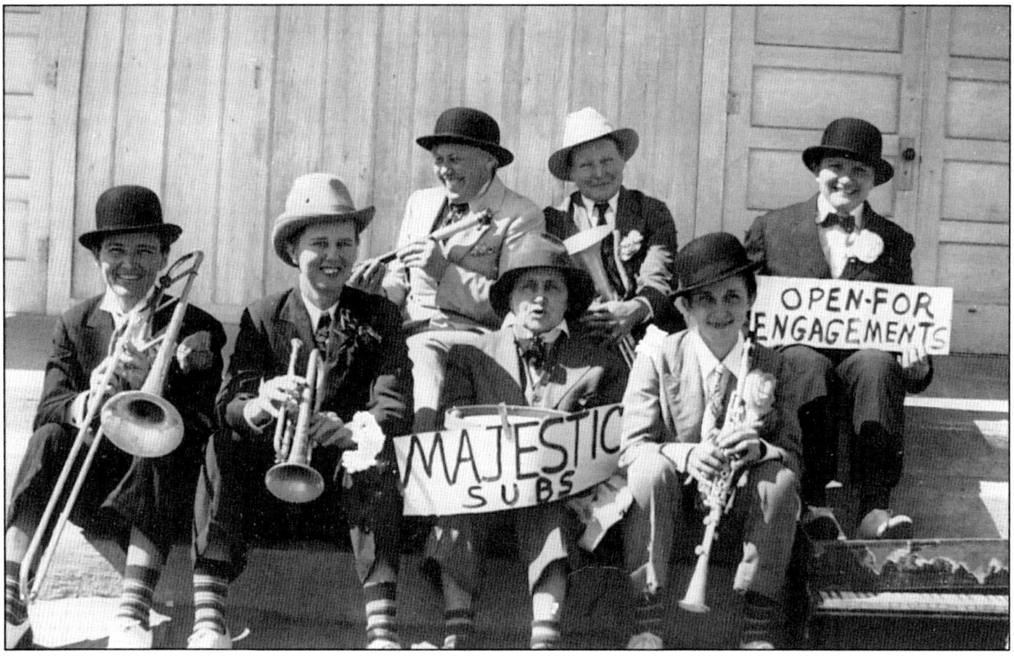

During the Nordheim Golden Jubilee Parade, some local women impersonated the Majestic Dance Band. From left to right are Helen Garbe, Malinda Peters, Ella December, Gussie Jutz, Miss Sachtleben, Anita Huck, and Thelma Estill.

Another local Nordheim band in 1919 was, from left to right, (first row) Carl Bolting, Paul Koerner, and Herbert Stoever; (second row) Henry Buesing, Edgar Koerner, and Herman Garbe. (Courtesy Lindbergh and Georgie Voelkel.)

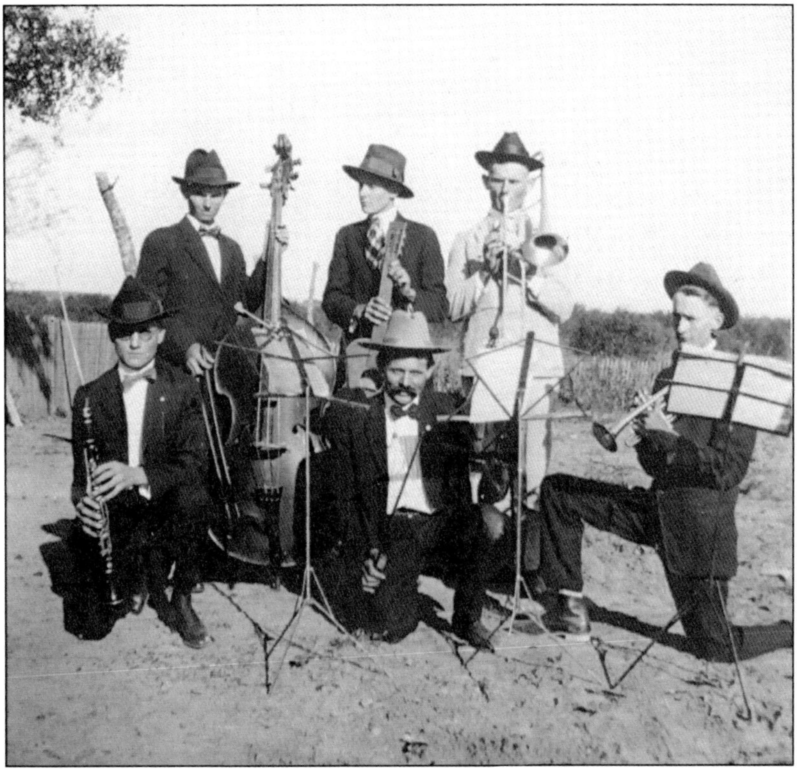

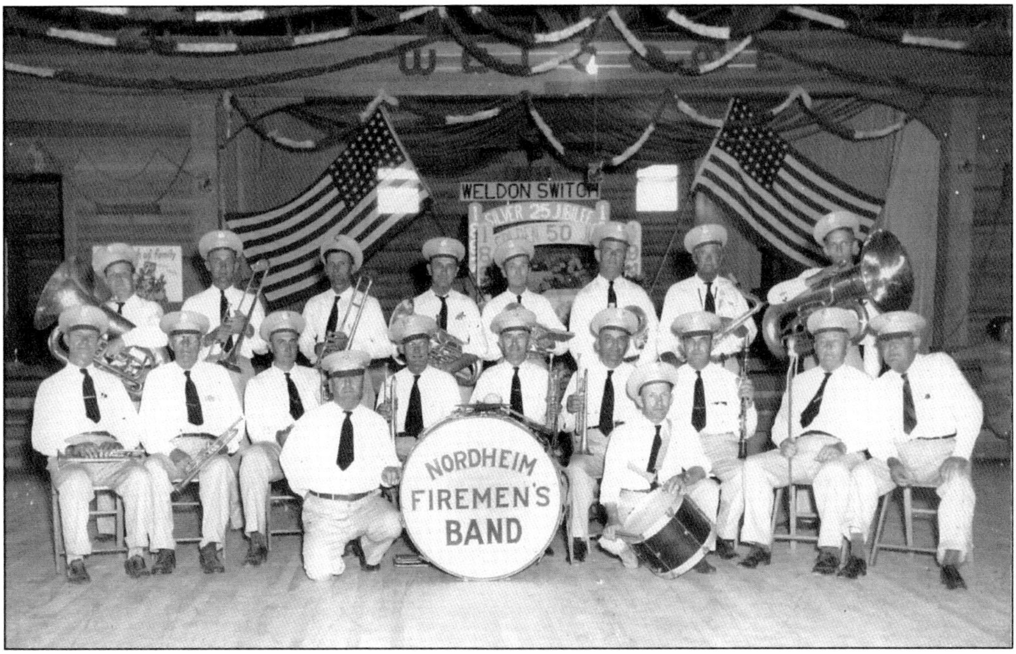

The Nordheim Fireman's Band was, from left to right, (first row) Osmar Audilet and Bennie Klaevemann; (second row) Alfred Schroedter, Willie Klaevemann, Ben Meichen, Edwin Klaevemann, unidentified, Afred Butschek, and three unidentified; (third row) Roy Brunkenhoefer Sr., Louis Stoever, Eddie Stoever, Albert Stirl, Fred Stirl, Herman Garbe, Bruno Morrisse, and Harold Stirl.

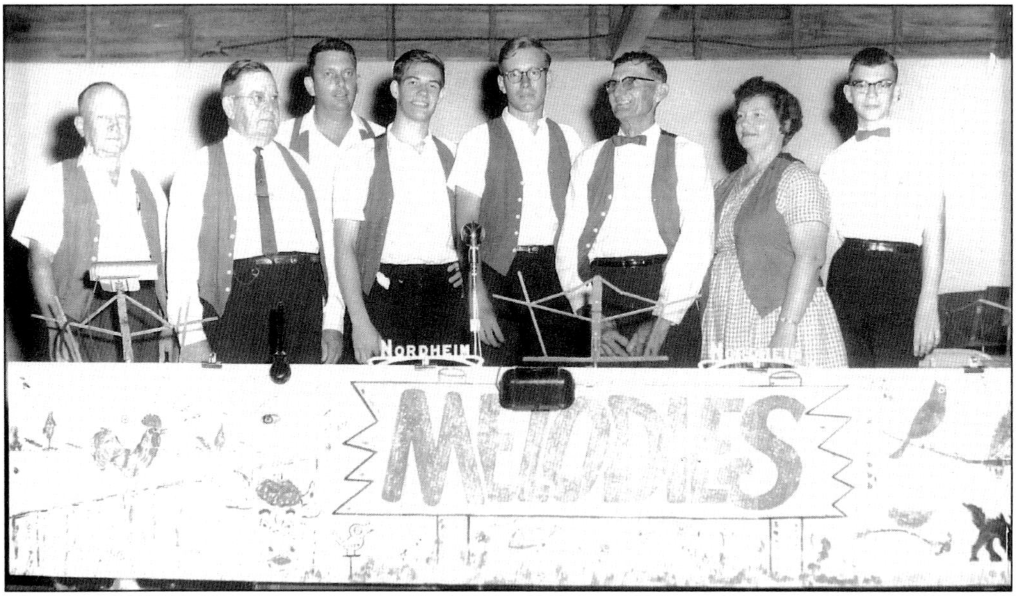

The Melodies played and entertained at events in Nordheim for many years as well as in other towns in South Texas. The band was made up of locals. From left to right are Bennie Klaevemann, Ceasar Metting, Harold Stirl, Daniel Potcinske, Glenn Sachtleben, Eddie Stoever, Georgie Voelkel, and Bruce Weise. (Courtesy Lindbergh and Georgie Voelkel.)

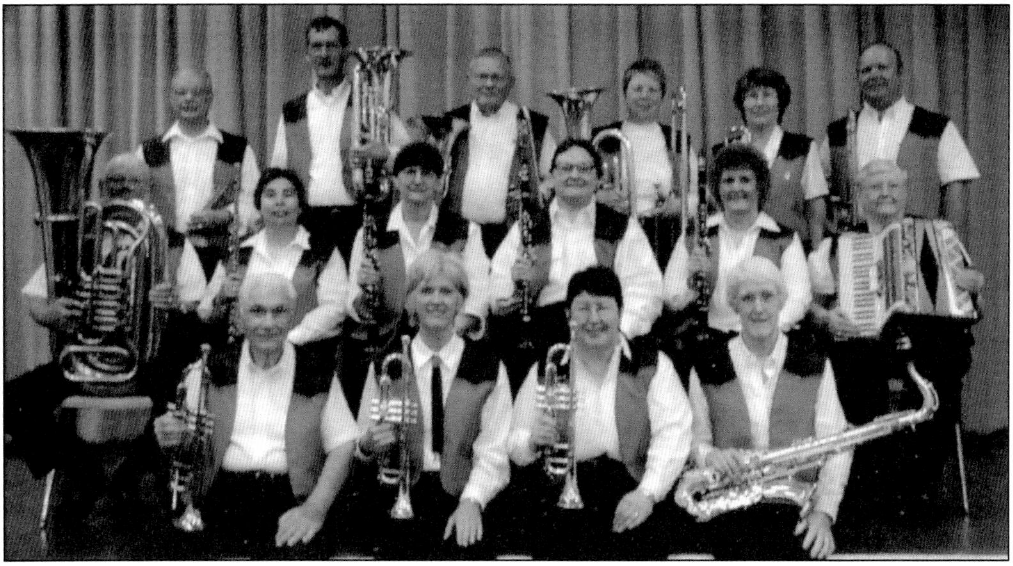

In the fall of 1990, the Nordheim School faculty came together and decided to form a musical group. They invited NISD graduates to play. They named themselves the Nordheim Faculty and Friends Band. The members of this band are descendants of the famous Nordheim Brass Band and are asked to perform at all local activities and at many other events throughout South Texas. Pictured here are, from left to right, (first row) Floyd Nicholson, Lynette Stirl, Rhonda Westfield, and Connie Harbers; (second row) Larry Wolf, Snookie Nesbitt, Anna Marie Garcia, Joyce Ann Warwas, Kay Klaevemann, and Georgie Mae Voelkel; (third row) Rene Garcia, Dalton Harbers, Gilbert Pargmann, Carol Johnson, Wilma Cagle, and Royce Pargmann. Not pictured is member Ernie Stirl. (Courtesy Rene and Anna Marie Garcia.)

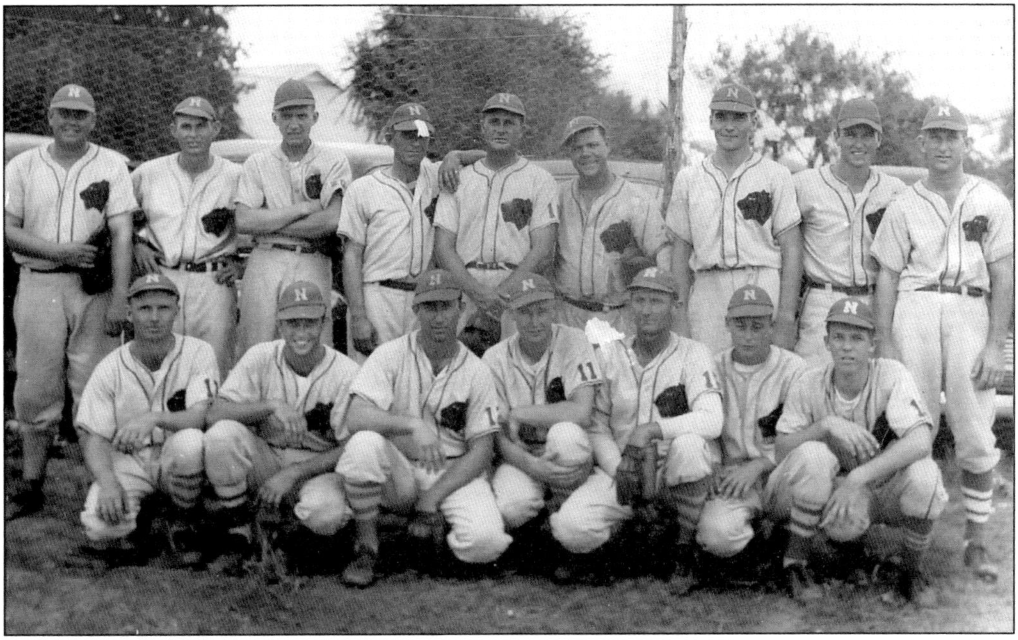

Baseball is important to Nordheim. Pictured here is a Blue Bonnet League team of 1946. From left to right are (first row) Edmund E. Mueller, Travis Semper, Sim Landry, O. J. Janssen Jr., Eddie Stoever, Ray F. Voelkel, and Rudy Jarzombek; (second row) Harry Gips, H. T. Voelkel, Bruce Morisse, Chunky Payne, Sugar Gips, Dave Woods, Vernon Riebschlaeger, Dan Simmons, and Elmo Neutzler. (Courtesy Lindbergh and Georgie Voelkel.)

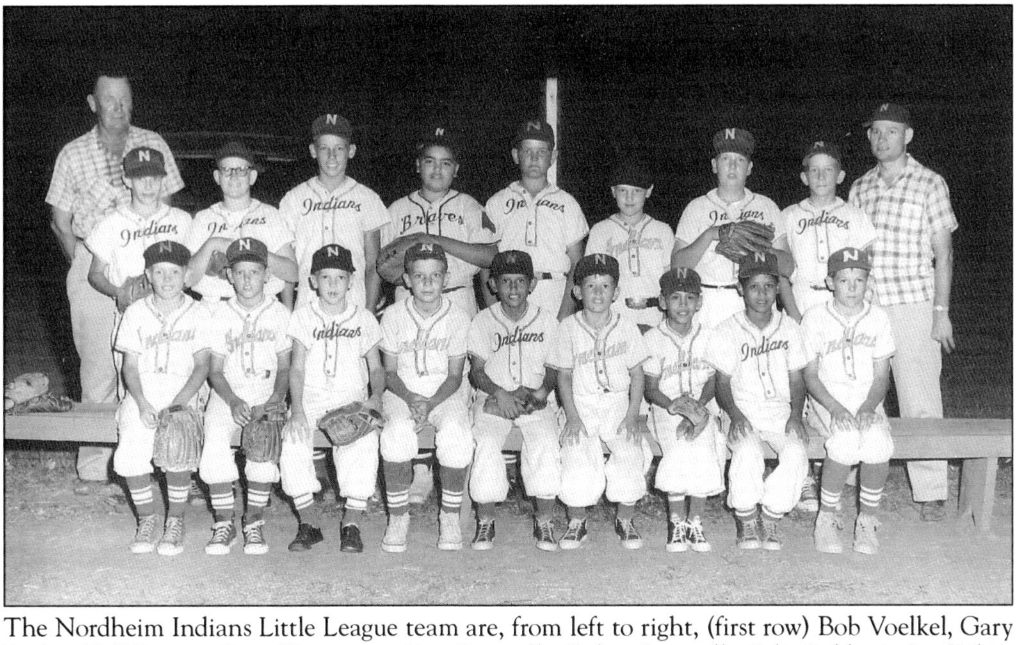

The Nordheim Indians Little League team are, from left to right, (first row) Bob Voelkel, Gary Butler, Cliff Semper, David Baumann, Greg Jaramillo, Robert Jaramillo, Felix Saldania, Joe Eribia, and Oliver Theime; (second row) Coach Edgar Klaevemann, Glenn Voelkel, Davis Schuenemann, Donnie Buchhorn, Gilbert Gonzales, Billy Weise, Gary Wisian, Barry Klaevemann, Roger Huck, and Coach Lindbergh Voelkel. (Courtesy Lindbergh and Georgie Voelkel.)

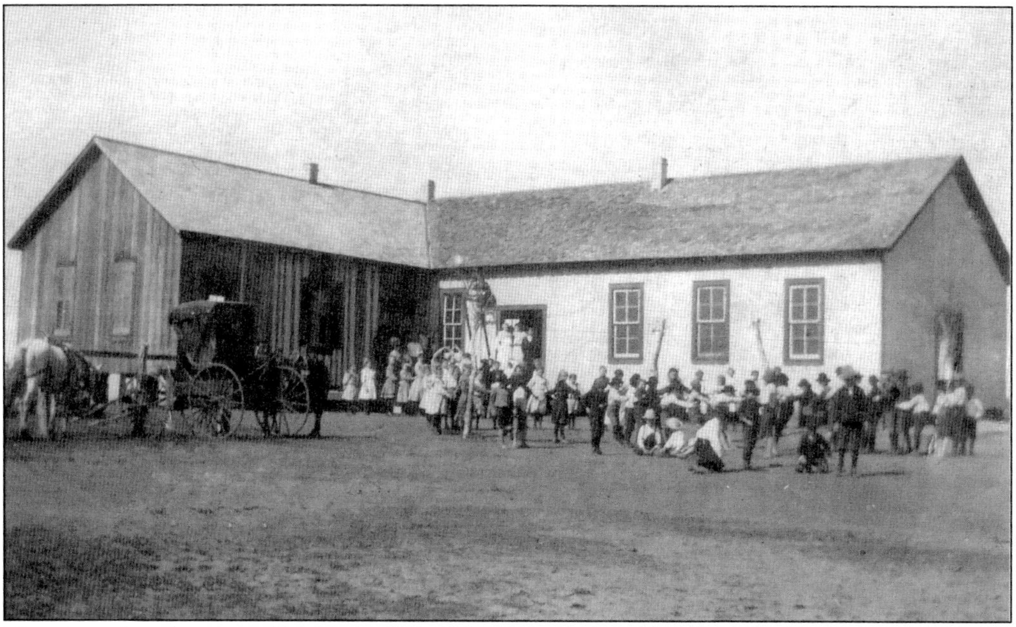

This first schoolhouse and horse shed was constructed of wood in 1897, and the school remained until 1909. This school was taught in German for many years. In this picture, children are playing in the schoolyard. The first full term left a three-week break during the spring so the children could help with the cotton crops.

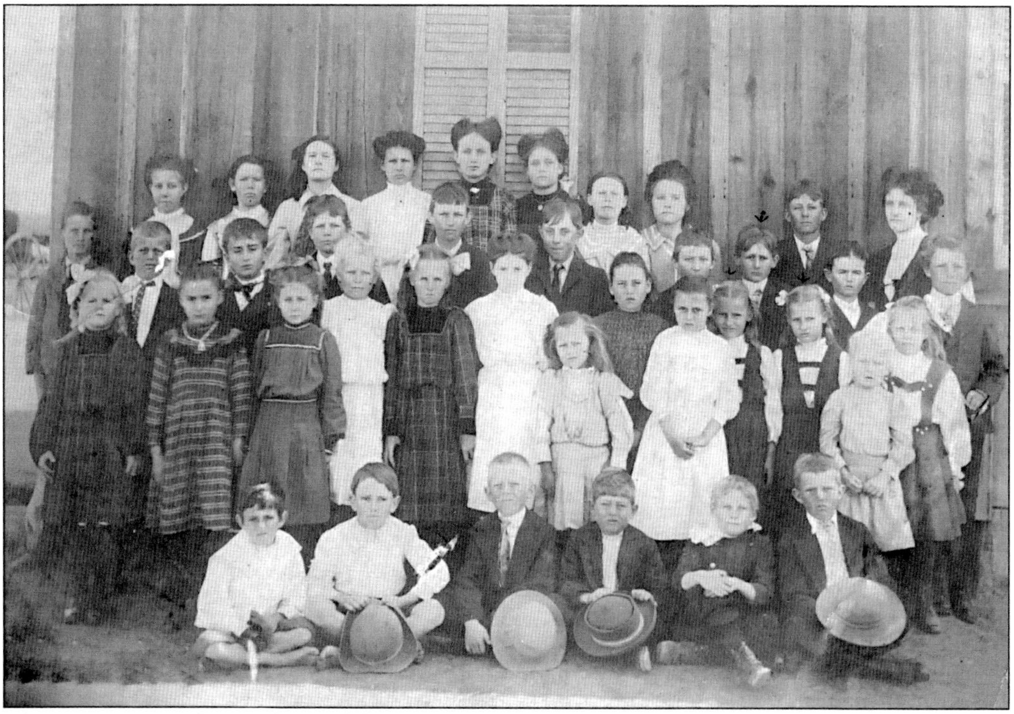

This picture was taken in front of the first schoolhouse in Nordheim. The school was a two-room building, and all the students were taught together in those rooms. The cost for these children to attend school was $3.10 per student each year.

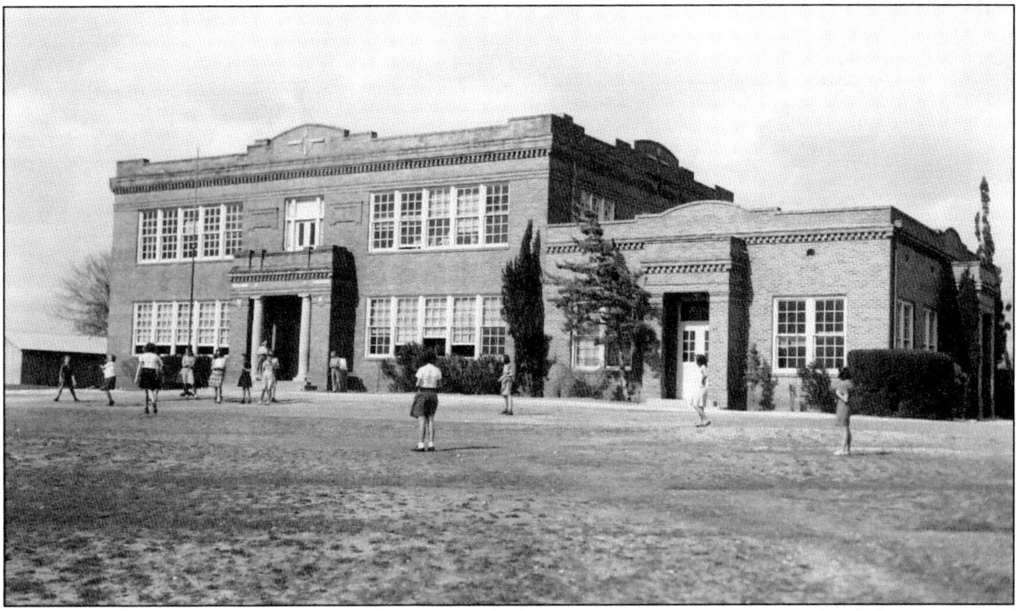

In 1910, when the school expanded to 10th grade, a larger school was built. This brick two-story building was constructed in 1913. Under compulsory laws in 1916, a separate facility was built for Latin American and African American students. This changed by 1954 when all students in Nordheim attended one school. (Courtesy Lindbergh and Georgie Voelkel.)

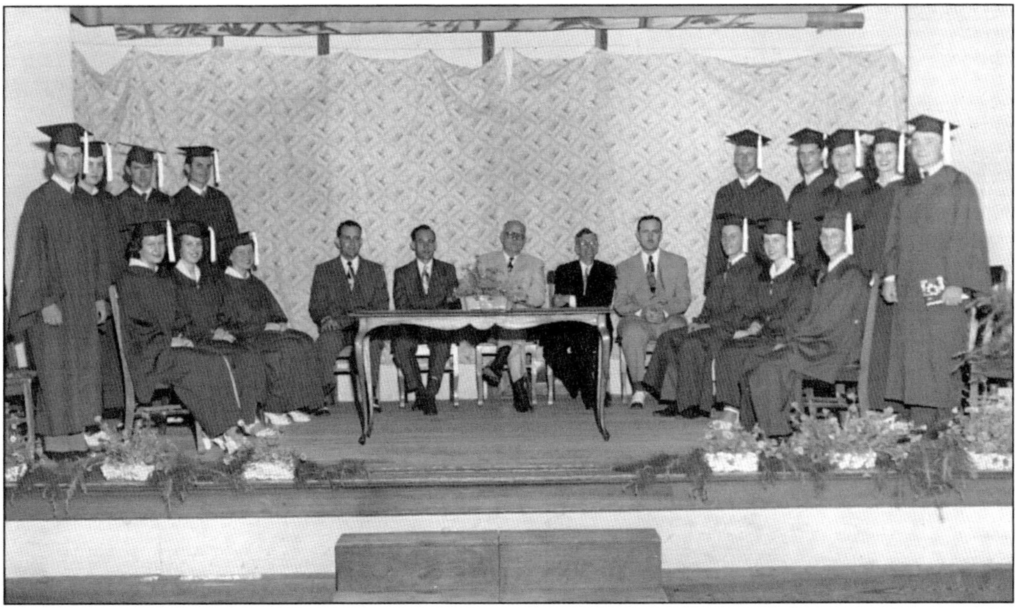

This was the last class to graduate from NISD's first brick school, in 1949. From left to right are (seated) Betty Mae DeReese (St. John), Olga Wunderlich (Hughes), Georgie Mae Stoever (Voelkel), teacher Vernon Osterloh, superintendent Marvin Schnelle, unidentified guest speaker, unidentified, school board president Dr. D. C. Scheffer, Lamar Koehler, Wilma Butchel (Billings), and Ferdinand Neuman; (standing) Jimmy Johnson, Della Mae Boerm (Sauer), Chester Lyssy, Charles Feller, J. Kenneth Neuman, Douglas Lemke, Audrey Jean Stratmann (Parsons), Aileen Bohach (Kenne), and Don Estill. (Courtesy Lindbergh and Georgie Voelkel.)

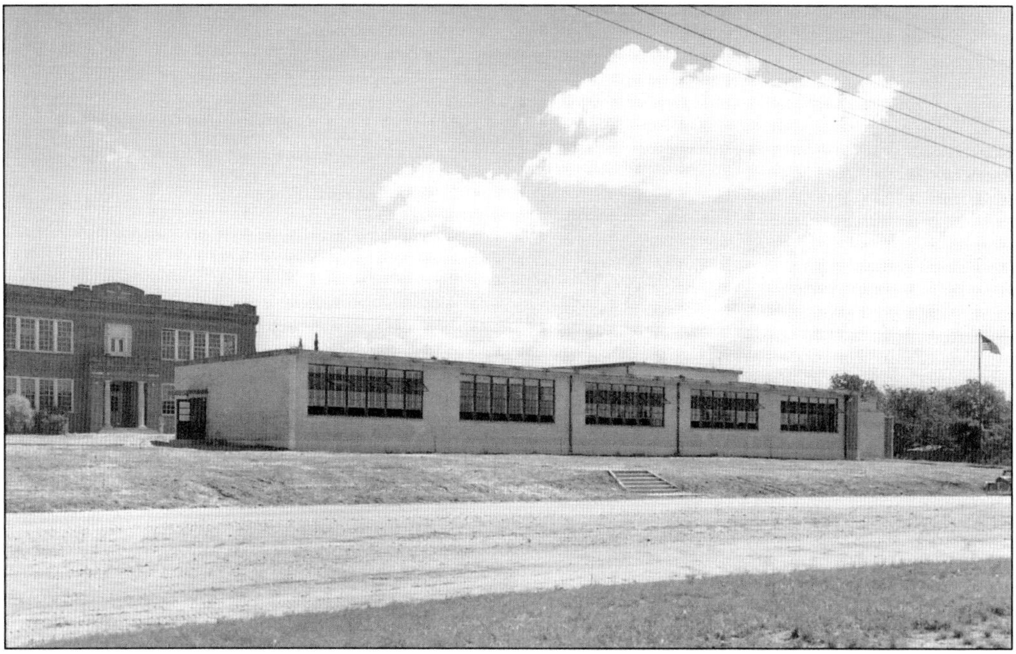

In 1949, a new brick school building was constructed, with a gymnasium and three classrooms added in 1950. This is the school as it is today. The Talk School, which was used for the lunchroom, was formerly one of the commons schools in the area until it was moved into town in 1946. (Courtesy Lindbergh and Georgie Voelkel.)

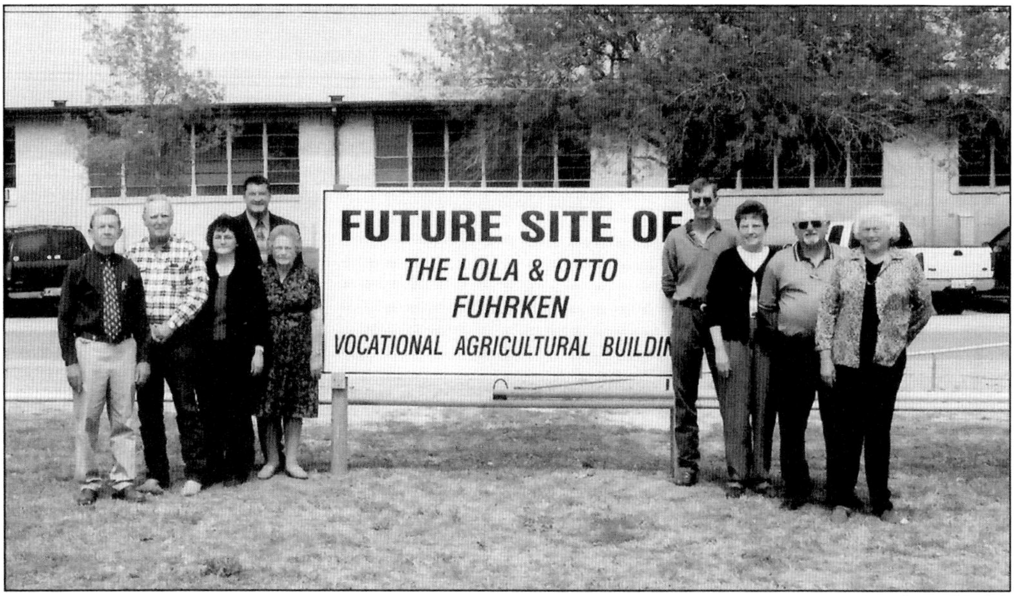

One of the biggest supporters today of the Nordheim ISD and the education of Nordheim's children is Lola Furhken. She has made great donations to help improve and educate the children of Nordheim. She is seen here in 2002 with the school board at the groundbreaking of the Otto and Lola Fuhrken Vocational Agricultural Building. Pictured are, from left to right, Pat Hull, Jim Lane, Pam Stehle, Superintendent Peter Running, Lola Fuhrken, Tim Voelkel, Caroline Pfeifer, Glenn Mueller, and Alma Jean Goehring. (Courtesy Nordheim ISD.)

Eight

Rural Communities

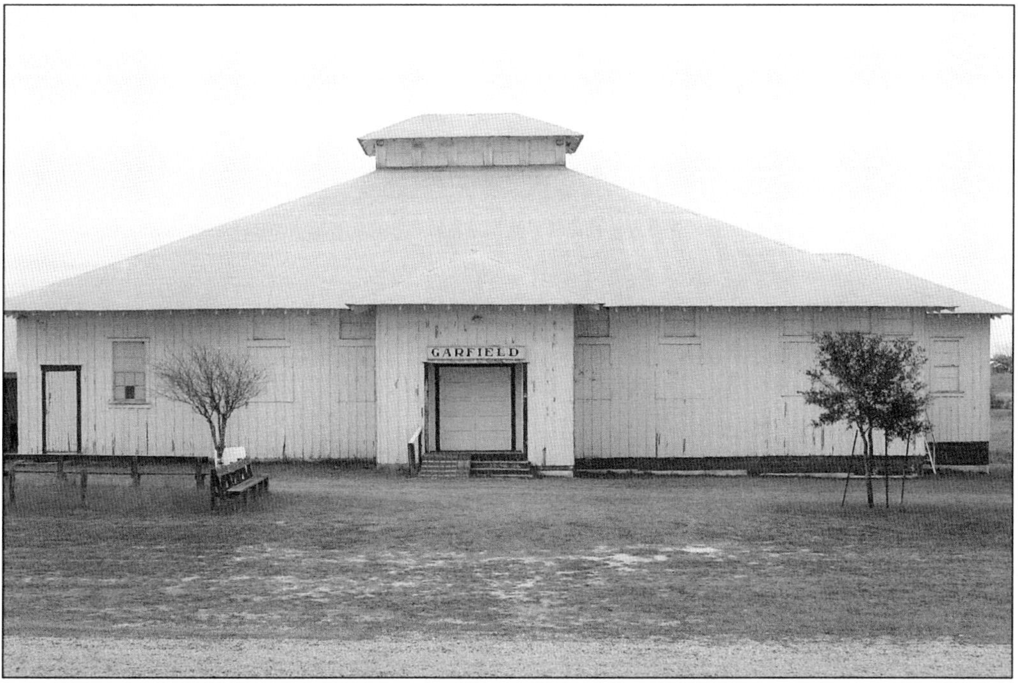

The Garfield Gun Club began in 1892, and soon after, a dance hall was built. The dance hall, named for Pres. James A. Garfield, is located 10 miles west of Yorktown on Farm Road 2656. Today the hall hosts sausage feasts twice a year for the public. It is also used for wedding receptions. In 1891, a school opened in the Garfield community with J. G. Guenther as the teacher. It had a store in 1918, but by 1940 the store appeared to have closed. (Courtesy Cathy Voelkel.)

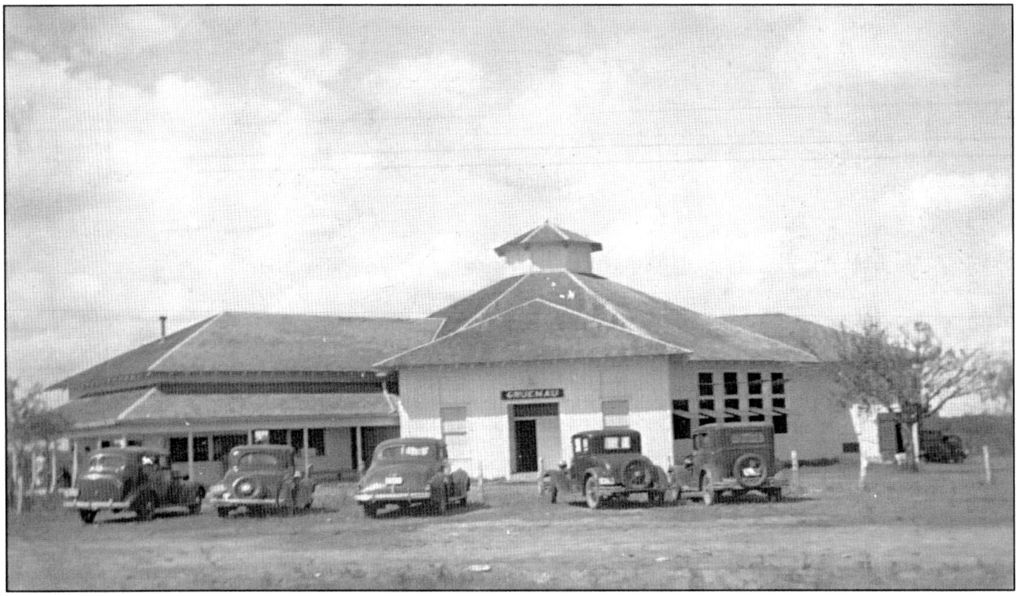

Gruenau was settled by Germans who named it after Grünau in Oldenburg, Germany, from where many have immigrated. Gruenau Hall was built in 1900. It was used as a community center hosting dances, rifle team activities, and feasts. The original building was demolished in 1927 and replaced by the one pictured. However, this building burned down on January 17, 2007, but the perseverance of the members helped resurrect a new building that opened in the fall of 2010. (Courtesy Robert Muschalek.)

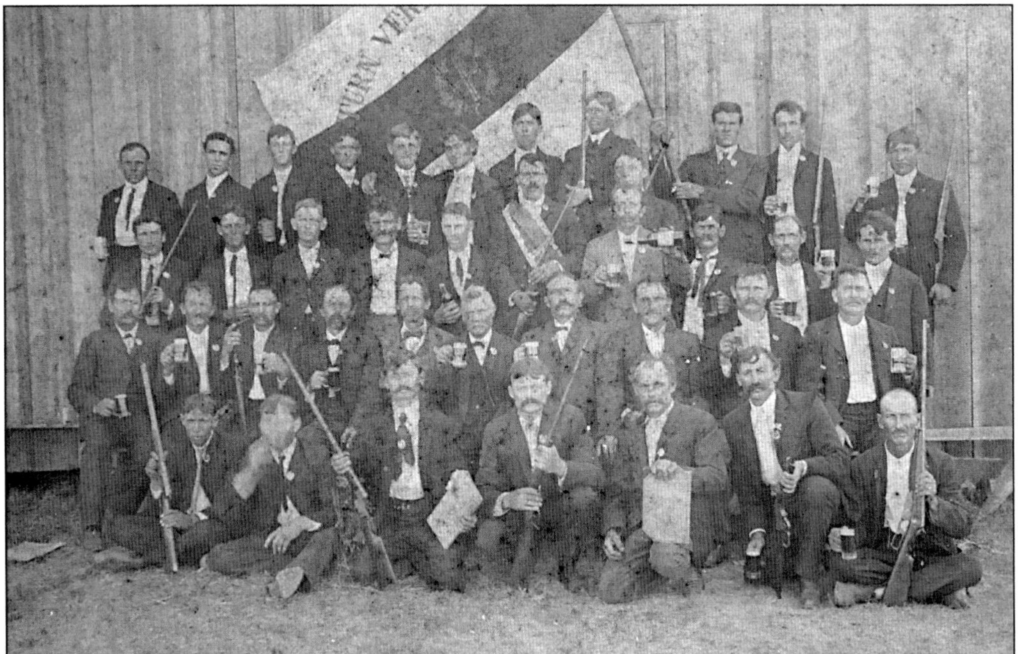

Around 1897, Gruenau started a Schuetzen Verein, or shooting club. The men depicted here are displaying the rifles they used in the shooting competition. Often the event was called a turkey shoot. (Courtesy Robert Muschalek.)

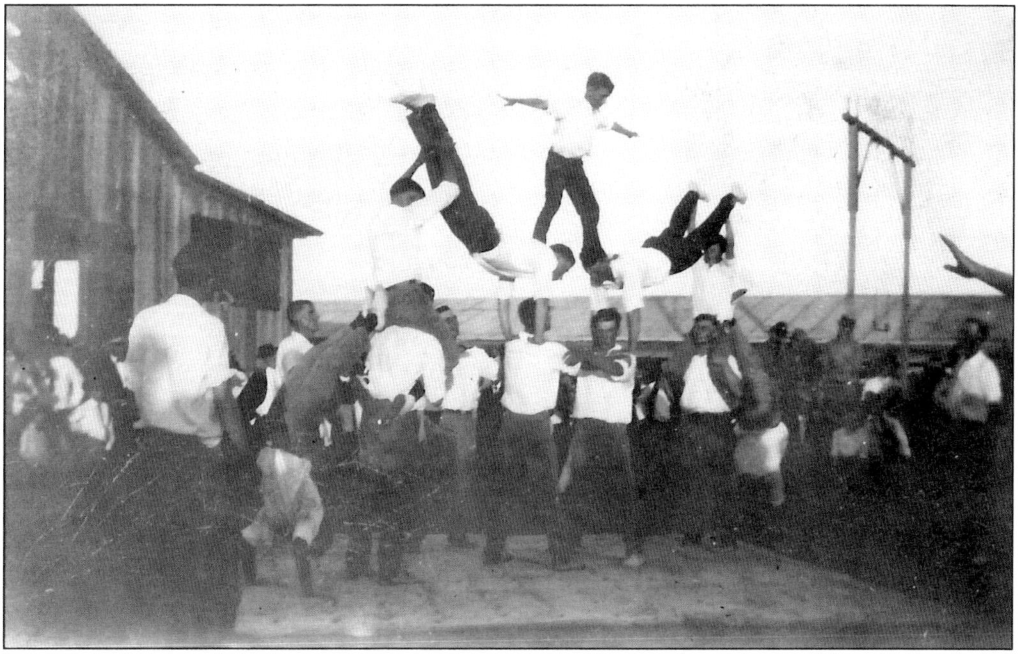

Gruenau also organized a Turnverein, or athletic club, in 1897. In this club, boys and girls participated in athletic training. This continued until 1910, but it resumed in 1924 when Edo Hoepken resurrected the club. Here the boys are going through their routine at a gymnastics competition. (Courtesy June Buchhorn.)

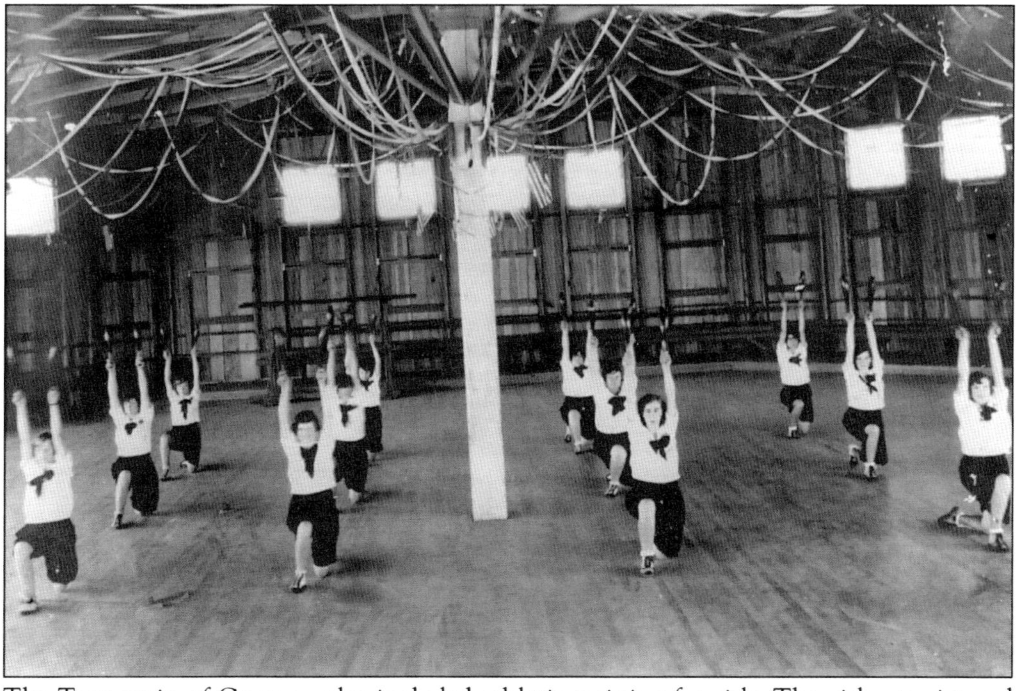

The Turnverein of Gruenau also included athletic training for girls. The girls are pictured exercising with dumbbells in each hand. Notice that they are wearing uniforms. Classes for the men and women were separate.

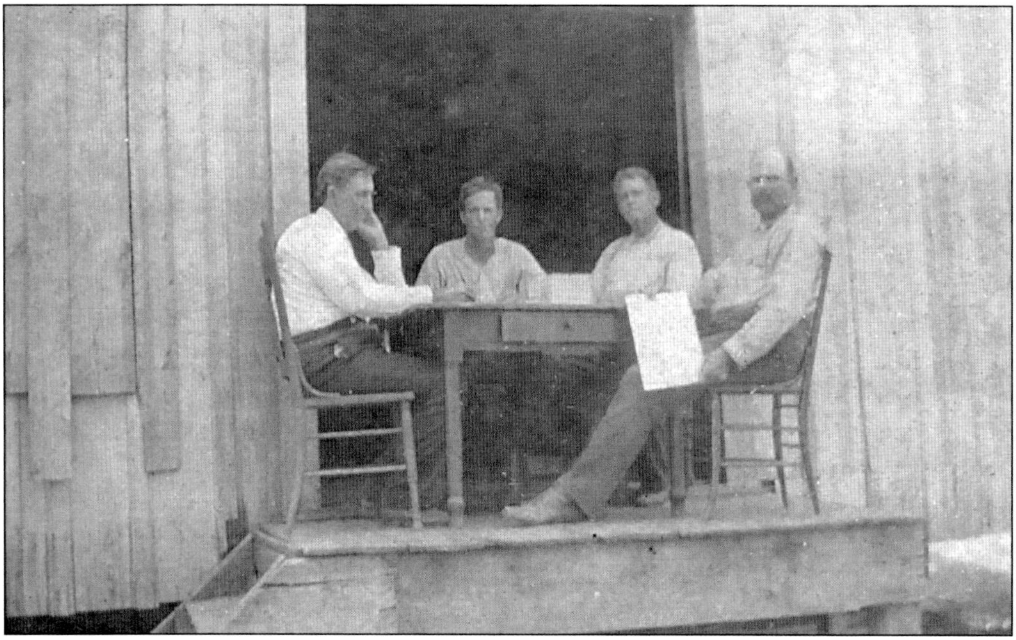

Cabeza Congress was the governing body for the community. In the early 1900s, the community consisted of the Rutherford Store, Dr. Rushing's office, a two-story schoolhouse with the Woodman's Hall upstairs, Mrs. Murphy's store, Langley's Store, Pierce's Blacksmith Shop, and the Grape Arbor Camp. Other residents in the community were the John Butlers, William Browns, and Christian Buendels.

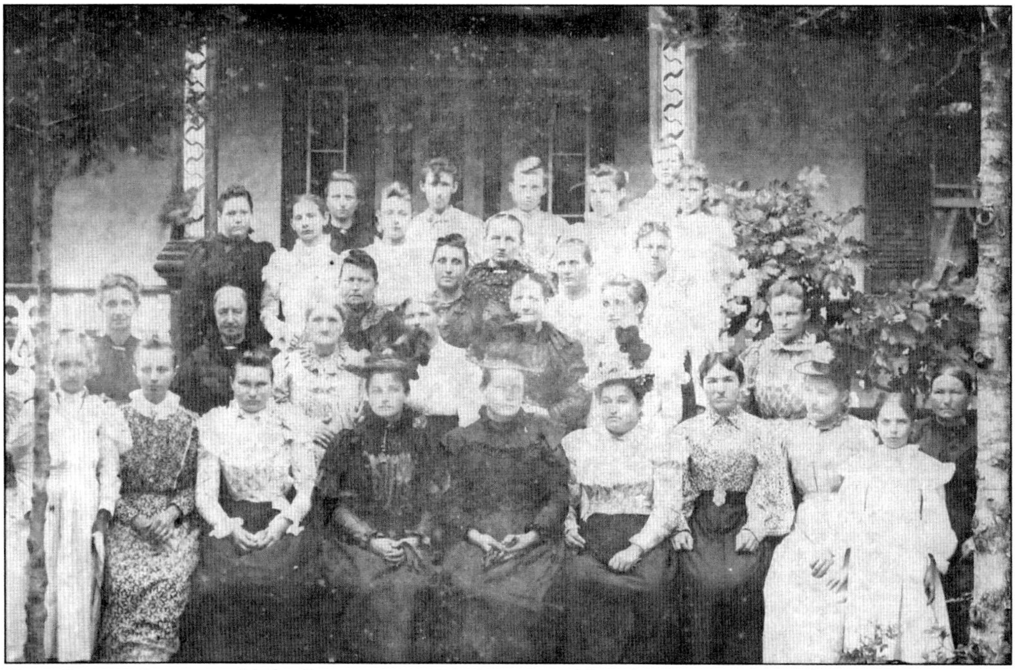

To enhance their social life, the women of Cabeza would gather at someone's home to visit, quilt, sew, play cards or games, cook, or bake. This gave them time to catch up on the news of what was happening in each other's lives.

Standing on the porch of the Cabeza School, District No. 11, is Miss Rushing. She was teaching there in 1938. (Courtesy Lindbergh and Georgie Voelkel.)

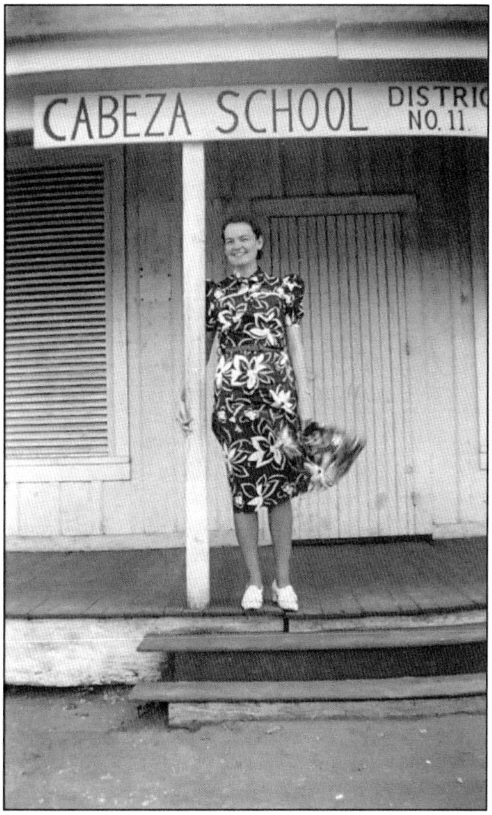

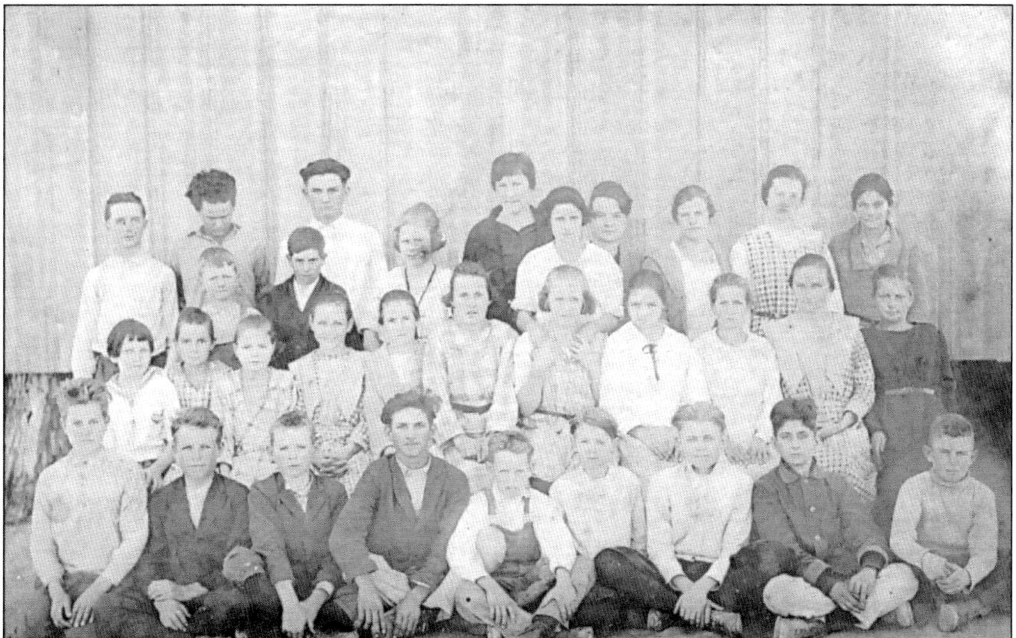

Lined up in four rows are students of the Cabeza School. Notice the shoes of the boys sitting in the front row.

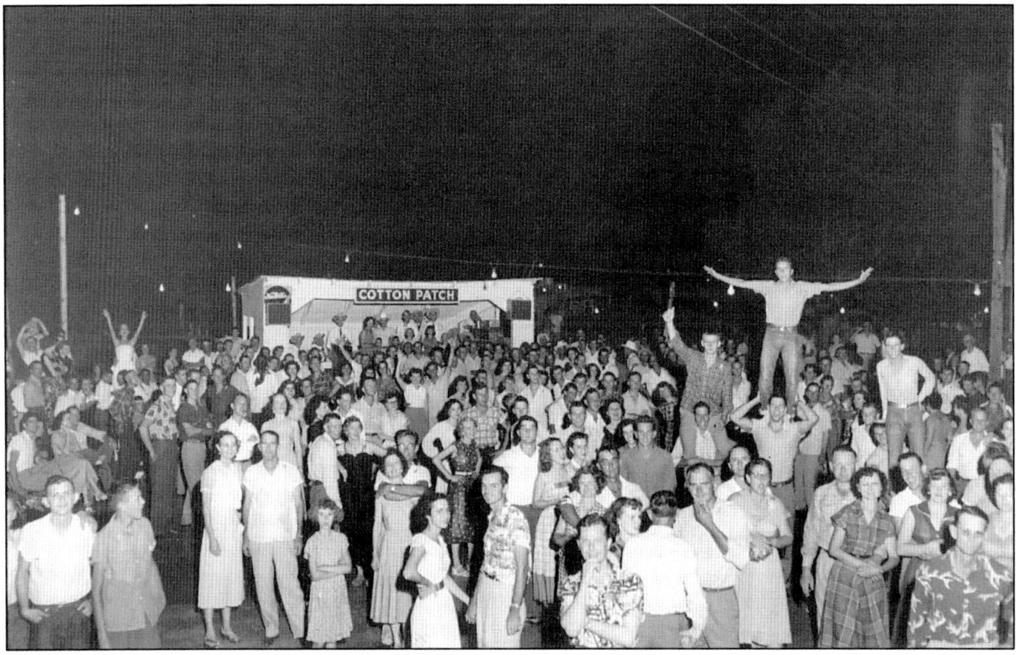

When Henry Morisse sold 1 acre of his cotton patch, the rural community of Cotton Patch came into existence with the building of a grocery store and gas station by Fritz Ehlers in 1930. In the 1940s, George Morisse added an open-air dance area with a small stage for live music and dancing. Large crowds flocked to Cotton Patch to dance. (Courtesy Esther Puente.)

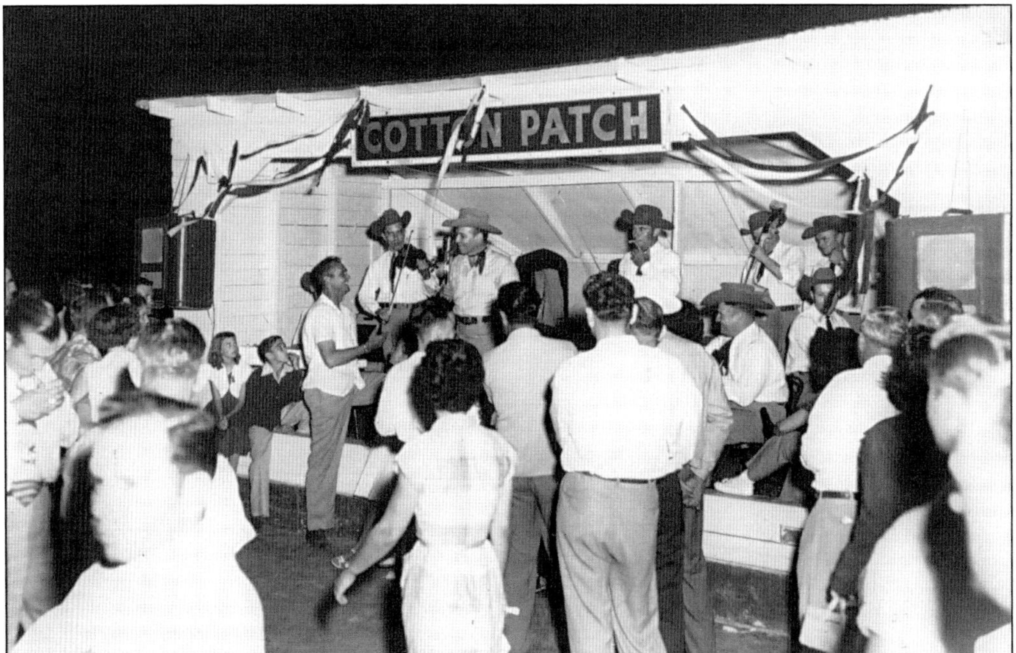

Music for dancing was provided by local talent as well as country singer Bob Wills and his Texas Playboys. In 1977, the Cotton Patch store closed, but in 2008 Michael and Esther Puente bought it and brought new life to the area, hosting parties and live music on weekends. (Courtesy Esther Puente.)

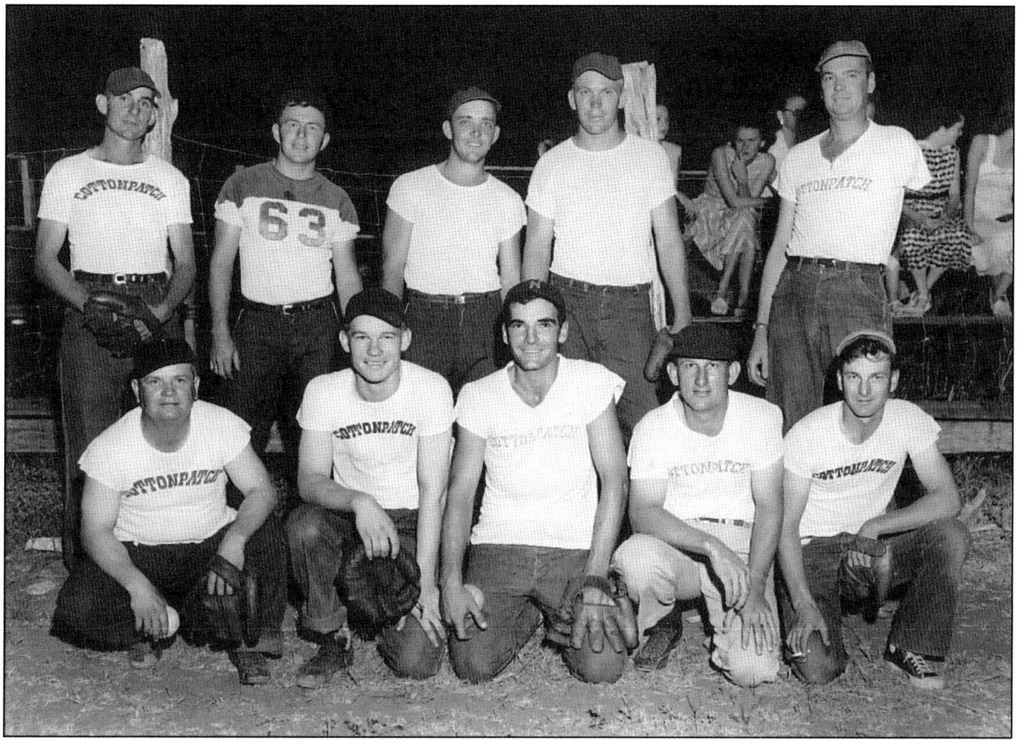

The Cotton Patch baseball team played against other area baseball teams. Members of the team are (first row) Gus Mueller, Elmer Neumann, Vernon Riebschlaeger, Elmo Neutzler, and Pete Styra; (second row) Ray Voelkel, three unidentified, and George Morissee Jr. (Courtesy Esther Puente.)

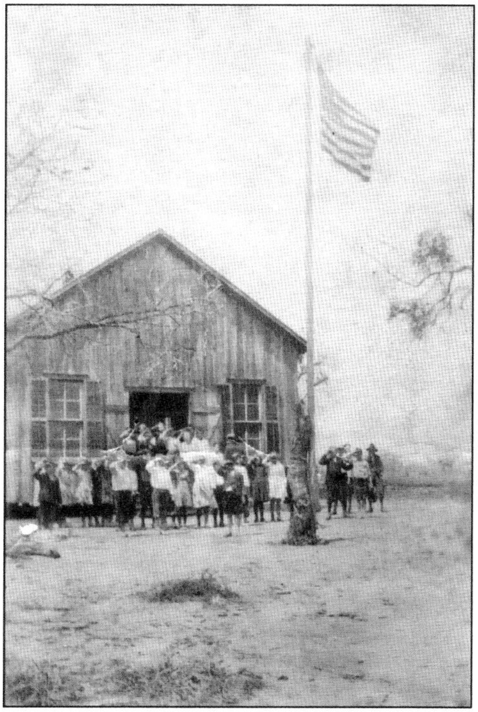

Henry Buesing donated land in the Cotton Patch community in 1914 for a one-room schoolhouse. The Buesing School operated until 1950. In this picture, the American flag is flying above the playground as the children salute it. Willie Buesing is the second child from the right. (Courtesy Bernice Geffert.)